'A must-read for anyone at
as an organiser. It's the exact kind of accessible text we
need to understand the connections between national and
global justice movements and to bridge the gaps between
organisers in the anti-racist space, working-class-led
movements, LGBTQ+ organisations and climate justice.'
Hannah Francis, Race Equality Researcher

'There is an important tradition of experimentation for
social justice and *Changemakers* contributes to that canon. It
is a gift: an offering to the radical, transformative organising
that has come before it and all that will come after. I already
feel like a stronger organiser having read this book. Every
page is an energising call to action – it demands we get to
work but generously shows us the possibilities of how.'
**Emmanuelle Andrews, Social Justice, Abolition
and Queer Liberation Campaigner**

'This book should have been written 20 years ago. If it had,
my understanding of my craft would have been much easier
and faster. It is a must-read for anyone wishing to challenge
the greedy and the powerful. The book takes you on a journey
through the key organising theories that inform and influence
the movements of today [and] presents a range of case studies,
showing how the theory applies. This provides the reader with
a rich understanding of the application of deep organising
theory – what works, what doesn't and what we can learn.'
Jon Clark, Trade Union Educator

'This excellent social, political and organisational history
is as fascinating as it is wide-ranging. The themes on
power, theories of change and the vested interests in the
status quo will be of particular interest to sociologists.'
Roger Yates, Animal Liberationist

'Packed full of insight based on years of experience at the coalface of organising. This book is a treasure trove of organising insights.'
Brendan Cox

'This book is essential for mapping the pathways through progressive mobilising and social organising. It brings together up-to-date insights into organising, community engagement and mobilising, with detailed experiences and case studies grounded in actual events and campaigns. It is a highly original and thoughtful book that maps how questions of social justice and participation can be developed on the ground across a range of communities and workplaces. The book is not just a "how to" guide but is in itself a way of reimagining and rethinking how mobilising and campaigning are key to deepening communities and democratic struggles.'
Miguel Martinez Lucio, The University of Manchester

'This is the book I wish I'd had when I was a young activist. Drawing on decades of experience leading and being part of many campaign organisations, Holgate and Page are generous with their insights, analysis and reflections. Organising is never easy, but it can be fun and is crucial to building hope for the future. This book makes us ask all the right questions to understand and build our collective power.'
Mel Simms, The University of Glasgow

'Building on a lifetime of activism and reflection on activism, Jane Holgate and John Page have created an incredibly useful resource for future changemakers. In their words, "the real 'magic' happens when new generations of organisers interpret what has been gifted to them by history, and then go beyond these principles to create something genuinely new". This book is a contribution to that magic, and I would recommend it to trade union and community organisers alike.'
Gawain Little, General Secretary of the General Federation of Trade Unions (GFTU)

CHANGEMAKERS
Radical Strategies for
Social Movement Organising

Jane Holgate and John Page

First published in Great Britain in 2025 by

Policy Press, an imprint of
Bristol University Press
University of Bristol
1–9 Old Park Hill
Bristol
BS2 8BB
UK
+44 (0)117 374 6645
bup-info@bristol.ac.uk

Details of international sales and distribution partners are available at
policy.bristoluniversitypress.co.uk

British Library Cataloguing in Publication Data
A catalogue record for this book is available from the British Library

ISBN 978-1-4473-2881-0 paperback
ISBN 978-1-4473-2882-7 ePub
ISBN 978-1-4473-6569-3 ePdf

Cover design: Nicky Borowiec
Front cover image: Adobe Stock/vlntn

Bristol University Press and Policy Press use environmentally
responsible print partners.

Printed and bound in Great Britain by CPI Group (UK) Ltd,
Croydon CR40 4YY

To those, too many to mention, who throughout the whole of human history have dared to run against the storm and whose efforts, in the words of Ella Baker, have carried us through the gale. To those who today are using every opportunity to shine a light so that others will find a way, and to those who read this book hoping to better their chances of bringing forth a world where everyone enjoys the freedoms that every democracy has promised but has seldom delivered.

Contents

Abbreviations

AAM	Anti-Apartheid Movement
ACAS	Advisory, Conciliation and Arbitration Service
ALF	Animal Liberation Front
ARC	Asbestos Research Council
BA	British Airways
BMA	British Medical Association
BNP	British National Party
CRED	Commission on Race and Ethnic Disparities
CWU	Communication Workers Union
EDI	Equality, diversity and inclusion
EDL	English Defence League
FBI	Federal Bureau of Investigation
GLA	Greater London Assembly
Hackney TUC	Hackney Trades Union Council
HR	Human resources
HSA	Hunt Saboteurs Association
IAF	Industrial Areas Foundation
IPPR	Institute for Public Policy Research
NAACP	National Association for the Advancement of Colored People
NHS	National Health Service
NUM	National Union of Mineworkers
ODA	Olympic Delivery Authority
RMT	National Union of Rail, Maritime and Transport Workers
SCLC	Southern Christian Leadership Conference
STST	Stop the Seventy Tour
TSSA	Transport Salaried Staffs' Association
TUC	Trades Union Congress
UKIP	United Kingdom Independent Party

Acknowledgements

I would like to acknowledge the various organisations who have over the years employed me as an organiser at one time or another. In addition, I want to acknowledge the learning I received from my involvement in the Liverpool committee of the Anti-Nazi League, the Hunt Saboteurs Association, Sea Shepherd and many more organisations, for welcoming me as an active changemaker and teaching me the basics of organising. Some of these collaborations ended well, others less so, but I learned from them all, and it is that learning that I hope has found expression in this book.

I would like to thank the members of Hackney Unison who, in 1999, elected me and a slate of 'reform candidates' to officer positions within the branch: it was an honour and a privilege. There are too many individuals to name that I have worked alongside over the last four decades, but I was never prouder than when I worked as part of the 'dream team' supporting communities to organise against the far-right.

I don't believe that we learn how to organise simply by reading books, but they can help to frame experiences and provide space for reflection. I would very much like to thank Jane McAlevey (a friend and fantastic organiser who sadly passed away on 7 July 2024), Marshall Ganz, Janice Fine and Arnie Graf, not just for their incredible writing, but for the times when we shared dreams and explored tactics.

Finally, I would like to thank Jane Holgate for a lifetime of love and comradeship.

John Page

Access to books and libraries at a young age provided the opportunity to think critically about the world and to understand that change can and does happen as a result of what we do as individuals – and even more so when we act collectively. As such

I would like to acknowledge the importance of libraries and access to reading, without which I think I would be a different person. Reading led to my first social justice activity when I joined Friends of the Earth in my early teens and attended an anti-nuclear demonstration in my hometown – and cemented my belief that we need to be well organised.

Since my early days of work, I have been active within the trade union movement where I have learned lots of good (and sometimes not so good) organising practice from a wide range of people. Undertaking a postgraduate degree in labour and trade union studies with the wonderful and insightful Mary Davis set me on a course of academic study where my research has focussed on trade unions for the last couple of decades. Along the way I have been fortunate to work with and have discussions with many smart people thinking about organised labour, including Janice Fine, Jane McAlevey, Amanda Tattersall, Melanie Simms and too many others to mention.

I have also had a particular interest in community organising, and seeing ordinary people making things happen with their neighbours is always inspiring. The campaigns around planning issues in Hackney have been challenging, frustrating – and wonderful when we have won. I've made so many friends as a result and I would like to acknowledge how much I've learned from organising in different ways with a diverse group of people. Su Forrester-Brown, my neighbour and great friend, didn't see herself as an organiser or a leader, but she could persuade anyone to do as she wished! She is dearly missed.

My time as an organiser in the hunt saboteurs and the animal rights movement taught me that there are so many different ways to organise, and about the importance of strategy and power. I give thanks to all the people who I worked with on those campaigns – again too many names to mention.

On a personal level, I have spent over 40 years discussing organising with John Page. You might think that all has been said over those years, but we are still learning and analysing the wins and defeats of campaigns around us. Thank you for your love and comradeship – the feeling is mutual.

Jane Holgate

Introduction:
What's this book about?

You may have picked up this book because you are angry about injustice and inequality, and, if so, you're not alone. Millions of people from around the world are involved in countless protests against the failure of governments to respond adequately to climate change, labour exploitation, discrimination, poverty, political marginalisation and many other causes that lead to social injustice. And even though there are many successes, there are also many defeats. While there is never a guarantee of victory in any campaign, there's a better chance of winning if we are organised, when we have a sound and well-thought-out strategy and – of vital importance – an understanding of power resources: those we have, or can access, and, of course, those available to our opposition. As Nelson Mandela once said: 'we can change the world and make it a better place. It is in our hands to make a difference.'

To change the world it's important to think about the reason it is the way it is, what has shaped it, and what forces are currently determining its direction. Whether it is climate change, LGBTQ+ rights, discrimination and inequality in the workplace, the killing of animals for sport, the casualisation of work or the unaffordability of housing, there's a reason why the societies we live in permit injustice – and it's almost invariably as a result of an imbalance of forces where some powerful groups benefit and, not surprisingly, seek to maintain their benefit, while others suffer and, equally unsurprisingly, seek to organise to effect change.

Our aim in this book is to engage with key organising concepts and theories of how to achieve social change, and to relate these to real examples to explore what has worked, but also what hasn't. We will consider the ideas of leading theoreticians and practitioners who have been involved in changing society for the

1

better to understand what we can learn from social movement theory that's been relevant to past campaigns and organisations – many of which we've been involved with in some way or another, either as organisers or as members.

The book is, in some way, a modern response to political theorist and community organiser Saul Alinsky's well-known book *Rules for Radicals* (1972). Saul Alinsky was a fantastic organiser, and tens of thousands of people have gained insights into how they can change the world through engagement with his ideas. Yet, despite its popularity, *Rules for Radicals* is not even his best work – that accolade goes to his early book *Reveille for Radicals* (1989 [1949]). *Rules* was written towards the end of his life, and its objective was to challenge the counter-culture movements at the beginning of the 1970s. It is, perhaps, so often cited because people feel the need for a step-by-step guide to organising, and his 13 rules are undoubtedly useful. But George Orwell (1946) once wrote a guide to written English with six rules, the last of which was 'break any of these rules sooner than say anything outright barbarous'.

It's now over half a century since *Rules for Radicals* was published, and its title, unfortunately, has encouraged it to be mistakenly read as if it were a proscriptive, universal blueprint for organisers. Too many people who have learned how to organise through these 'rules' tend to judge their actions according to what the theory says, not what the reaction is to their actions. We think that Saul Alinsky would have disapproved of this. He was, ultimately, someone who was intensely attentive to what was going on around him, looking for strategic opportunities to change the power dynamic to his advantage. He would happily break any rules that obstructed the path to winning. We argue that the development of a body of fixed ideas referred to as 'Alinskyism', and the treatment of *Rules for Radicals* as a 'bible for organisers' is a mistake for several reasons. Among them is that Alinsky had only limited engagement with the African American Freedom Struggle, and his work doesn't reflect the many lessons available from the movement building within that struggle. Wherever there is oppression there will always be resistance, sometimes it will be disparate and weak, at other times it will be phenomenally strong. In the UK we have a rich legacy of organising from the

Chartists to the Suffragettes, from the Tolpuddle Martyrs to the 1888 matchwomen strikers. However rich that legacy is, any discussion of organising must recognise the immense contribution of the African American grassroots community leaders such as Ella Baker, E.D. Nixon, Bayard Rustin, Septima Clark, Fannie Lou Hamer and many, many more – people who, through their actions and reflective learning, systematised the process of building power both in the community and in the unions. Alinsky was a keen supporter of those struggles but, unlike his friend Myles Horton, he had no first-hand knowledge of them.

This book is therefore, both a tribute to and a reaction against *Rules for Radicals*. Rather than suggest that there is *a* blueprint for successful organising, we believe that while there are some broad principles, the real 'magic' happens when new generations of organisers interpret what has been gifted to them by history, and then go beyond these principles to create something genuinely new.

Also, the world has moved on. Alinsky's organising precedes the widespread use of fax machines and domestic telephones, let alone the internet, mobile phones, and social media, and while Alinsky delighted in baiting his enemies so that they would respond in a way that was actually destructive to their agenda, today's politicians, companies and other decision makers with whom we might be in battle have PR professionals whose job it is to save them from themselves.

Those who benefit from inequality and divided societies have studied how people resist, and developed counter-tactics, which means that every generation needs to create new tactics relevant to specific social, political, and economic circumstances. Further, Saul Alinsky talks very little about movement building in and of itself, and instead focuses on individual campaign tactics – at which he was an undoubted expert. Yet, ultimately, if we are looking for fundamental change for the many, then movement building must be a central focus for organisers.

In contrast to providing a set of rules or step-by-step guide, this book will seek to constantly review real-life campaign experiences – messy and confused as they often are – to illustrate the complexities and contradictions that are part of the journey of a successful campaign. There aren't fixed rules when it comes to organising, but we can reflect and learn from the many and various approaches to organising – allowing us to consider what 'fits' best in the specific circumstances of a particular campaign.

Another key difference with many of the excellent books on organising theory and practice is that we don't focus on just one particular social justice cause, or form of organising. While books on organising tend to be rooted in the specifics of, say, union organising, Black Lives Matter, the peace movement, or environmental campaigns, in our case, we hope to show – using the specifics of real-life examples – that an understanding of the 'fundamentals' of organising practice will allow the formulation of strategies that can be applied in many different and varied circumstances. By drawing upon specific campaigns from our own experience – some successful, but others not – we hope to provide an insight into the inter-relationship of theory and practice, and the value of applying theoretical tools to the strategising of campaigns.

In essence, the book is less of a manual on 'how to do' social movement activism, but more of a 'how to think' about planning, resources and strategising to achieve movement-building goals. It encourages reflexivity – the process of 'stepping back' to think about a campaign's 'theory of change'. What's working well, what's not? Why not? What rethinking needs to take pace? What course of action needs to be altered? What is the response from our opponent? Why has conflict developed within our organisation and what do we need to do to fix it? How *did* we manage to win against all odds? This process of constant critical and honest reflection throughout campaigns and struggles should ensure we don't continually repeat the same mistakes or adopt the same previously unsuccessful tactics, hoping that we just might be successful the next time. A regular mistake is to fall into the trap of using a great tactic that worked previously because it surprised your opposition; next time, it is unlikely to come as a surprise and your opposition may now be fully prepared.

Many campaigners, ourselves included, have reacted to events that we feel need urgent attention – and sometimes this is just what is needed. But often campaigns or protests start without much thought about how specific actions will contribute to winning. We generally know what we want, but don't necessarily have a plan, nor have we strategised the stages we need to go through to be effective changemakers. Instead, we are moved to act because we feel the need to respond – often in a very visible way. We leaflet, we petition, we march, we chant, we sit down and occupy, but often this is what our opponents expect. They have planned for this – it was on their risk register – they can wait it out, or they have accurately assessed that our actions won't change the power dynamic, which means they won't be forced or persuaded to change their course of action.

The odds are often stacked against us, so we need to be smarter if we are to be effective, but if we take the time to plan then there are a whole host of tactics and strategies that we can use that will give us a better chance at winning. We need to know our opponents as well as they know us, but we also need to go off the 'risk register' – to do the unexpected – so as to create an element of surprise. More thinking, more planning, more strategising, more playfulness and more involvement of wider groups of people is often what is needed for effective social movements, and in this book, we will be looking at examples, as well as theories, of how this can be achieved.

The themes we will develop in the book include: understanding a theory of change and its importance to campaigns; leadership and the development of leaders; mapping power – where it is and how to build and then use it; how small groups break through to become big networked organisations; equality as central organising practice; mobilising as an organising strategy; developing a story of 'us'; the art of negotiations; communication and the changing of dominant narratives through a process of reframing.

Many people baulk when they read the phrase 'theory of change', either because it's unfamiliar and they don't know what it means or because it *is* familiar and has been used as a form of words to disguise the fact that a campaign or initiative doesn't have any idea about how it is going to win, or as a tool to block any discussion about why victory seems to be elusive. But the first and most important lesson we hope you will take from this book, is that organising is an art. While there are some fantastic frameworks that can help us think about strategy, organising and winning is a creative process, and, where possible, it's great to inject some fun into campaigning.

5

How to read this book

It is often said that, with fiction, the reader is the co-creator of the story, that while the book may be written by an author, the story is not solely created by them. The reader of a novel brings three important tools with them when they begin this process. First, they bring their own lived experience: of joy, of loss, of friendship, successes, defeats and so on. Then, they bring their cultural experience: the legacies of other stories they have read, songs they have listened to and movies they have seen. These histories explain why no two people reading the same book ever experience the same story. Finally, the reader brings their imagination: they can visualise the story, they can see the characters and feel their emotions.

This process of reading fiction is a creative one, and a good writer will create a narrative that guides our imagination through a series of challenges, choices and resolutions that befall the characters, but our experience of this journey will be uniquely our own.

Non-fiction is seldom read with the same licence to create your own unique version of the book. Please accept our permission to bring your whole self, your history, and your imagination into the process of reading this book.

After over 40 years as organisers in the community, anti-racist and trade union spaces, we look forward to innovation coming from the only place it has ever come from: young people taking the traditions of resistance that they have inherited and reinterpreting and remaking them to meet their own immediate needs. When you read this book, there may be things you wholeheartedly agree with, and times when you strongly disagree. Both of these can be valuable learning opportunities: why does something chime so closely with your thoughts or, alternatively, why does a particular suggestion grate so much? But a word of warning: certainty, for an organiser, is an unreliable comfort! Challenging ourselves to constantly rethink that which we have assumed is one of the ways in which we learn and grow to be better organisers.

Writing this book has reminded us of how much we don't know, and of how much of which we are uncertain. It is likely that if we were to write this book in a couple of years' time, it would be different. It is possible that things we have argued here, would be things with which we might later disagree. If you are not constantly re-evaluating your 'truths', then you will be less equipped to organise in a world of uncertainty and change.

If, when you finish this book, you assume that you now know all you need to know to be a great organiser, then we will have failed, but if, instead, you come away with a framework for thinking through some of the big questions that organising poses, then we will have made a useful contribution.

We hope you enjoy the journey and look forward to hearing of the positive change that you create.

1

The two souls of organising: above and below

What is meant by 'organising' and who is 'an organiser'? These seem like relevant questions to be asking at the start of this book, particularly as there are probably as many different answers as there are organisers. The word has many everyday meanings, for example, you might organise a petition, a boycott, a protest march or a strike, and these are all tactics that you might use in a campaign. They often require a process of people coming together, discussing and evaluating potential and competing strategies and agreeing on specific steps, and to that extent they involve organising, but organising is a more specific and mindful practice. We prefer to think of 'organising' as a shorthand for 'organising for transformational social change', which perhaps goes beyond the mechanics of the day-to-day practices we have just mentioned. It's strategic, planned, and connected to a theory of change to achieve the goals we are looking for.

The process of organising tends to take place in specific circumstances – most often where there's a widely perceived wrong that needs to be righted, and where there's an imbalance of power, and an abuse of that power. But it's not always related to remedying a widely perceived wrong. Those who have wealth and privilege also organise, to keep that wealth and privilege. As Woody Guthrie, the legendary folk singer who sang about American workers' struggles, socialism and anti-fascism, once said: 'the employers always have their own union, they just don't like it when we have ours'.

When something is wrong in the world, whether that be poverty, exploitation, discrimination or the climate emergency, it's almost always the case that the reason the people who have the power to stop it don't is because either they benefit from the injustice or they're heavily influenced by those who do. Simply petitioning, lobbying or protesting about the issue, without thinking about the power imbalance that's created the injustice, is unlikely to effect the change we want. Therefore, we need to change the balance of power, either by becoming more powerful so our voices can't be ignored or by making the decision makers less powerful – and we do this by strategic organising.

Organising starts with people, and there's an old saying which goes, 'there are two forms of power in the world, organised money and organised people'. We don't have the money, so our job as organisers is to organise the people. This isn't just a question of convincing people of desired change and getting them to come along to a public meeting or a protest march; organising people involves surfacing their latent agency and convincing them that they are the architects of the change they're looking to make. As the song from Sweet Honey in the Rock – the a cappella group that grew out of the African American freedom struggle – so accurately affirms, 'we are the ones we have been waiting for'.

In society, the poor, the dispossessed, the oppressed and the marginalised are led to believe that their problems are either bad luck, or their own fault. Working-class communities, robbed of relatively well-paid industrial jobs by deindustrialisation, are told they haven't adapted to the changing world, or they're not agile enough, or don't have the right attitude when, for example, they refuse to work for the minimum wage jobs in the service or care industries. Communities blighted by poverty, discrimination, poor health and anti-social behaviour are told that there's something inherently wrong with their community, rather than there's a lack of opportunity for those within it. This is why those who succeed from disadvantaged backgrounds so often have 'imposter syndrome' – also referred to as the 'hidden injuries of class'. In contrast, the children sent to Eton and other private schools – those who are almost predestined to attend Oxbridge universities – are raised in a system where they are encouraged to think they can be whoever they want to be.

There was a period in the late 1960s and early 1970s in the UK when there was a real sense of the possibility of change.

Even under Conservative governments of the time, standards of living for working-class families improved over a generation. Meanwhile, revolutionary upheavals around the world, and as close as in Portugal in 1974, were ending the shameful era of direct colonial rule, and in the context where change was so obviously possible, there was a thirst for ideas about how to effect change in the world. From the late 1960s, a generation of industrial working-class people believed they were entitled to improvements, not just in wages and job safety, but also in wider society. However, by the mid-1970s power was already shifting away from the working-class and towards the elites. This power shift is perhaps best characterised in the English-speaking world by the rise of politicians like Ronald Reagan in the US, and Margaret Thatcher in the UK, and the neo-liberal economic agenda they delivered – most graphically illustrated in the UK by the militarisation of the police, first in majority Black communities, and then during the 1984–85 miners' strike. This militarisation was at its most brutal at the 'Battle of Orgreave', where striking miners were led into a trap, brutalised, beaten and then systematically framed, leading to almost a hundred prosecutions, all of which eventually collapsed at trial. Michael Mansfield, the lawyer defending these workers, described the subsequent failed attempt to criminalise the miners at Orgreave – on charges that would have carried ten-year prison sentences – as: 'the worst example of a mass frame-up in this country this century' (Seton 1985). The defeat of that strike contributed to the trade union movement adopting 'new realism', a philosophical approach that argued that unions could no longer win through industrial muscle. A practical consequence was a loss of collective class consciousness as unions attempted 'partnership' to resolve disputes with employers. The theory was that if unions couldn't beat employers, they could make themselves useful to employers and urge concessions in exchange. As the 1980s progressed, the post-Second-World-War consensus around a welfare state was broken, with Prime Minister Thatcher claiming: 'there is no such thing as society', as she decimated local services and starved the National Health Service (NHS) of funds.

Today, there perhaps isn't a widespread belief that if we get organised, we can win. The confidence we saw in past decades of struggle has been replaced, for many, with a sense of powerlessness – a feeling of being at risk in a tumultuously changing world. Consequently, one of the first tasks in organising is to impress upon people that they *can* shape the world around them if they act collectively. Only when they believe it's possible are people able to act to force the boss, the local council, a big company or even the government to change their mind. The most radical thing that we can do today in terms of facilitating a complete or dramatic change in the balance of power in society is to encourage our communities to believe that they can, and indeed should, take it upon themselves to shape the society around them. Ella Baker (1969), the African American civil rights activist, once said: 'I use the term radical in its original meaning – getting down to and understanding the root cause. It means facing a system that does not lend itself to your needs and devising means by which you change that system', and this is the context in which we use it here.

Organising blueprints: don't treat them as gospel

Many organisers have been schooled in the principles of Saul Alinsky's methods of organising. Saul Alinsky, American community activist and political theorist, learned how to organise communities when he was a sociology student studying the Mob in Chicago in the late 1920s and seeking to address what was then referred to as juvenile delinquency, which he and his colleagues believed was often a direct consequence of the adverse circumstances in which young people were growing up. There's no doubt he was a brilliant changemaker, and many of his original insights remain powerful today, but very often the practice of his latter-day supporters denies, or limits, the agency of affected communities, as his approach relied on direction by 'organisers' – often from the outside of communities. He wrote a great book which was, perhaps unfortunately, called *Rules for Radicals*, where the title has contributed to many of his supporters treating his ideas as a form of universal blueprint, rather than as a place to take inspiration from. As Myles Horton, founder of the Highlander Folk School that trained social justice organisers, observed – in defence of Alinsky against his acolytes – 'you don't try to imitate people who know more than you. You try to learn from them' (Horton, Kohl and Kohl 1998: 178). There's much to be learnt from Alinsky's approach, but rigidly following tactics without regard to specific times, context and changing circumstances is not transformational organising.

Organising from above: leading from the outside

Within the Alinsky current, there is a school of practice where personal testimony is used to draw attention to wider social issues facing a community. This can be a great tactic to highlight a problem as it personalises the issue – it takes it away from being an abstract concern. This testimony is generally built upon by an upstanding member of the community – often a faith leader who can add moral authority to the need for those in power to act. In the modern Alinsky approach, a directly employed organiser, for example working for a housing advocacy group, might find a local faith leader, who would introduce them to, say, a single mother, perhaps on benefits, whose child is suffering ill-health because of damp and mould in their flat. The organiser would then appoint this person as a 'leader' and ask them to 'give testimony' in front of the press and politicians, or perhaps even at a large community meeting, with representatives of the landlord/ council present, to focus attention on the issue. In such situations the faith leader highlights that there's a moral duty to care for the poor in our society. The person or organisation who is the target, for example a landlord or local authority, are asked to exercise their power and to commit publicly to resolve the problem.

This approach can work over small specific issues, particularly if, as in this case, there's also a legal duty to address the problem. However, it seldom challenges the power dynamics that created the circumstance in the first place. It may be that the individual is moved to a better home, but the systemic problem – the power balance – remains largely untouched, and unresolved. It may also be the case that the individual is co-opted by the landlord/ local authority to tell a new story of how much better life is because of the intervention. In *transformational* organising, the question we need to ask is: when the organiser moves on to the next issue, what level of agency is left behind? Is the community better able to fight its own struggles? The answer is likely to be 'no' unless new leaders were developed in the process. The issues related to structural defects on the estate may still be there and, once the professional organiser has moved on to create new headlines somewhere else, the previously appointed 'leader' from the community whose testimony appeared so powerful may be left without their newfound voice, or the ability to build power without the external direction. This is why leadership development is central to transformative organising, something discussed in a later chapter.

The approach outlined here – which we have perhaps caricatured a little to give an insight into its deficiencies – is sometimes referred to as 'instrumentalism'. What can happen is that the story of the person with lived experience, and indeed the person, and their community, are used (in a non-pejorative sense) as an instrument by a skilled expert, to exert pressure for change. Even if the outcome is successful, this won't mean that the balance of power has necessarily shifted in favour of those living on the estate – and, having been schooled to behave as if their only source of power is their authentic voice, the community member may have gained few transformative organising skills to equip their people to address injustice when the spotlight has moved on and those in power are no longer listening.

Organising from the base: putting people at the centre of organising

An alternative approach places the community at the centre of resolving their own problems. Going back to the housing estate example we just mentioned – it's run down, it's in need of repairs, the lifts often break down, there's damp in people's homes, there are high levels of worklessness and significant deprivation. A community that was once stable has been fragmented as those people who could move out did, and have been replaced by people with fewer ties to the area, often new migrants. Meanwhile, the stairwells of the flats are used by gangs to sell drugs to the more affluent people from across town. Let's imagine, in this scenario, that within this community there are also multiple divisions, perhaps between the older residents and the young families with children, perhaps between the new migrants and the established community, and there might also be other divisive issues.

An organising-from-below approach would start by asking: 'What are the shared interests of this community?', 'What stories bind them?' and 'Where can they find their agency?'. Or, put another way: who is the 'us' in this story, and who is the 'them'? In a real-life example, an experienced campaigner organised on just such an estate. It was a relatively small estate, but it had one additional problem over and above those listed previously: it was on the edge of an 'night-time economy' area with many clubs and bars, and late at night revellers would use the estate's communal grounds as a toilet. The organiser began with door-to-door meetings, and she quickly found out that, in the main, people didn't know their neighbours. A key issue was that the estate garden was being abused, so she worked with the tenants to organise a barbecue to which everyone on the estate was invited. This created the opportunity for people to meet and speak, share their concerns, and think about what they needed to do to change things. There was no predetermined plan, just a strategy to stimulate a desire within this community to build the power they needed to effect the many changes they wanted to see.

In this version of organising, the organiser is not the strategist, they don't pick the issues, they simply ask people: 'What would you like to see changed?', 'Do you think anyone is going to do it for you?' and, most importantly, 'Do you think your neighbours feel the same way?', before moving on to ask 'Do you think there might be value in calling a community meeting?'. Jimmy Reid, the legendary trade unionist who led the Clyde Shipbuilders' 'work in' which saved the Govan shipyards in Glasgow, gave a speech on alienation in 1972, where he talked about people who feel themselves the victims of economic forces beyond their control. He said alienation is '… the frustration of ordinary people excluded from the processes of decision making. The feeling of despair and hopelessness that pervades people who feel, with justification, that they have no real say in shaping or determining their own destinies' (Reid 1972).

The point Jimmy Reid was making is that this feeling of despair and hopelessness is not uncommon and it's not an individual failing. Society can be alienating for many people. It's also a rational response to a world in which individuals are systematically disempowered. Yet despair and hopelessness are demobilising for individuals and communities. If people feel that nothing can change, and no one will listen, then it makes no sense to invest time, emotional energy and, at times, risks to your livelihood to challenge injustice. As transformational organisers we aim to help people to see they do have agency and can create change. The Industrial Workers of the World used to refer to this hopelessness as the 'policeman in your head'. They argued that workers, due to the work of the 'head fixers' – the press, official spokespeople, and reformists within the labour movement – sometimes convinced themselves that they couldn't win: the way things are is natural, inevitable and perpetual. This 'policeman in the head' was more of a brake on social activism than any riot squad on the street.

Believing what's possible

Perhaps an organiser's primary task at the start of any campaign is to make people believe in themselves. It is worth noting the contrasting approaches of Saul Alinsky, founder of the Industrial Areas Foundation (IAF), and that of Myles Horton, founder of the legendary Highlander Folk School where students included Martin Luther King, Rosa Parks and many other leaders of the African American freedom movement. Alinsky and Horton were friends and had a mutual admiration, they had different approaches to organising, yet this didn't lead to animosity. It's perhaps a lesson for us today that we can learn from each other – even when we disagree.

Saul Alinsky was always chief strategist and undisputed leader. He also expected to be funded before he entered a community and brought financial resources and often powerful allies with him into his initiatives. His model was not one that a neighbouring community could easily replicate. Myles Horton, on the other hand, believed that developing people's vision of themselves as agents of change and unleashing their capacity was more important. What he brought to the organising table was the ability to inspire people to become the best version of themselves.

We have tremendous respect for Alinsky's integrity and ability, as well as the contribution he's made to organising theory and practice, but we feel the Alinsky approach too often doesn't result in self-sustaining organising within communities. His end goal was to win a specific issue – which was fine for a particular campaign – but transformative organising is about what is left behind in terms of the strategic capacity of the community: to what extent are ordinary people combat-ready for the inevitable next issue? Myles Horton said that his approach to organising was different from Alinsky's because if he had to make a choice between achieving a specific goal and utilising the struggle to develop and radicalise people, his choice would be to drop the goal and develop the people. On the surface, both Alinsky and Horton had the same goal – to win for working people – but they differed in the method they adopted. Alinsky's was often short-term while Horton believed in building sustainable leadership in unions or communities for the long haul. For Alinsky, winning on a particular issue was *the* most important thing, and sometimes he would be gleeful about how a sleight of hand had allowed him to win. However, for Horton the question was if you win for or on behalf of people, what do they learn from that experience and how does it equip them for ongoing struggles? His view was that while it's true that you can learn from mobilising, and you can learn to manipulate people to achieve a goal, a better organising practice is to learn to educate your own people. He said: 'We taught them our own way, and the reason we did that was because we wanted them to be educators as well as organizers. Instead of just mobilizers we wanted them to educate the people' (Horton and Freire 1990: 123).

While acknowledging that the Highlander Folk School was responsible for producing leading organisers in both the labour and the African American freedom movements, Horton disputed it was an organising school:

> There were so many organizing in the labor movement who came from Highlander that people called it an organizer's school ... [but] Highlander was not a school for organisers. It was a school to help people to analyse and give people values, and they became the organisers. The reason so many of Highlander people were successful organisers was because of that ... not

[because] we trained them in techniques of mobilising and organizing, because we didn't do that. (Horton and Freire 1990: 123)

The focus on educating for organising was thus central to the approach of Horton and the Highlander Folk School. He believed that an organising experience should be educational, and as a radical democrat, this process of organising had to have a cornerstone of democratic community decision making. Here was his departure from Alinsky. Horton said having people participate in the process of developing and delivering the action rather than having just one authoritative 'messianic' leader was essential for transformative organising.

There is a parallel in the different organising approaches to be found in an article by Marxist writer and socialist activist Hal Draper (1966) titled 'The Two Souls of Socialism' – although here it is expressed much more starkly. In essence, Draper argued that while socialist groups were constantly disputing who was most socialist – often in terms of the leftist credentials of their take on obscure elements of Marxist doctrine – the most important divide was not between left and right, or between so-called 'revolutionary' and 'democratic' socialism, but between socialism from above and socialism from below. What unites the many different forms of *socialism from above* is the belief that socialism (or their image of it) must be *handed down* to the working-class in one form or another by a ruling elite who are not subject to their control; this elite could be Fabian reformers, armed guerrillas or the central committee of a so-called vanguard party. On the contrary, at the heart of *socialism from below* is the view that socialism can be realised only through the self-activity of the working-class, reaching out for freedom with their own hands. In essence this requires a process that sees them moving from passive acceptance, however bitterly, of their condition, to being agents of their own destiny, as actors – not merely subjects – on the stage of history. This approach is summed up in the first sentence in the Rules written by Marx for the First International, and the First Principle of his lifework: 'the emancipation of the working classes must be conquered by the working classes themselves'. Hal Draper is scathing in his criticism of the well-meaning proponents of socialism from above when he says that they implicitly adopt a view – consciously or otherwise – that

> [the] mass of people are congenitally stupid, corrupt, apathetic and generally hopeless; and progressive change must come from Superior People rather like (as it happens) the intellectual expressing these sentiments. This is translated theoretically into an Iron Law of Oligarchy or a tinny law of elitism, in one way or another involving a crude theory of inevitability – the inevitability of change-from-above-only. (Draper 1966: 29)

But Draper doesn't romanticise the working-class. He asks, How does a people or a class become fit to rule in their own name?

> *Only by fighting to do so.* Only by waging their struggle against oppression – oppression by those who tell them they are unfit to govern. Only by fighting for democratic power do they educate themselves and raise themselves up to the level of being able to wield that power. There has never been any other way for any class. (Draper 1966: 26)

This of course builds on Marx's concept of a 'class in itself' – a class that is objectively defined by its relationships with the means of production – moving to becoming a 'class for itself' – a class that is self-conscious and recognising its class position, organises, as a class, to effect change. Perhaps the consequence of the difference in these approaches is best exemplified by Eugene Debs, one of the founding members of the Industrial Workers of the World, when he told a group of supporters:

> I do not want you to follow me or anyone else; if you are looking for a Moses to lead you out of this capitalist wilderness, you will stay right where you are. I would not lead you into the promised land if I could, because if I led you in, someone else would

lead you out. You must use your heads as well as your hands, and get yourself out of your present condition. (Debs 1908: 71)

This concept that oppressed people must 'do for self' is not limited to the Marxist tradition. The second-wave feminist movement organised 'consciousness-raising' groups as a political practice, and the disability rights movement has long had a slogan: 'nothing for us, without us'. The Combahee River Collective, a Black lesbian feminist socialist organisation active in Boston, Massachusetts from 1974 to 1980, made a statement that became famous in which they articulated a detailed analysis of what would later be termed intersectionality. They said, 'we believe that the most profound and potentially most radical politics come directly out of our own identity' (Combahee River Collective 1988). Within this approach is the belief that what is essential to good organising practice is the varied and multifaceted lived experience of participants. It's in the process of struggling for their own liberation that participants disrupt the damaging socialisation they've been subjected to and collectively create the opportunity for a new socialisation, new norms of thinking and feeling that reflect their collective self-interest, rather than that of their oppressors.

Organising: unleashing inherent capacities

While the concept of 'two souls' that we've been discussing in this chapter originates in Marxist analysis, it's also found a resonance in many other social movements and it can be used to help us understand that organising is about unleashing people's inherent capacities, and making them aware of their ability to effect change. Organising is not about the ritualisation of a set of campaign tactics – its dynamic is ever-changing depending on the specific circumstances in which people are operating, but some organising practice has become ritualised or based on a set of rules. In part this has come about because of a misreading of *Rules for Radicals*. Myles Horton, who urged organisers to think creatively, and not to think of organising as merely a set of tactics, was scathing of this ritualisation of Alinsky:

I have great resentment today toward some of the people who trade on Saul Alinsky's name and train organisers by what they call the Alinsky Method, when it is often only mechanically and technically Alinsky's. They think it's a matter of gimmicks. What made him such a good organiser was his tremendous sense of humour, his brilliance, and his utter disregard for what anybody said about him. He could have organised in half a dozen different ways and it would have worked, though some people think it was the particular method that was responsible. (Horton, Kohl and Kohl 1998: 178)

These were the 'rules' that Alinsky talked about in *Rules for Radicals*:

- Power is not only what you have but what the enemy thinks you have.
- Never go outside the expertise of your people.
- Whenever possible go outside the expertise of the enemy.
- Make the enemy live up to its own book of rules.
- Ridicule is man's most potent weapon. There is no defence. It is almost impossible to counterattack ridicule. Also, it infuriates the opposition, who then react to your advantage.
- A good tactic is one your people enjoy.
- A tactic that drags on too long becomes a drag.
- Keep the pressure on.
- The threat is usually more terrifying than the thing itself.
- The major premise for tactics is the development of operations that will maintain a constant pressure upon the opposition.
- If you push a negative hard and deep enough it will break through into its counterside; this is based on the principle that every positive has its negative.
- The price of a successful attack is a constructive alternative.
- Pick the target, freeze it, personalise it, and polarise it.

These make a great starting point for any discussion, or training, on mobilising and organising, and some are deeply insightful. They are a useful checklist for any campaign, whether 'top down' or 'bottom up', but none of these rules requires a transformational organising approach to be valid and Alinsky's own varied practice suggests that even he did not believe in 'rules' in organising. As you will have gathered from this chapter, we are advocates of transformative organising that goes beyond the mechanics of the day-to-day practices: organising that is strategic, planned and connected to a theory of change to achieve our goals. This is what we will look at in the next chapter.

Developing your theory of change

Consider a campaign, organisation, or movement in which you are involved.

Who are 'your people', the people most affected by the issues (make a list of the different categories)? For example, if you were concerned about the housing crisis, you might think that it disproportionally impacts on young people, people from racialised minority communities, older women, people with disabilities and so on.

Think about to what extent these people are 'leading' the campaign. Are they visible in the decision-making bodies, among the paid staff or among the leading lay activists? If not, what efforts are being made to change this?

How do the ideas of those most affected about how to organise their communities get surfaced and put into practice?

Consider how much energy is spent on developing the capacity of your people. What training do you provide, and what is its purpose? To what extent does it support people to develop their capacity to be changemakers?

Ask yourself whether this is a 'top-down' or 'bottom-up' campaign/ organisation/movement, perhaps giving it a score on a scale of one to ten (with one being a typical advocacy organisation that uses professional staff to advocate on behalf of its constituency, and ten being a self-sustaining grassroots activist movement).

Once you have made this judgement, do you think this is the optimum place on the spectrum for your campaign/organisation/movement to be and, if not, how could it move towards being more inclusive and empowering of your people?

2

Understanding theory of change and its importance to effective organising

When we are first motivated to act to change the world there's an understandable tendency to either copy what other people are doing or do what is already familiar. Common forms of action are starting a petition, holding a protest, writing to our local Member of Parliament or councillor, calling for a boycott or, in a workplace context, balloting for industrial action. Often, in a hurry to get started, we don't give enough thought as to *why* the problem – for example, anti-social behaviour on an estate, climate degradation, exploitation of child labour, bullying at work, low wages, the housing crisis or institutionalised discrimination – exists, and what forces sustain it. If we do stop to analyse the situation, we often find the problems we seek to address endure either because they meet the needs of a powerful lobby, or because the actions needed to mitigate them conflict with the interests of the rich and powerful. Naturally, when we talk about power, it may operate at different scales, for example, the reason why an employer turns a blind eye to the bullying of a particular manager will be on a different scale to a systemic international failure to address climate change. However, at almost every scale, from the hyper-local to the international, those with power have proven adept at using their influence to prevent the change required to eradicate the variety of injustices that impact upon our lives, anger us or are just plain wrong. If we are to be effective at ending a particular form of oppression or changing adverse circumstances and winning a better world, rather than merely protesting at injustice, we need to think strategically and seek to understand the forces reigned against us and in doing so develop a 'theory of change'. Put another way, we need ask ourselves: how might we shift the balance of power in our favour?

The development of a theory of change is the building block to strategic choice. Once you have identified which decision makers you need to persuade or, more often, force to take a different approach, you can then begin to ask: 'What would make this decision maker exercise their choices in a way that was less damaging?' And then: 'How can we establish a plan to marshal our forces, those we have, and those that we can build, to destabilise the current equilibrium of power?' Many of us have of course been subjected to 'strategic plans' at work, with key performance indicators and other constraints. But planning for liberation is a different game altogether. Rather than trying to constrain people's activity we are seeking to encourage their creativity and imagination. This is not about managerialism, but rather co-creating a plan within which we each contribute both ideas and actions. If you have come to this book looking for a set of strategic blueprints, then you will be disappointed. What this book offers is a series of useful questions, but the choices you make will depend on too many variables to be reduced to a 'how-to' or 'step-by-step' guide.

We will explore examples of strategic choices that emerged from theories of change in this chapter, but let's remain with the issue of power for a moment. There is something called the 'information deficit model' of change that implies that a particular injustice exists almost as an oversight: 'if the people in power only realised just how bad things were, surely, they would act to eliminate it?' While there may be a limited number of examples of where new information has, by itself, secured change, in the main the decision makers we are challenging know what they are doing, they know the consequences of their decisions, and yet they are still doing it, so 'evidence-based' representations seeking to remedy the injustice will often go unheeded.

Information deficit model vs power deficit model

While very few people would articulate their theory of change in this way, the dominant approach to calling for change, illustrated by the *actions* of aspiring changemakers, is often the *information deficit model.* This approach leads to people thinking perhaps we need some compelling new research, or some heart-rending case studies where people living with the consequences of the problem testify as to the adverse impact on their lives. Unfortunately, because a problem is so seldom based on an information deficit, simply amassing more research, testimony and information about the issue generally doesn't lead to change. There is also a real issue about the role of testimony from people with lived experience. With an information deficit model, the more harrowing the story, and the more incapacitated the 'victims' of this injustice are, the more compelling the need for others to act on their behalf. The whole process risks feeding what – borrowing from psychology – has become known as 'saviour syndrome', where the oppressed are seen as objects of our compassion, rather than agents of change. In contrast, in a *power deficit model* of change, our objective is not to reduce the subjects of this injustice to the role of begging for help, but to support them to develop and exercise their inherent change-making capacity. It's not that evidence isn't necessary, merely that it isn't sufficient to effect transformational change. A well-reasoned argument might help to build your base, inoculate your supporters against misinformation, or help you to mobilise, but that's a discussion for another chapter.

In the power deficit model of social change, we recognise that those of us who experience a particular injustice tend to have less power than those who wish to sustain it. An example is Amazon, where the chief executive, Jeff Bezos, is the richest man in the world; he was the world's first 'centibillionaire' – someone whose net worth is more than 100 billion pounds – yet the same company advertises jobs working unsocial hours in its UK warehouses at £10.40 per hour. In the case of Amazon, there's clearly a power deficit. The level of exploitation of workers is high, which is why the CEO is so rich and powerful. It can't be the case that Bezos doesn't know that the reason he is outrageously rich is because his company employs over a million people, many of whom are living in poverty, on dismally low wages. For wage rates to go up and exploitation to go down what's most needed is not a heart-rending video of Amazon employees talking about how hard it is to make ends meet, but a union that is able to take action to force Amazon to pay a better wage. Making a video about the condition of Amazon workers might be a *tactic* you use to help workers realise that their problems are not because they 'aren't very good with money', but because they are paid a shamefully low wage. Doing this might also help to build public support for any action. But in a power deficit model, the value of such a video is measured by how much it encourages individuals to collectivise and act, not its potential to alert the decision maker to the consequences of their decision.

Thinking about power

This therefore brings us to the question of how we build our movement's relative power. How do we build our power, and how do we reduce the power of our opponent? Of course, there will be other factors at play, such as issues of leadership – ours and theirs, opportunities that arise without warning, and moments when our concerns are unexpectedly thrust into the spotlight, but ultimately the question of social justice is about rebalancing power. Once we evaluate the different sources of both actual and potential power, then an effective strategy may be built by asking ourselves a range of questions, such as: How do we challenge our opponent at the points where they are weakest? How do we bring new forces into play that will support our cause? How do we persuade or, if necessary, force, supporters of our opponent to withdraw from the conflict?

Marshall Ganz, a veteran of the civil rights movement's Mississippi Summer of 1964, was for 16 years the lead organiser with the United Farm Workers (UFW) in the USA. He joined the union in 1965 working alongside its leader, Cesar Chavez. He has since worked with many grassroots social justice organisations, played a strategic role in the first Obama presidential election campaign, and is currently employed at Harvard University in the Kennedy School of Government where he teaches leadership, power, organising for change, and public narrative. Ganz has written extensively on the importance of adopting a 'theory of change' at the start of any campaign (see for example, Ganz 2009b; 2011b; 2016b). He says that theory of change is a clear and compelling strategy that lays out a believable path to change. Unfortunately, while the terminology of a theory of change has been utilised by many campaigning charities and social justice organisations, it's often used without sufficient reference to the question of power. A theory of change that doesn't analyse the balance of power will almost inevitably, whether consciously or not, fall back into an information deficit model. As a result, many people's experiences of the concept of a theory of change are such that they perceive it as mere jargon designed to make a funder feel happy, but which has no practical value in advancing a particular cause. To repeat, there can be no effective 'theory of change' that doesn't include power analysis and power mapping.

Marshall Ganz learned how to organise as an ally of the African American freedom movement. As part of the Mississippi Freedom Summer of 1964, organised by, among others, Fannie Lou Hamer, Bob Moses and Ella Baker, he learnt that the people who are experiencing a particular form of oppression will contain within their cumulative lived experience all the knowledge they need to find a way to win. This was a principle the civil rights leaders developed out of their own experiences and their relationship with Myles Horton and the educators at the Highlander Folk School, the social justice leadership training school established in Tennessee in 1932. To get to your theory of change – a strategy for achieving your goals – you need to talk with your people and surface the understandings you collectively have about *why* things are as they are and *what* needs to change before you will be able to win the change you need or desire. This isn't, however, a single discussion. Ganz says you need first to surface the assumptions/ideas about change through discussion, and then make them explicit so they can be 'examined, evaluated, and, if necessary, replaced' with a more realistic set of assumptions. This is important as too often campaign groups will assemble a panel of what they describe as their 'experts by lived experience' and assume that their campaigns have validity because they've been endorsed by these 'experts'. Unfortunately, the first time you ask someone to think about the form of oppression they've experienced, they are likely to explain it in terms of the dominant narratives about that oppression. If they are being asked by a middle-class campaigning group looking to 'help' them, they may also simply give the answers that they believe the questioner wants to hear.

Changing the resources you have into the power you need

It is the process of collective reflection that probes the validity of people's first assumptions, and moves their answers from what the philosopher and Marxist writer Antonio Gramsci would describe as 'common sense' (reflecting the dominant narrative) to 'good sense' based on an analysis of their own lived experience and that of people they know. Once you have established your theory of change, it becomes the foundation of your strategy – 'how to change the resources you have into the power you need to get what you want' (Ganz 2011a: 15–16). Although we might want to add here that in transformational organising, you don't just rely on the resources you already have, because one of the most important things that happens in transformational organising is that you are constantly aiming to increase your resources.

Again, Ganz is an organiser whose work builds on knowledge developed by activist educators, such as those from the Highlander Folk School, and Paulo Freire (one of the most influential philosophers of education of the 20th century), who practise what has become known as experiential learning – using the students' lived experience as the basis for their education. It is often said that 'people don't know what they don't know', but perhaps a more insightful observation is that our people often don't know what they do know. In other words, people are often unaware of the deep wells of knowledge they contain, and one of the roles of a movement is to encourage our people to surface that knowledge, evaluate it and make explicit what is often implicit. Developing this knowledge is, in Paulo Friere's conception, 'coming to know what we know differently'; it is one of the ways in which we increase our capacity and is a powerful resource for change.

An integral part of developing a theory of change is to ask why the problem has not been solved already? Why have you, and perhaps those who went before you, not been able to resolve this issue? Is it through a lack of information, a lack of understanding of what is wrong, a feeling that, no matter what, it can't be changed – the powerful are too powerful, your people are too divided, there isn't consensus about what would be an appropriate solution to the problem, or is it that leaders have been bought off, or scared off, in the past? The answers to these questions will help you shape your theory of change and hence the tactics you adopt. As regards tactics, one particularly important question might be 'What does the target expect us to do?' and, just as importantly, 'What do they not expect us to do?' Thinking through these and other questions in a systematic way will help you develop a strategy that is designed to build the power you need to win, and to deploy it successfully.

Unless we are mindful, we can approach campaigns with an unacknowledged set of assumptions or simply act in a familiar way because it feels like the right thing to do. But if these assumptions are erroneous, they will set us off on the wrong path, wasting time and resources that could be more appropriately deployed if we had invested time in the necessary pre-planning strategic groundwork. As Ganz (2011a: 20) said: 'making a "theory of change" explicit can help you strategize how to turn the "world as it is", seen clearly, into the world as it "should be".' Once you and your people have surfaced the collective knowledge, done the analysis and developed a theory of change, you're able to develop the necessary tactics to organise and then mobilise your resources to achieve your goals.

Strategic choices when challenging racism directed at refugees

As we were writing this book, the UK was experiencing a surge in racism directed towards asylum seekers. The press has been prefixing the term 'asylum seekers' with 'bogus' for a generation. Some of those on the right of politics have been agitating to 'send them back' for more than a century, but at the time we had a Conservative government who looked determined to fight the election not on their record on the economy, housing or health, but on how much more of a hostile environment they would create for asylum seekers. This included explicitly repudiating international human rights obligations to more effectively 'stop the boats' and repel the so-called 'invasion' of asylum seekers. The Conservatives lost the election, but immediately afterwards, the resentment was exploited by the far-right leading to racist, anti-migrant riots across the UK. As ever, when mainstream politicians play the race card, the street thugs of the far-right are emboldened and are organising attacks on hostels and hotels housing asylum seekers. Meanwhile, communities are becoming increasingly infected by a racist and divisive narrative that blinds people to the steps needed to address the real issues, such as the cost-of-living crisis.

A typical, and entirely understandable, response to a far-right mobilisation is to organise a counter demonstration. It's a familiar tactic, it appears to be doing something, and it shows solidarity, even in the face of physical threats, to asylum seekers. But a more detailed reflection might start with a series of questions:

- Why did the government decide to make hostility to asylum seekers an election issue?
- What did they hope to achieve by doing so?
- Why were many of our people persuaded that asylum seekers are a bigger problem than low rates of pay, a housing crisis and job insecurity?

You might conclude that the then Conservative government wanted to use fear and hatred of asylum seekers as a 'wedge issue' at the election. Making hostility to asylum seekers a key determinant of how people vote was an issue they might have won on in a way they couldn't on the economy, the NHS or the housing crisis. As it turns out, they couldn't even win on this issue, as they were outflanked by Reform UK, who gained from being seen as a party that would be 'tough' on migration. But the result should not distract us from considering whether, if we want to stop politicians launching attacks on asylum seekers, we need to reverse the electoral advantage they hope to gain from it.

When asking why so many of our people are influenced by this narrative, we might think after a generation in which real wages have stagnated or shrunk, where employment has become increasingly precarious, where even rental accommodation is now unaffordable, and when we have entered an unprecedented cost-of-living crisis, that many people in working-class communities are feeling frightened for the future and disempowered. They are hoping for someone to promise to wave a magic wand and solve all their problems. From this you might – or might not –

decide that the key focus for a strategy should not necessarily be physically confronting the fascist agitators, but engagement with the wider community in an attempt to build people's sense of agency. You might then start to look for institutions and networks in your community with whom you could work. It may be that organising with food banks, concerned as they are with food poverty and in daily contact with people experiencing it, are a key partner to start a process of inoculating your community from a narrative that blames asylum seekers for all our country's ills, and consequently dents our ability to address them.

This isn't meant to be a fully formed theory of change for addressing the challenge of anti-asylum-seeker rhetoric in our communities, merely an illustration that when we begin to *think* about the fundamental causes and how to address them, we may get very different answers than when we merely react to the manifestations of a particular problem. A theory of change isn't static – very little that happens in the world is – so it's important to constantly revise and revisit and respond to changing circumstances. This is what your opponents will likely be doing, so to win, we must constantly reflect and rethink our strategy and tactics. We need to be flexible, dynamic and responsive if we are to achieve our goals.

Relational organising and your base

For a social justice movement an essential part of campaigning is remaining credible to its base and to involve that base in strategic discussions and decision making. As we shall see in later chapters, effective leaders don't create followers, or just hand out tasks to be completed. Instead, they work to create increased capacity for action by developing and building relationships and the skills, knowledge and experience of their base. Effective organisers organise in ways that surface the knowledge and creativity of their constituency and enable them to turn the resources they have – including their often underutilised social capital – into the power that's necessary to achieve the goals they want.

Almost every organising theorist talks about 'relationship building' or 'relational organising' as being key to organising success (Alinsky 1972; Ganz 2009b; Han 2014; McAlevey 2016;

Graf 2020). Sometimes we mistakenly think of our numbers of supporters, or worse still, the number of likes we get on social media, as a measure of our power, or at least influence, and while this is by no means unimportant, it's not the same as building strong and sustainable relationships *among* our supporters. These relationships are what holds a movement together, particularly at times of the inevitable periodic setbacks that occur in campaigns. It creates a sense of 'us' and ensures that there are sufficient people willing to undertake the less glamorous tasks without which the movement stops moving. If we connect with people on an individual level – understand how their passions and self-interest connect to the common interest around which we are coalescing – then we are creating an identity, a bond or a 'social glue' which binds us together, carries us through the difficult times when our campaigns face setbacks and takes us beyond a fleeting connection. This relationship building is essential to sustaining the engagement of supporters because it creates a sense of commitment to each other as well as to the issue: it builds solidarity. That collective commitment allows us to act consistently, over a prolonged period, to create the pressure necessary to effect the change we are determined to achieve. Also – and this is an issue we will be covering in more depth in Chapter 7 – by involving a wider pool of people in decision making we are not only increasing our supporters' sense of agency – an understanding that what they think and do is important – but we are drawing upon a wider pool of lived experiences and accumulated knowledge. From this diversity of views, knowledge and experience arise new insights and innovative approaches to problem solving. It also means we are far less likely to make the self-defeating mistake of inadvertently excluding people from different backgrounds and demographics because of toxic and often unquestioned cultural norms that can arise within groups.

Movement building

Why have we not managed to convince more people to join our movement? Is it because there is little confidence in our theory of change? Put simply, do people feel: 'I agree, it's terrible, but honestly, nothing can be done'? If so, perhaps more work needs to be done to develop and communicate a credible vision to achieve some clear and measurable change – and, equally importantly, to ensure the issues that people have are recognised as issues for the community – however defined – rather than merely an aggregation of individual problems.

John Kelly (1998), a leading industrial relations academic and union activist, has used social movement theory to help understand how and why people come together to act to change their experience and treatment in an employment relationship. He says that there are four key processes that bind groups of people together. Firstly, there must be a *sense of injustice*. If people feel, for example, that it's just bad luck that housing has become unaffordable, then they are less likely to do anything about it. If, however, they feel that the housing system has been rigged against them, and that buy-to-let landlords are becoming unjustly enriched at the cost of tenants, they are more likely to do something: even more so if a rip-off landlord, by failing to undertake necessary repairs and maintenance of the property, does not keep their side of the bargain.

Secondly, people need to *attribute blame* to someone or some organisation – by this Kelly means there must be a decision maker whose actions are either creating or sustaining the injustice, someone who has the power to effect the necessary change by choosing to make a different decision. Of course, attributing blame to the right person/organisation is of vital importance in devising campaign tactics (and your theory of change), and it's not always the case that campaigners get this right. Without an understanding of the underlying power dynamics, it's easy to mistake a figurehead as the person who has the power to make the change you require, whereas, in reality, power may lie elsewhere.

A good example of this might be when a local authority reluctantly chooses to make cuts to a service, increases council housing rents or increases the council tax. Residents might be furious at the consequences of the decision, but if the council's budget was restricted, or reduced by central government, to what extent were they the primary decision maker? This does not mean that the local council should be given a free pass, but it might mean that campaigners ask: 'If we want to win, how can we exert pressure on central government to reverse these budget cuts?' This is why Jane McAlevey (2016) in her book *No Shortcuts* talks at length about undertaking a detailed power analysis of allies and adversaries at the start of any campaign. This way you can correctly identify different levers of power and who the people are you need to shift, or target, to achieve your goals.

The third process that binds people together in Kelly's theorisation is *social identification* – the factors or characteristics that mean we identify, and are prepared to act collectively, with others. Most obviously this might be a group of workers working for a particular employer, or in a particular industry, but it could also be people who live on a particular estate, or on estates managed by the same authority. Organisers often draw upon existing social identity to promote group cohesion to move people from self-interest to collective interest, #BlackLivesMatter is an obvious example. But sometimes it is necessary to create a new 'story of us', to literally create a new identity. An example would be in New York City, where there was a Latino migrants centre. People who joined came from all over Latin America; some of them were fleeing left-wing regimes, others fleeing right-wing regimes, and some were simply economic migrants. They were, on the face of it, a group of people who had many points of difference, but they began to organise based on their status as migrants and their relationship to the employment market, where, irrespective of their skills or education, they were all working in low-paid service sector jobs. They soon built a shared sense of identity as 'Latino/Latina migrants' that was more powerful than the issues that separated them, and that carried them through many struggles for economic justice.

The fourth of Kelly's necessary processes concerns the notion of *leadership*. Leadership is not just about formal or positional leaders. In organising theory and practice it also includes informal leaders – Saul Alinsky referred to them as 'grassroots leaders', while Jane McAlevey calls them 'organic leaders'. Getting these grassroots/organic leaders onside is crucial because they can transmit your narrative, and theory of change, because they are known and already trusted in their community – people look up to them and respect them. They are people to whom people listen, they are persuasive and they promote group cohesion and identity – all the characteristics that can pull people together to act collectively. These organic leaders have already built relationships of trust and are thus precisely the people you need on your side in campaigns. However, sometimes, perhaps often, these leaders may not initially be convinced of your campaign, perhaps because they are used to solving their own problems rather than needing to organise with others, or because they might even be in opposition to your 'demands' for any number of reasons. For the same reason that these organic leaders can bring such a benefit to your campaign, if they oppose you, they can be a substantial obstacle to your organising and mobilising efforts. You will then need to figure out if it's possible to persuade them to switch to supporting your cause. Again, this comes down to relationship building, understanding both self and collective interest, attribution of blame, an effective framing of the issues and a credible theory of change. If you can't bring them over, you may want to consider if it's possible to reduce their influence over the community. One way of doing this is to find and develop new leaders within the community. A famous example of this would be the Montgomery Improvement Association, founded in 1955 by the trade unionist and race equality activist E.D. Nixon. He was concerned that the local clergy were too compromised to lead a consistent opposition to segregation, and understood that, to win, they would need to develop new leadership among the majority Black churches. He sought to develop the leadership of a young pastor – Martin Luther King – who was unknown at the time. There are many inspirational leaders in our communities – our job as organisers is to find them.

Organisers are always on the lookout for informal leaders *within* groups who have the ear and trust of their local communities, or fellow workers, as these people are often best placed to articulate, or frame, issues to promote a sense of injustice around the issues of concern. Kelly (1998: 26) says: 'Injustice (or illegitimacy) frames are critical for collective organisation and action because they begin the process of detaching subordinate group members from loyalty to ruling groups (or in Marx's 1847 terms, converting a class-in-itself into a class-for-itself)'.

In other words, issues benefit from being framed in a way where both the injustice is clearly articulated and the attribution of blame is such that it is understood that someone – some human agency – is responsible. Not only does this focus existing anger, but it also helps build that necessary 'story of us' that contributes to a realisation that 'if we stick together, we can force things to change'.

Who are your people, and what's the structure you are hoping to organise?

When seeking to effect change, we often begin by looking for people who feel the same way as ourselves. This is clearly a useful place to start, but if you don't move beyond organising your base and don't seek to engage people within a 'structure', then you are in danger of speaking to yourselves or becoming a well-organised, vocal, minority that is largely ignored or ineffective. An innovation in organising thinking is the distinction Jane McAlevey makes between organising your base and organising a *structure*. Jane had decades of organising experience, particularly in the trade union movement, and she argues that by organising in a structure – for example, a workplace, an electoral district, or a housing estate – you can accurately measure the level of power you have built for your cause. Within a structure you know how many people there are: think of your workplace, where you know there are, say, 50 workers. You can then track how many are with you, how many are ambivalent and how many are hostile to your demands for change. This way you can figure how much, or how little, power is at your disposal which, almost by definition, also tells you what work is still necessary to build an overwhelming majority in support of your cause. Remember that power is always fluid, you can build it, it can occasionally drop into your lap, it can be taken from you, and you can lose it.

A great example of this distinction between your base and organising a structure is from a direct-action campaign to stop blood sports, and, specifically, the Holcombe Hunt in Lancashire, England. For several years, as members of the Hunt Saboteurs Association (HSA), we had found as many people as we could who opposed hunting, but these were mainly people living in the cities or urban areas where many hunt saboteurs lived. Activities included going into the countryside to seek to disrupt the hunt, to ensure they were unable to kill wildlife. Whistles, hunting horns and rattles were used to distract the hounds, and to issue mis-directions to the hounds – shouting 'leave it' when they were onto a quarry, and 'on, on, on' when they were heading in the wrong direction. Inevitably, this led to conflict with hunt supporters, some of whom were intensely violent. After a while hunt members and followers got to recognise hunt saboteurs' vehicles and would often slash tyres on their vehicles or smash windows to intimidate. It's not surprising that the hunt saboteur group began to think of the countryside, and particularly the hunting territory, as hostile. As a group we unconsciously and naively assumed that almost everyone who lived there was pro-hunt – until a particular incident.

On one occasion, a hunt saboteur vehicle had been parked while group members entered the field to disrupt the hunt and on return to the van found that all the tyres had been slashed. Fortunately, there was a friendly garage that came out with four part-worn tyres and got us mobile again. While our group was waiting – wet and bedraggled – a woman came out of her house to asked what had happened. We learnt from her that she didn't like the hunt, and that many of her neighbours in the area were of the same opinion. She talked of how they often chased across land where they had no permission, and the constant fear that the hounds would chase and kill a domestic pet. She was, in short, 'one of us' – in opposition to the hunt. This led our group to radically rethink what it meant for our campaign if there were people hostile to the hunt amid the hunt's territory. Discussions led to thinking about how to use this to our group's advantage. If we could organise the anti-hunt supporters in the countryside, maybe we could change the power balance in the campaign against blood sports.

A great triumph was in the small village of Ainsworth, halfway between the towns of Bury and Bolton in north-west England. It was a very traditional meet for the hunt, where they met regularly during the hunting season. We decided to test our theory of taking control of their territory. The week before the hunt's meet, our group leafleted every door in the village of about 500 homes. We asked people to join us to 'occupy' the pub forecourt where the hunt planned to meet on the Saturday morning. We were expecting a violent reaction from the hunt supporters when we arrived, but instead there was already a large crowd of people, who were very supportive, along with plenty of police officers. There was no sign of the hunt and we learnt that they had tried to meet about a mile away but were soon spotted and eventually gave up and went home – the hounds having never left the hound vehicle. Suddenly, our hunt saboteur group was in a position where we could mobilise local opposition to cancel the day's hunting. This was the ultimate prize: no hunting meant no wildlife killed and the hunt being weakened as an institution.

Local supporters were ecstatic, and a short rally on the pub car park confirmed that people would come out again. Up until this point the police had always been hostile to us, seeing hunt saboteurs as outside 'agitators' whose very presence could be construed as 'breaching the peace' because we were interfering with the perfectly legal 'sport' of killing wild animals. But their reaction was very different towards this local population. Whatever their personal views on hunting, they recognised that this was a community that had come out to say 'no'. Now there was a switch – the hunt had suddenly become the 'outsiders' disrupting the peace of the village community.

Naturally, the group sought to repeat this success, and equally understandably, the hunt responded to the new approach by evolving their tactics. They stopped publicising where they would meet each week, so activists and supporters couldn't pre-leaflet the nearest homes. The group had to rely on one supporter who had joined the hunt to get that information. However, the hunt soon became aware that we had an 'insider' and that we were getting advance notification so they began to tell only trusted members where they would be. Their hunting territory spanned a vast area, and we knew that if we kept up the pressure, we could limit their activity. But we needed to find where they were going to be, even though they were not even telling their members! We needed a new strategy and a change of tactics.

The group's new strategy was to leaflet villages and settlements across the territory seeking to build a database of pro-wildlife (anti-hunt) supporters, and to our initial surprise we soon constructed a significant web of 'hunt watchers'. These were people in local communities in the villages within the hunt's territory who would let us know when the hunt was heading towards a particular meet. Given that the hunt would start to arrive about two hours before they began hunting, with good luck and great planning we often found ourselves arriving at the meet before they started – even though, just a couple of hours earlier, we had no idea where they would be hunting.

This occurred in the days before mobile phones or email, so our group had a complex system of using telephone boxes to relay information to the saboteurs in the field from a central 'home base' telephone number known to all our supporters. The result was that we could find the hunt, and disrupt their attempts to kill wildlife, even if they had not told their own paid-up members where they were going to be on that date. Consequently, the hunt supporters were now more aggressive than ever, and we needed to travel in large groups because their threats were becoming ever more violent. Indeed, our infiltrators were sharing discussions of supporters debating whether to hospitalise anti-hunt supporters as a 'lesson' to the rest. This merely confirmed that our group had them under enormous pressure and the power had shifted in the hunt saboteurs' favour. Of course, the system didn't always work perfectly, it was based on supporters tracking the direction of horseboxes that travelled early on a hunt day, and on one occasion, we ended up being directed to a particular gathering which turned out to be a gymkhana!

In summary, rather than focussing on organising already existing supporters, we had begun to organise the people living in the territory or communities within which the hunt was operating. This was transformative. Not only did we find incredible new resources – a key indication that we were undertaking transformative organising – but we also undermined the narrative of the hunt being the 'norm' and hunt saboteurs being the outsiders and, instead, replaced it with the hunt being the 'outsiders'. The theory of change was to organise within the hunt's territory to challenge the dominant narrative that it was normal, traditional or cultural to kill animals for fun; and to build an active local resistance to their unfettered permission to kill at will. It was about rebalancing power.

As an aside, at the time there were two national anti-blood sports organisations. There was the well-financed League Against Cruel Sports that didn't participate in direct-action campaigns.

It had a significant number of employed staff, in London, and a reputation for being a bit 'old fashioned' and 'stuck in its ways', although in reality it was doing a vast amount of unseen work. Then there was the direct-action group to which our group was affiliated, the Hunt Saboteurs Association, which had no offices, no staff and was in many ways the cutting edge of the anti-blood sports movement. Despite the success of this new organising approach – combining direct action and community organising – there was less support and even opposition from within the local Hunt Saboteurs Association groups, some of whom were unenthusiastic in embracing this new approach of reaching out and including non-saboteurs in the campaign strategy. Some saboteurs, who were used to the particularly high-adrenaline approach of confrontation with the hunt, found the systemic organising work of leafleting doors, or even celebrating with locals when a day's hunting was abandoned, quite tame in comparison.

Meanwhile the League Against Cruel Sports could see the potential and political capital for involving the wider public and, just 12 months later, the League launched a very similar initiative down in the south-west of England working to organise those residents in the territory of the various stag hunts to build resistance. It had repurposed our initiative to an area where traditional support for the barbarism of stag hunting was being eroded. This, combined with their long-term strategy of buying up the hunting rights over land as it came up for sale and offering free legal representation for people whose pets had been killed, or whose land had been trespassed, meant the League was able to squeeze the hunts from a number of different angles. Its multifaceted, if perhaps less exciting approach, undoubtedly reinforced the work that the direct-action campaigns were doing and eventually led to the long overdue legislation that officially banned hunting with hounds, although it has so many loopholes that most hunts carried on regardless.

A campaign around equal pay: how a theory of change can result in success

To further illustrate the value of a theory of change, we will also draw upon a couple of examples of trade unions seeking to address unlawful unequal pay suffered by their members: one in a trade union where there was no effective theory of change, which resulted in failure, and a second where theory of change resulted in success. In the first case, the union represented workers in management grades, and one of the key employers was a well-known telecoms company where the senior management team bought into 'free market' beliefs about individualism and performance-related pay that they mistakenly believed incentivised workers. The company had moved away from the standard public-sector approach to pay whereby a particular job attracts a standardised rate of pay following a formal job evaluation. Instead, management introduced 'pay bands' that were so broad that someone at the top of a pay band could be paid double the amount of someone at the bottom. In other anomalies, someone could be paid less than the person they managed. These anomalies were seen as a benefit of the new pay structure because, coupled with a performance-related pay structure, it was thought it would encourage staff to work harder. It gave managers the freedom to pay individuals in their team whatever 'felt right', which was a recipe for favouritism, cronyism and unlawful discrimination.

You might think that because the UK has had equal pay legislation since 1970, which prohibits sex discrimination between employees in respect of their contractual pay and their terms and conditions of employment, there would, by now, be no systemic unequal pay. The law requires that men and women get paid the same for doing the same job, different jobs that are objectively of equivalent value and different jobs that are graded as equivalent under a job evaluation scheme. But having a right in law isn't the same as being able to exercise that right, and equal pay cases are complex and the legal route tends to individualise the problem – despite some recent excellent collective successes (for one example see BBC 2022).

The UK had guidelines produced by the government-appointed Equal Opportunities Commission – later reconstituted as the Equality and Human Rights Commission – on how to create pay structures that reduce the risk of creating unlawful gender pay inequality. However, the pay structure at the telecoms firm at the time – and to be fair across most of the FTSE 100 companies to this day – could almost have been designed as the exact opposite of that advice. In the case we are discussing this included overly long and overlapping pay bands, with huge amounts of arbitrary power given to local managers to set individual pay.

The union had plenty of evidence, in the case of one large employer, that women members were being paid substantially less than male colleagues for doing the same job. Indeed, they were often approached by female members asking for advice. The problem was systemic, and to have rectified this and paid women the same as men for doing the same job would have required a significant investment of cash, which the company was unwilling to commit. However, the employer did agree every year to 'hold back' a percentage of the annual pay award to redistribute to particularly extreme cases, referred to as 'outliers', where individual women's pay was objectively and grossly unjustified – in effect a slush fund to pay off women who might otherwise have considered taking their case to an employment tribunal. The union's research suggested that it wasn't individualised acts of discrimination at work – indeed on average, women were judged by their managers to score marginally higher on performance than their male colleagues – but was the result of a pay structure that was simply out of control. No one had any clear idea why a specific person was paid what they were paid. It was the result of sometimes decades of arbitrary decisions by their manager – or series of managers. It didn't help that women were often appointed into management grades from lower-paid roles than men, and an unjustified assumption that a fair starting rate of pay was 'a little bit higher than your pay in your last job' – acted to reinforce gender pay discrimination.

The union had, as many unions that represent managers have, limited industrial power because, at the time, managers didn't generally think of themselves as 'industrial militants' and had some difficulty imagining themselves standing on a picket line. As such, the traditional 'industrial dispute' approach was dismissed by the union as not an option. Women suffering unlawful unequal pay could, of course, always take an industrial tribunal case and seek to have their pay discrepancy addressed. The problem was that this is an individualised approach, and an individual woman must identify a 'comparator' – a man doing either the same job or one of equal value who is paid more – and be able to argue that her work is of equal value as her comparator's. Finding a comparator is not always easy, particularly when, at the time, many employers viewed it as a disciplinary offence for an employee to discuss their pay with colleagues. A woman submitting a claim would also know that the only defence the employer has would be to say 'oh, but you are not as good at the job as the men'. In other words, to advance an equal pay claim is often to invite your professionalism and competency to be brought into question. And there was another factor. Many women believed – not unrealistically – that taking their employer to tribunal would see them labelled as 'trouble', and the phrase 'career suicide' was regularly used in the same sentence as 'employment tribunal'. The union had a brilliant *analysis* of the problem, and indeed regularly made informative presentations on it to employer representatives, but they had no theory of change or strategy to overcome it.

The second example, where there *was* a theory of change, was a union also representing management grade members, this time at a leading transport company – an organisation that was quasi public sector but had a pay structure inherited from a failed company that had once been a part of a nationalised industry, and which had since been privatised. The industry is very male-dominated, and the union's members were overwhelmingly male. Women were under-represented within the union's structures at that time. The company's pay structure was very similar to that of the telecoms company we've just discussed, but with the added complication of using 'forced ranking' within the performance-related pay. In performance-related pay, you first rank people's performance: for example, as outstanding, very good, good, acceptable, or needs improvement. Most performance-related pay systems allow the manager to simply make a judgement and award a grade to each member of staff based on their ability or performance.

With forced ranking there is an expectation that a certain percentage of staff will be at the very high end of performance, most will be in the middle, and another predetermined percentage will be in 'needs improvement'. The problem is that if a manager has a team of five excellent members, they cannot score each of them 'outstanding'. Instead, they would probably have to allocate one to each of the five categories – even though this has no relation to their actual performance. A worker's annual pay award was therefore decided by arbitrary placement within one of these categories. The union regularly represented members appealing their performance ranking, including examples where their manager had stated: 'there is nothing wrong with your performance, but I am forced to place someone in the category of "needs improvement"', but these weren't often successful.

Following pay negotiations in 2012, the union worked hard to build a campaign for a 'yes' vote in a ballot for industrial action, and to see the forced ranking system abandoned. The union used the evidence of gender pay inequality as a way of illustrating how arbitrary the outcomes of the pay structure were – 'you are not paid for what you do, but for who you are', and argued convincingly that men as well as women were disadvantaged by an arbitrary pay structure. Given that this industry was predominantly male, the union had recognised that if it wanted to make progress on gender pay equality, then it needed a way to frame the issue in a way that made it a *workplace* issue, rather than a *women's* issue. The ballot for industrial action came back, with a 'yes' vote for 'action short of strike', which gave the union the ability to call a work to rule, overtime ban and so on, but a 'no' to strike action; a muddled result that meant there was no realistic chance of forcing the employer's hand through industrial action. Any action would be 'tokenistic' as it simply could not create the power necessary to effect change. Despite the defeat at the strike ballot – which wasn't entirely surprising given this was a management group and, as we have said, many managers find it hard to imagine themselves out on the picket line – the employer's senior management team were shocked that the majority of their managers who had voted had voted to take industrial action.

However, the union had a problem; it needed a theory of change to win on gender pay inequality and having decided not to use the mandate for action short of strike action, it needed a win to avoid demoralising its activist base and its most loyal members. From the result of the ballot, it knew that industrial action in the form of 'action short of strike' was not going to be successful. The union had to figure out a way to force the employer to say 'yes' when they wanted to say 'no'. It did this through a power analysis of the issue of unlawful unequal pay. They knew that their members – now including the men – were supportive of an initiative around this, and they knew that the employer was nervous about losing the loyalty of its management – the next stage was to figure out how to change the power dynamic.

The union realised that the employer understood that it would take millions of pounds to fix the problem of bringing women's pay up to equal that of men, and to introduce a pay structure that was objective. Meanwhile, while rare, equal pay cases can generate huge liability. A woman who wins a claim can be entitled to up to six years' back pay, and interest on the unpaid wages. Yet, despite this huge legal liability, only a tiny trickle of legal cases were brought by women employees each year. As is common across many leading FTSE 100 companies in such cases, the employer's approach was to refuse to admit liability but contain the problem by responding to the individual cases by paying off the women with a small pay increase accompanied by a confidentiality agreement or 'gagging clause'. However, the union, at that time, had a significant commitment to advancing the equality agenda. It wasn't just that gender pay equality was a 'nice to have' for union members, it was a mission of the union to rectify the problem. The union worked backwards from thinking about how the employer could get away with ignoring its statutory responsibility and thought about each link in the chain and whether it could do something that would change the balance of power, which in this case meant the balance of cost. The union recognised that to win it had to make doing nothing about gender pay inequality more expensive than addressing the problem. The plan that emerged was very simple.

The union anonymously surveyed all its members after the implementation of the pay round, and asked them their gender, their job title, their grade, their pay, their performance rating and their pay award. The results took a couple of weeks to analyse, then the union called a meeting with the employer and presented the findings. On average women within the management grades were judged to have marginally outperformed their male colleagues – they got a higher performance rating – but, despite this, they got lower wage increases. It was found that, on average, women within each of the four management grades were 20 per cent worse off than their male colleagues. Therefore, the union concluded, the employer had an unlawful, horizontal, gender pay gap – women were getting paid less for the same graded work as men. The pay system generated arbitrary, unjustifiable and unlawful outcomes. Yet the response from the Director of Industrial Relations was short and terse: 'That's just your survey, and we don't recognise those figures.' This response would have been more convincing if the employer had agreed to release its own analysis of gender pay differentials but, not surprisingly, they wouldn't.

The union had also considered the employer's potential response and knew that the most common comeback from employers facing trade union negotiators seeking to address gender pay inequality is to suggest that they would have to reduce the pay of men to make them equal with women. The reps were inoculated in advance of negotiations that this was bound to be raised at some point by the employer, and when it was, it was met with derision. This data gathering was, however, helping the union build its theory of change. A newsletter was produced informing members of the findings of the first survey and then informing them the union was moving into more detailed surveys of *individual* job roles. The plan was to submit multiple employment tribunal cases for both women and men who were being paid less than counterparts of the other sex. This survey was designed not to be anonymous, and members were asked to indicate that they would be happy to be *either* a claimant if they were underpaid, *or* a comparator if they were paid more than their colleagues for doing the same work. This was very important, as one of the biggest challenges for any equal pay claim is to identify a comparator – someone doing work of equal value who is of the other sex and who is paid more.

The first results came back, and it was evident that women and men doing the same job were being paid substantially different salaries. In more than one case, the highest-paid man was paid twice as much as the lowest-paid woman for doing the same job. There was a substantial take-up of the union's offer to pursue equal pay claims on members' behalf – the majority of course from women, but also a significant number from men – something the union viewed as a huge advantage given this was a male-dominated workforce. The union adopted what was termed 'strategic litigation' – using the law to create collective change, rather than winning individual compensation on a case-by-case basis. The union informed the employer that unless it had an immediate commitment to addressing gender pay inequality – and the wider arbitrary nature of the pay structure – it would be submitting a minimum of 30 equal pay claims per month as part of a rolling programme of analysing each role within the company. The union didn't get a response from senior managers *until* the third tranche of 30 claims was lodged. The union's theory of change was that once its strategy started to affect the company's finances then the power dynamic would shift, and it was likely that the employer would want to negotiate. At this point the big questions were: what was the union's ask, and what might it need to 'give' in the negotiation process?

Let's start with the 'ask'. The union knew that designing a pay structure would take two years of detailed negotiations, and it needed to have an agreement, in principle, in the short term to frame the context of those negotiations. The union sought a commitment that the employer would work with them to develop a pay structure that was consistent with the Equalities and Human Rights Commission's guidance on eliminating 'high risk' elements of a pay structure. This included minimising arbitrary decisions, avoiding long overlapping pay scales, having a consistent and justifiable policy on starting pay on appointment/promotion, and so on. This was a great 'ask' because it was clear and simple, every member could understand the union wanted a new pay structure that met an external standard of fairness. Yet it also sounded like a very small ask: after all the union was merely asking the employer to adopt a pay structure that was lawful and consistent with good practice. You would have to understand the complexities of equal pay quite well to recognise just how big an ask this really was: it appeared that the employer did not.

As to the 'give', this was simple: the union would agree that it would stop proactively harvesting employment tribunal claims if the employer agreed to cooperate. It knew it had opened a Pandora's box and that it would be difficult to put the lid back on this issue. The more momentum the initiative gained, the harder it would become to reel it in, so the employer was under a time pressure and the power dynamic was shifting. It took three months and over 100 employment tribunal claims lodged before the employer collapsed and agreed to renegotiate the pay structure in exchange for the union halting the harvesting of legal claims.

As is so often the case when a union wins a negotiating demand, there then follows a certain degree of massaging of the employer's collective ego. It is a fundamental of negotiations, that when you win, you are gracious, and provide a route for the employer to save face. The narrative inevitably changes, and the union and the employer were now 'working together' to create a fair pay structure. An oddity of this enforced 'partnership' working was that there was joint training of both reps and human resources (HR) staff about equal pay. For the trade union reps delivering the training to the HR professionals, there was an important insight when, time and again, the HR professionals used language very similar to trade union reps to say: 'we know this is wrong, we have been saying it for years, but no one has been listening.'

Irrespective of the tone of communications, managers across the company knew that their union had forced the company to say 'yes' when it wanted to say 'no'. There was increased pride among union members, which resulted in new members and reps coming on board, as well as a culture change in negotiations across the company. What's interesting is that this approach to gender pay inequality would work across most of the FTSE 100 companies' management grades where very few companies have objective pay structures, where gender pay gap reporting illustrates substantial gender pay inequality, and where employers unanimously insist, without producing convincing evidence to support it, that the gap is wholly related to vertical inequality – where women are in lower-value roles – rather than horizontal inequality with women and men doing work of equal value but women being paid less.

To summarise then, a theory of change makes it far easier to devise an appropriate strategy and relevant tactics. Spending time at the start of any campaign thinking through the questions we have discussed here will help you be more effective in marshalling your resources in the right direction.

Before we close this chapter, we should say that things are a little more complicated than perhaps we have implied. Another great theorist is Myles Horton, introduced in Chapter 1 as the founder of and inspiration for the Highlander Folk School. Myles Horton and Saul Alinsky very publicly, and fraternally, disagreed about the art of the possible. Saul Alinsky, the master tactician would often find ways to 'win' either by disorganising his opponent, or through being outrageously opportunistic (or should that say 'tactically agile'?) and, to a certain degree, because he was very careful only to ask for what his power analysis revealed as being achievable. Myles Horton was not afraid of losing (in the short term):

> If you don't push to the place where you might fail, you've missed a wonderful opportunity to learn to struggle, to think big and challenge the status quo, and also how to learn to deal with failure. If you analyze them, you can learn more in some ways from failures than from successes. Now, all this is predicated on learning from analyzing your experience. An experience you don't learn from is just a happening. (Horton, Kohl and Kohl 1990: 176)

But Horton's most important insight into organising was this: when you start organising, you begin to build power, possibly not a lot at first, but every step changes the power dynamic, and your vision of what is achievable should be constantly evolving. As you organise, you change not only what is achievable in the short term, but also what change is believable in the eyes of your supporters in the longer term. In a famous phrase, he said: 'you make the road by walking'. In other words, while it's important to undertake power analysis and develop a theory of change (we would not have written a chapter about it if it wasn't) it's important that you don't let the cold reality of the limitations of what can realistically be achieved *today* frame your dreams of what can be possible in the future. Equally, we should not confuse our vision of our destination, with the steps we need to take to get there.

> One of the dynamic aspects of a social movement as opposed to an organization is that quite often in the

latter, you'll bargain down to make concessions in order to survive. You have a limited goal, and you might say, 'Well, we want to get ten street lights', and you'll get together and figure that you won't get ten, but you probably can get five. So you decide to tell them you want ten in order to get five. In a social movement, the demands escalate, because your success encourages and emboldens you to demand more. (Horton, Kohl and Kohl 1990: 115)

What we can take from this is that, as changemakers in the social justice movement, irrespective about the limitations of our immediate demands, we should be bold enough to think about how we escalate our demands as we grow in power.

Finally, we should say something about inertia. In any organisation there is often a resistance to change. In campaign organisations a cultural change is particularly difficult. People may have become active because they felt comfortable with the existing approaches. In the previous examples, it was hard to convince people who were genuinely committed to winning change of the need to change strategy. Jeremy Waddington's detailed and extensive research into the 'turn to organising' within the public sector union Unison illustrates how reluctant players can be to change their behaviour even when they are convinced of the need for change (see Waddington and Kerr 2015). Any realistic theory of change, as well as analysing the external environment, will need to address the need for internal changes in culture and practice to deliver to the plan. Perhaps one of the hardest challenges for changemakers is that when an existing strategy is failing, unless there is a practice of reflection and evaluation, there is often a continuing commitment to a strategy that is failing. This is sometimes known as the 'sunk cost fallacy'. It's a bias that is particularly common with committed activists who fear any admission that the strategy is not working is the equivalent of abandoning the objective of winning. Sometimes to achieve our objective we have to acknowledge that the strategy we have adopted is not working, analyse why it is not working, and then consider what we can do differently to overcome the obstacles.

How to develop a theory of change

Think about an issue in which you are involved in terms of the following questions:

- Is the demand for change led by an individual organisation or a movement?

- How clear is everyone about the change you want?

- Where does your target get their power from (power can be multifaceted, and can come from legitimacy, as well as force or wealth)?

- What resources – people, institutions, narratives – are available to your side to build power, and how could you increase these resources?

- What relationships are you nurturing that will make your campaign sustainable?

- What power dynamics must you disrupt to succeed?

- What does your target care about, such that if you could realistically threaten to influence the outcome on that issue, it might make them change their course of action?

3

Without power we have no movement

Understanding power and how to leverage it is vital when considering how to effect change, because, as many key changemakers have noted, power is seldom conceded without a struggle. Change most often happens when the balance of power shifts, yet analysing the power dynamics between us and our opponents is seldom the starting point of many campaigns. There's a natural tendency to leap in and get started, eager to challenge the injustice, but vital time, energy and resource can be lost if we lack an understanding of where power lies, different forms of power and how we might utilise these to our advantage. Power analysis is part of the process of developing a theory of change, as a good understanding of power will inform the strategy adopted in a campaign. But what do we mean by power and how does it change?

Firstly, it's useful to understand that power isn't a 'thing': it doesn't exist outside of relationships – it *is* a relationship. Like all relationships, power relationships are complicated: power can be difficult to understand, it can be both positive and/or negative, it can be authoritative and controlling, but it can also be liberating. It is dialectical and changeable – it's all these things (and more) and dealing with it can be messy. Despite this, if we accept the power deficit model of change then we need to engage with and harness our collective power if we are to win. A starting point for social movement activists is to understand what power we can build and draw upon through our collective strength and how we can reduce the power of our opponents. A simple, but well-known definition of power is that advanced by Martin Luther King when he said power was the ability to get someone to say 'yes' when they would rather say 'no'. Robert Dhal, theorist on the concept of power, describes it this way: 'A has the power over B to the extent that he [sic] can get B to do something that B would not otherwise do' (quoted in Lukes 2005: 16). The question is: how and why does this happen – how does A acquire power over B, and how can circumstances change to shift this balance of power?

Power operates through the ways in which society is structured as well as through the conscious actions of powerful individuals or organisations. As these authors note: 'power will always exist in a complex contingent tension between a capacity to extend the freedom of some to achieve something or other and an ability to restrict the freedoms of others in doing something or other' (Clegg, Courpasson and Philips 2010: 191). Sometimes power is acquired or inherited through positions of influence, sometimes it's gained by the acquisition of money, or other resources, and access to this power puts people in a position of domination over others. Historical, social, cultural, economic and political circumstances will contribute to whether you are 'A' or 'B' – although, of course, power positions aren't fixed, as relationships are apt to change depending on circumstance. For example, you can be subject to power from above, while still exercising power over others – a middle manager being an obvious example.

Sometimes power is exercised in such a way that it isn't always recognised by the powerless. For example, Steven Lukes (2005: 1) says that 'power is most effective when it's least observable', by which he means that the powerful are able to control or rule in ways that are disabling to those who are being 'controlled'. The powerful can sometimes obscure their authority and influence and create the impression that the way things are is just the 'natural order of things', and as a result people are sometimes unaware that they are being manipulated, oppressed or exploited – they know things are bad, but they don't feel that it is someone's fault. They may even conspire against their own interests. This is one explanation of why people don't act when their own interests are not met. This inability to challenge power may arise from a lack of confidence, a fear of negative consequences, or not having access to alternative ideological frames that can provide an understanding of the nature of exploitation. Without a sense of injustice, of abuse of power, which is the same thing, there is little incentive to act to change the balance of power. Understanding *ideological* power, then, is often an important first step for changemakers.

One source of ideological power can be found in popular narratives and discourse that are transmitted through social networks within society. This type of power is often in the hands of those that have control of media (in its broadest sense) or information, who can instil certain ideas of what are accepted ways of being – or a 'natural order' – which in turn creates societal norms that act to constrain individuals with dissenting views from speaking out or challenging accepted opinions or behaviours. While this ideological power is exercised at a societal level, it can also be detected within small campaign organisations where a fear of dissent creates what has been described as 'group think'.

Paul Edwards (2006) in his article titled 'Power and ideology in the workplace' explains that workers, as well as bosses, society, the state and media, also produce ideologies or sets of beliefs that both express and reinforce a particular set of power relations. These will often contradict each other, but they create 'frames of reference' that provide us with ways of thinking about the world. They're often taken-for-granted understandings of the way we think things are or should be. For example, many workers have accepted managers' 'right to manage' and this therefore constrains their ability to challenge their exploitation. Union stewards, however, may draw upon 'collective solidarity' and 'fairness' among *their* frames of reference to build power in the workplace. Ideology can therefore be a formidable tool for those wanting to control or maintain their power, but on the other hand, it can be enabling for workers (or others) to initiate change in the power dynamic, if an alternative frame of reference gains currency among the constituency you are organising.

Ideological power – much more than direct coercive power – can have a strong effect in that it suggests that the current situation is 'natural' or unchangeable (or both) and therefore prevents people from even trying to challenge those in power. It's because of its subtler nature that individuals or communities may not fully realise how or in what ways they are controlled and prevented from acting in their own interests. Antonio Gramsci – a key Marxist thinker – has written about how ideology, or – to use his term – 'hegemony', is the way that class rule has largely been secured by consent rather than force. Perhaps there is an inbuilt bias that suggests that the world as it is, is the natural order. If you can reinforce this through a near monopoly over the ideological apparatus, for example through the control of education or the media, you are able to instil in most people an acceptance of a particular social or political order. Then acceptance rather than rebellion is the more likely course of action.

Gramsci (1971) says that 'it's only in times of crisis, when control through such hegemonic structures fails, that power is exercised directly, and forcefully in order to restore control' (Holgate 2021: 23).

If dominant ideology is a problem ordinarily, it's even greater in times of crisis. Marxists have always argued that racism is a deliberate tool used by the ruling class to divide and rule workers: a process of 'othering' that divides worker from worker and prevents them acting collectively to challenge their oppression. In the UK today we see that traditional, naked, racism is less effective than it was a generation or two ago, except perhaps against Gypsy Roma and Traveller communities, but that it resurfaces as hostility to Muslims, who are constantly dehumanised in the press, or to asylum seekers and refugees, who are systematically portrayed as 'bogus'. These narratives directly damage the lives of those dehumanised by them, but they also prevent people with common problems and aspirations 'seeing themselves in the other' and coming together to build power to address their shared problems.

The need to challenge dominant ideologies is one reason why political education – perhaps better termed political literacy – is an essential tool for organisers. It's important that people in communities are not only aware of the power of ideology exercised by their opponents, but are able to create, share and discuss alternative value frames that create the ideological space in which we can build alternative sources of power. But stepping outside of dominant ideology and societal norms can, at times, be uncomfortable and can risk ostracisation from colleagues or peers; indeed, this is an example of the power of dominant ideologies.

Dominant ideologies can be pervasive, but they can also be shallow. It might be that something is 'common sense', and 'everyone knows that'. Yet these ideologies are often built on sand, and while people in our community might accept a racist characterisation of a section of our community, they are equally likely to acknowledge that people they know from that group 'are not like that'. As organisers, we need to make people feel secure and have the confidence to hold differing opinions from the dominant ideology and to be able to challenge that dominant ideology or group think. This is why education and learning spaces are central to effective organising. When workers or community campaigners create the opportunities for discussion and reflection, they can challenge the dominant narrative by encouraging people to draw upon their own lived experiences to create counter-narratives that are shared with their peers. This process of generating counter-narratives can also be provoked by action, including street theatre that parodies, or ridicules the dominant narratives.

Challenging dominant narratives: the society of the spectacle

In 1957, an obscure group of avant-garde artists, intellectuals and political theorists formed what became known as the Situationist International. In the late 1960s they produced two publications that are relevant to us: *The Society of the Spectacle* by Guy Debord and *The Revolution of Everyday Life* by Raoul Vaneigem. While they claimed to be Marxists, their work owed more to the artistic movements of surrealism and Dada than it did to more traditional sources. One of their central theses was that everyday life was a fiction, a 'spectacle' generated by mass media and what Gramsci would have called 'capitalism's hegemonic superstructure' to keep us consuming, and to keep us alienated from our true sense of who we are. These writers came to believe – in a somewhat elitist manner – that their role was to jolt the rest of us out of our sleepwalking and provoke opportunities for us to see life as it really was. This was known as the 'construction of situations' but might be more aptly described as the 'deconstruction of the spectacle'. An early example was when members of the situationists ambushed a live broadcast from Notre-Dame Cathedral in Paris. One of their number dressed as a monk, approached the rostrum, and began to give an earnest sermon, broadcast live, on the realisation that God had died and that the Church was involved in a 'diversion of our living strength toward an empty heaven'. It took some time before the authorities realised what was happening and a near riot ensued. The action, despite being perceived as shockingly disrespectful and silly, sparked a national debate in France.

The architects – or at least the promoters – of punk rock were heavily influenced by Situationist ideas. Malcolm McLaren's promotion of the Sex Pistols was an example in point. From the allegedly 'shocking' scenes on the TV programme, *The Bill Grundy Show*, where they reportedly acted like 'foul-mouthed yobs', to the deliberate breach of copyright for the cover of their 'Holidays in the Sun' single, which got more advertising value in the column inches for their 'flagrant breach of copyright' than it cost to settle the non-dispute. Most 'shockingly', after losing their lead singer, they recruited long-term fugitive and notorious train robber Ronnie Biggs to perform a deliberately offensive song. The song, now long forgotten, and utterly devoid of merit, reached number 7 in the charts.

This form of provocative 'action' is worth a little bit more exploration. Closely associated with the construction of situations is the concept of 'propaganda by deed'. This was originally an anarchist concept where 19th-century anarchists believed that if they were able to assassinate the occasional tyrant then this would initiate a revolution in which the masses would be encouraged to rise up and finish the job. It was a false hypothesis; nonetheless, the idea of a form of direct action that both chips away at the problem and influences the way the public feel about the issues, has grown, particularly after the examples of Mahatma Gandhi and Martin Luther King created a new and rich tradition of non-violent direct action. The Suffragettes were another example, and many other causes have benefited from this approach. In such actions the primary target of the protest is not the decision maker with the power to effect change, but the public, with the aim of provoking them to think about an issue to which they've previously not paid much attention, or about which they have been neutral. The Suffragettes' acts of sabotage could be seen in this tradition, as could their hunger strikes when they were convicted.

A more recent example would be the time in 1998, that Peter Tatchell and the LGBTQ+ group OutRage! occupied the pulpit and chanted gay rights slogans when the UK's Archbishop of Canterbury began to deliver an Easter sermon in Canterbury Cathedral. They were protesting about the Church's opposition to single-sex partnerships and 'gay marriage', and its refusal to support equal rights for the LGBTQ+ community. There was headline news coverage throughout the Easter weekend. The thing about these types of protests, as adopted by progressive movements, is that to be successful they must be non-threatening and, where possible, a lot of fun. There is normally some modest risk of arrest, but seldom any prosecution as there's little public interest in punishing those involved and even if there is a prosecution, it tends to be for the most minor public order offences.

In this case Peter Tatchell alone was charged with 'indecent behaviour in church', a previously unheard-of offence under the Ecclesiastical Courts Jurisdiction Act 1860. The prosecution alleged that any protest in a church was, by definition, 'indecent'. This gave rise to a vigorous defence campaign that saw more than 700 lawyers, professors, clergy, and human rights activists sign a petition calling for the Act to be repealed. This included support from a Church of England bishop, Bishop Holloway, who, while not enthusiastic about OutRage!'s tactics, recognised that they were in the tradition of non-violent, disruptive protest that had contributed significantly to social justice reforms in the past. Bishop Holloway was provoked to speak out by the prosecution of Tatchell, whom he saw as a non-violent, if irritating and irreverent, protester. Bishop Holloway's decision to speak up was the start of a process through which Church of England officials began to speak about the injustice of homophobia, a process that is on-going. Peter Tatchell, after successfully garnering acres of press coverage for gay rights, was eventually convicted and ordered to pay a fine of less than £20 – reportedly his only conviction in over 50 years of direct-action campaigning. While, at the time, the Archbishop of Canterbury was less than pleased by the intervention, he later said that the world was a better place because of Peter Tatchell and his campaigns.

OutRage!, as a campaigning group, had a theory of change. They were determined to confront homophobia particularly in institutions of control such as parliament, the police, and the church, but to do so with a smile. One of their most iconic actions was a mass 'kiss-in' in September 1990 at the statue of Eros in Piccadilly Circus. It's a mark of their success that today it seems unfathomable that, at the time, gay men kissing in public was considered criminal. The mass kiss-in was inevitably mobbed by press photographers and, almost as inevitably, no arrests took place. Further actions followed, and over the next four years, prosecutions of gay men for consensual activity fell by two thirds.

Another example of this type of 'propaganda by the deed' campaigning was through an organisation called Chicken's Lib, back in the 1980s – a group with which we were involved at the time. It was a small campaigning organisation that argued for the end of 'battery cages' for laying hens. The battery system was particularly cruel, and its use was banned throughout Europe in 2012, although there remain significant concerns around the systems that have replaced it. At the time most hens were kept in cramped conditions in battery cages, where they were often mutilated to stop them from attacking each other, and no major supermarket stocked free-range hens' eggs.

Chicken's Lib's theory of change was that if it could persuade market-leading supermarket Marks & Spencer to stock free-range eggs, then other supermarkets would follow, and once the public had the choice, they'd likely pick free-range, rather than intensively farmed eggs. The purpose of the campaign was to create sufficient pressure that Marks & Spencer would start to stock free-range eggs. This supermarket was chosen simply because, at the time, it was the market leader, and where it went other supermarkets would surely follow. Chicken's Lib had been lobbying, petitioning and producing evidence-based reports for some time, and now decided it was time to turn up the pressure.

In Greater Manchester at the time there was a range of Marks & Spencer stores, and there was a range of local newspapers. Our tactic to support the campaign was to hire a chicken costume, get some leaflets printed and a petition produced, and we began to work our way around the town centres where these stores were located, seeking to elicit public support. We got lots of public support, but we didn't receive any press coverage, so the message wasn't getting out – we had to rethink our tactics. The revised approach was to get the chicken to leaflet shoppers *inside* the store next to the aisle where the battery eggs were for sale. While most of the group were outside leafleting and petitioning, the 'chicken' went inside, stood in front of the egg counter, and started leafleting – as well as clucking loudly! Photos were taken to give to the press to add visual impact to any story they might cover. Soon enough the store security dragged the poor chicken away, creating some nice visuals of a 'chicken' being manhandled. However, on one occasion, the shelf-stackers largely ignored the chicken, thinking it was some kind of in-store promotion.

The local newspapers loved the story about the plight of the hen, and as we toured around local stores – each time with a different local newspaper – we knew not only that our message was getting amplified, but that Marks & Spencer's press office would see every one of those clippings. Similar mild provocations were taking place up and down the country, and it wasn't long before Marks & Spencer became the first supermarket chain in the country to stock free-range eggs and – not that much later – they became the first to stop selling battery-farmed eggs.

In another example, just outside leafy Harrogate in North Yorkshire, England, was a research laboratory where regular protests were held by animal rights campaigners. These were well attended and noisy. But even the local press paid no attention, despite being provided with details of some of the shocking experiments undertaken on primates – animals who tended to attract more sympathy than laboratory rats. The laboratory was set in its own grounds, and few passers-by were able see the protests. The local campaign coordinator decided on an approach to attract press interest. A monkey suit was hired, and two white lab coats were acquired that were conveniently splattered with blood-red paint. The press was then called and given a story which was that the group were going to return an escaped 'monkey' to the laboratory. The press sent a photographer, who was intrigued by the unfolding escapade. The 'monkey' was ceremoniously dragged across the grounds by the two 'scientists' and taken, kicking and screaming, into the reception – followed by the press. Still in character, the 'scientists' asked the bemused security guard for help returning the escaped monkey to its crate. The scenario produced great photographs and copy, which covered the front page of the following week's paper. The local campaign coordinator was quoted as saying, 'we have made a serious point, albeit in a light-hearted way, but there are monkeys in that building being experimented on today'. The press coverage transformed the campaign. What had been a small group of committed anti-vivisectionists was swelled by local people who were horrified at the experiments taking place in their town.

They have the money: we must have the people

There's an oft-used quote in campaigning groups that says in society there are two sources of power: organised money and organised people. Given that we very seldom have the money, we therefore must organise the people. One example of how people power can win is the campaign against the 'Poll Tax' in the UK in the late 1980s. The government abolished a 'rates' system that saw people contribute to local council finances based on the value of their home. In principle, the bigger your home, the more you paid in contribution for local services. It was a blunt instrument, but it generally meant the more well-off contributed more. The prime minister at the time, Margaret Thatcher, replaced it with a Community Charge – universally referred to as the Poll Tax after a hated law from 1379. It meant that both rich and poor would pay the same fixed contribution to the cost of local services. In effect, it was a massive shift in the burden of local taxation from the wealthy to the poor.

There was considerable opposition to its introduction and, consequently, local Anti-Poll Tax groups were established across the country. This was one of the few examples of political campaigns where campaigners went door-to-door and spoke to everyone. The aim, and it was often achieved, was that each individual housing estate or street would have its own organised Anti-Poll Tax group. These were largely autonomous groups with local leadership drawn from the estate or the streets where people were organising. A national Anti-Poll Tax Federation was set up.

Its main task was to call for a programme of non-payment and to organise a national demonstration.

In March 1990, local councils across the country were agreeing their annual budget and setting the rate for their Poll Tax. Every Anti-Poll Tax group was mobilising to protest to put pressure on the decision makers to demonstrate to the wider community that the campaign of non-payment would be widely supported. Many of these local protests ended with mild disorder as protesters heckled the councillors, and the police broke up the protests with varying degrees of violence. An internal police report in these demonstrations makes instructive reading:

> From the reports we have received there is no indication of national co-ordination of the demonstrations. The left-wing demonstrators seem likely to be the most vociferous and active where they are present, but it is evident from the reports we have received that they have been joined by other demonstrators wishing to show their disapproval at the setting of the community charge. (Quoted in Foot and Livingstone 2022: 124)

On 31 March 1990, the day before the tax became due, there was a large march comprising over 200,000 people in London. It was attended by many people who had been involved in local protests the previous week outside their own local councils. A small group of protesters staged a sit-down protest outside the gates of Downing Street, the Prime Minister's official residence and office. The police – perhaps expecting trouble to erupt – overreacted and began to treat the whole of the protest as a target that needed to be subdued and dispersed. Lines of police on foot and on horseback charged into the assembled crowd. But, penned in by police officers, they had nowhere to go and were hit with truncheons and run down by horses. Perhaps inevitably, fighting broke out and, once it did, it escalated quickly. There was serious disorder and the police couldn't contain it – it resulted in a widespread riot with significant damage, arrests and injuries.

On their return to their homes, protesters focussed on the key strategy of the campaign, which was mass non-payment of the hated tax. This was a relatively easy ask, given that for people short of money, a non-payment campaign was tempting. For those who could pay, but chose not to, they could put the money to one side and, if the campaign failed, could make the payment at a later date. There was a growing sense that this was a massive act of collective defiance, which created a feeling of collective solidarity – it felt like everyone was involved. There was also widespread anger at the police attack on the national protest, coming as it did in the shadow of the police attacks on the miners' picket lines a few years earlier. It's perhaps easier to ask people not to part with their hard-earned cash, than to attend a protest, or to get involved in some other way. But perhaps more important than anything was the fact that this was not the 'usual suspects' trying to substitute for their lack of numbers and support by a heightened level of militancy, but organised communities, in large numbers, saying 'we won't pay'.

The sheer simplicity of the strategy, and the huge headaches it caused, was brilliant. Local authorities began to issue court summonses to non-payers, and local Anti-Poll Tax groups provided advice and guidance as to how to delay and prolong these proceedings. It could take half a day in court to get one court order and there were millions of non-payers. Other people chose to take their name off the electoral register and 'disappeared' so were never billed for the new tax – a downside to this tactic, however, was that these people were disenfranchised as they could no longer vote in local and national elections. Whole streets were simply refusing to pay the hated tax – an estimated 18 million were involved in the Anti-Poll Tax campaign. At one stage, 88 per cent of the country was being chased by their local authority for non-payment. This was what union organiser and writer Jane McAlevey would describe as a super majority. With this level of active support, the campaign was going to be difficult to stop.

When, eventually, the courts began jailing people for non-payment, another problem arose for the authorities. Anti-Poll Tax groups were adept at challenging the rulings and providing support to non-payers in court. A consequence was that following judicial review of their cases, people jailed for non-payment were routinely released, sometimes within hours, as their imprisonment was judged to be technically unlawful. The law allowed the jailing of refusers but only as a last resort, and not as a punishment. Over 1,000 people were jailed, but most were released very quickly, with lawyers taking some cases to the European Court of Justice. Meanwhile the cost of collecting the unpaid 'Poll Tax' was estimated to be more than the cost of the total budget for local authorities' refuse collections (Piggot 1994). By this stage the tax was unworkable because organised people refuse to pay – the courts were clogged up and local councils, despite their efforts, were unable to force people to pay. In November 1990, just eight months after the new tax was introduced, Prime Minister Margaret Thatcher was deposed by her own party. The tax was abandoned, and the government was forced to write off billions of pounds of unpaid tax. The people had won.

No Nazis in Hackney

The mapping of power in campaigns is a vital part of a theory of change and the development of strategy, but it's not something that campaigns routinely do. Power mapping is a collaborative process where you consider who has power in a given situation, and the extent to which different 'players' are supportive or not. People who use power analysis don't jump in with a familiar tactic, but look at the balance of power, including latent power, and ask how we can increase the power of our side, perhaps by bringing new players into the field of conflict, and/or decrease the power of our opponents.

One example of where the process of power mapping worked well was in a local campaign in the London borough of Hackney. Historically, Hackney was a front line in the campaign to eradicate various Nazi organisations. The British Union of Fascists had repeatedly organised rallies in Ridley Road Market in the 1930s, and again in the 1950s, when pitched battles fought by groups such as the 43 Group had cleared them from the area. In the late 1970s and early 1980s, the National Front, another far-right group, established its headquarters in the south of the borough.

In 2008, Hackney Trades Union Council (Hackney TUC), a grouping of trade unionists in the borough, had long been concerned about the rise in support for the far-right, which at the time was expressed through the activity of the British National Party (BNP), which had been founded by an ageing Nazi who had been jailed in the 1960s for establishing a neo-Nazi paramilitary organisation. At this time the BNP had, at least outwardly, turned towards electoral politics, and in 2006 had won 12 seats in another London borough, Barking and Dagenham. The BNP's surprise electoral success was a clarion call to anti-racists across the capital, particularly as, in 2008, the London-wide elections for the Greater London Assembly (GLA) were to be run on a part proportional representation system. Hackney TUC coordinated joint trade union activity in the area and agreed a plan of work to promote voter registration and engagement in the run-up to the London-wide elections. Hackney had notoriously low rates of voter registration and engagement partly due to dissatisfaction with the local Labour Party, which was perceived (whether fairly or not) to have run the borough badly for decades. Hackney TUC campaigned to reduce the risk of a BNP candidate getting onto the GLA by encouraging people in Hackney to vote. In a proportional representation election, the strategy was that the more people in Hackney who voted, the less likely the BNP would achieve the necessary percentage of the overall votes cast to win a seat.

As was Hackney TUC's practice, it took out an advert in the local paper – endorsed by local faith and community groups – calling on people to make sure that they voted. A few weeks before the election Hackney TUC was notified that the BNP had commissioned adverts across London's local papers, including the Hackney's local paper the *Hackney Gazette*. The newspaper, although owned by a national chain, was a local paper, which understood and respected the borough it served. Hackney was a multicultural population, home to a large Jewish community, it was one of the historical areas of settlement for the Windrush generation, had a sizeable Muslim community, and was home to a Kurdish community, many of whom had been refugees from a government they would describe as fascist. Many of the elders in the borough had been participants in the struggles to rid Hackney of a far-right presence in the past and they were angry at the *Hackney Gazette*'s decision. Understandably, many people believed that they would be the targets, not just of smears and vitriol, but of violence, should the far-right re-establish a presence in the borough.

Hackney TUC had less than a week to persuade the newspaper to cancel the advert, but how? A knee-jerk approach might have been to launch a petition, organise a protest, or call for a boycott of the paper, but starting from familiar tactics is not a great way to identify the most effective way to achieve a win. Instead, people did a power analysis. Through trade union contacts, Hackney TUC knew journalists on the paper would be sympathetic, and while they clearly had some potential influence to bring the paper to reconsider its decision, there wasn't the confidence that union members at the paper would walk out on unofficial strike. Another approach was a consumer boycott. This also potentially had power to achieve a win as they knew the community would be sympathetic, but it wasn't considered possible to launch a boycott in a few days.

The paper relied heavily on advertising, including from the numerous estate agents who advertised regularly in the paper. The presence of a far-right group in the borough would hardly make it more attractive to homebuyers, but it would take a lot of work to convince individual businesses to boycott the paper, and again, that wasn't possible to organise in less than a week. A protest was suggested, or even an occupation of the newspaper's offices – again it was hard to see how either of these would force the paper to change its stance on the far-right advert, and indeed, it risked entrenching their position.

However, the power analysis revealed an intriguing possibility, identifying an influential group that might be able to effect the change Hackney TUC were looking for: the newsagents who sold the paper. Most newsagents in the area were run by minority ethnic businesses, none of whom were likely to be sympathetic to an avowedly White supremacist party. The sales of the *Hackney Gazette* were not a large part of their weekly income, so it was thought that an approach to persuade them to put pressure on the paper to withdraw the advert would be possible. Hackney TUC had an extensive email list of trade unionists throughout the borough, and because of its work around anti-racism, it had good working relationships with local faith leaders and community groups.

From this idea a campaign strategy quickly emerged. A template fax, a now-defunct form of digital communication, was produced and delivered to newsagents. It asked them to fax notification to the publisher, that if they published the advertisement from the far-right, then the newsagent would cancel their order for that week. Hackney TUC thought a personal approach was likely to be more effective, so it asked everyone on its mailing list to take a copy of this template fax to the newsagent where they bought their newspaper. As a valued customer, and where they and the newsagent already had a level of relationship, this was thought likely to be more fruitful. Within days, Hackney TUC estimated that at least half of the borough's newsagents had faxed over the ultimatum to the publisher. It was a very targeted intervention, with several hundred people each undertaking one important structured conversation with a key influencer, and it worked. The *Hackney Gazette* cancelled the advert and instead wrote an editorial in which it said:

> Our decision on whether to publish or not is based on the nature of the local community. Our editors have to balance the need to be consistent in our approach with a desire not to damage the community in which they operate, a process which has been made more difficult by a clearly orchestrated campaign of complaints. We have concluded that it is not in the best interests of the community to publish the advertisement in the *Hackney Gazette*.

Hackney TUC and the local community were proud of the achievement and the backhanded compliment about a 'clearly orchestrated campaign'. Without undertaking a detailed power analysis at the start of this campaign and recognising that the newsagents were the 'choke point' and that they could be quickly mobilised, the campaign wouldn't have been a success.

Clearing the backlog of rubbish

A rather different strategy emerged from applying the process of power analysis to an unofficial industrial dispute between refuse workers and their employer Hackney Council in the 1990s. No one can quite remember the details of the dispute, but this was a highly organised group of workers who, rather than ballot for official industrial action, had embarked on an unofficial go-slow for weeks. They ensured that at the end of each day they didn't finish that day's collection, and therefore had to complete this outstanding work the next day, which naturally meant that each successive day they got further and further behind. Eventually collections were a fortnight behind schedule, and residents were beginning to get angry. Rubbish was piling up, there were reports of rats and other vermin, and a stalemate was reached. The employer wasn't prepared to concede to the demands of the workers, and because the workforce wasn't losing pay, they were prepared to continue their action indefinitely, causing considerable disruption.

A group of residents met with their neighbours to discuss how they should respond to the problem of the build-up of rubbish in their streets. They talked about what they might do to force the council to act, but initially couldn't figure out what leverage they could draw upon. The council appeared to have decided on a policy of sitting out the action and it seemed the council was unconcerned about the level of anger among residents at the backlog of refuse collection. There wasn't an imminent election, where elected councillors could be threatened with losing their seats if they didn't respond to residents, so what would make the council say 'yes', when it seemed it wanted to keep saying 'no'? Suggestions of collecting the rubbish and depositing it at the town hall, or even in the front garden of elected councillors were considered and rejected.

Lateral thinking about pressure points helped the group of residents reach the desired outcome. It was noted that local authorities have a statutory duty to provide refuse collection services. The UK's Environmental Protection Act 1990 provides a route for an 'aggrieved person' to serve notice on 'the person responsible' for creating a nuisance – defined as including 'any accumulation or deposit which is prejudicial to health or a nuisance'. But before bringing any action the aggrieved person must serve notice in writing on the person or persons responsible for the nuisance, of their intention to bring the proceedings.

From this, a plan emerged in which residents served notices on each of the elected councillors, the council's chief executive, and the council as a legal entity. This notice stated that they were responsible for the accumulation of waste that was building up across the borough and this provided harbourage and food for pests – all of which was prejudicial to health.

It was clear that there was a statutory nuisance as rats had been seen among the uncollected rubbish, but the group was uncertain whether or not a court of law would hold individual councillors responsible for this failing. Nevertheless, the residents banked on the idea that elected councillors would be nervous about receiving a legal document holding them personally responsible. The residents were confident that the notice would catch the attention of councillors and likely cause them to spring into action in some way – especially if they feared being served with a court order requiring the council to clear the backlog. The purpose of the action was to create a reaction, which until now individual complaints had not. The resident group was confident that the council would not want this to get to court. The tactics worked; there was a reaction.

Following receipt of the legal notices, the council quickly hired a refuse truck from a neighbouring borough to clear the residents' streets. The refuse truck, however, ignored surrounding streets, driving past piles of rubbish, and only cleaning the area where the residents had organised. Naturally, as good neighbours, the group shared their tactic with neighbouring streets, where residents planned to replicate it. Yet before the campaign escalated the council and the unions negotiated an agreement that saw service return to normal.

Instead of adopting traditional approaches such as lobbying councillors through their surgeries, the group of residents undertook a power analysis, and the tactic arose from that analysis. They asked themselves who had the power to make the change, what would force them to change their position, and how could they effect that change? It was only through this process that they were able to surface what they thought might be the most effective tactic. There are two separate concepts here: building power and exercising power, and as usual, while it is useful to separate them out for analysis, in reality in transformative organising, we often build more power by effectively exercising the power we already have.

Building alliances

If you undertake a power analysis, then you will often find that there are people who want the same outcome as you but for a different reason. For example, you might oppose a development of a large supermarket with a housing estate built on top of it because it would overshadow and impact on the environment in an adjoining nature reserve, because of the traffic chaos it would cause, because it would suck the life out of the local community shops, or because the housing did not include any affordable or social housing. All these are legitimate reasons to oppose a planning development, but sometimes it can be hard for the housing campaigners to engage with the local chamber of commerce, or the environmentalists, or traffic campaigners. In our individual campaign silos, we tend to prioritise the issues we care most about, and sometimes even compete to ensure our concerns are the ones that get heard. But if we take the time to bring all these disparate concerns together into a broad-based coalition, then we often find that, in terms of power, the coalition is much more powerful than the sum of its parts. Such coalition building is an art in itself. But it starts from taking the time to listen and understand other people's concerns and motivations and then agreeing a strategy that ensures that the concerns of each of the constituent parts of the coalition will get a louder and more effective voice working together. Sometimes you will find yourself in a working relationship with a group you otherwise have little in common with, but if there is a degree of honesty, and a clear commitment to the objectives and the limits of joint working, then it is a very useful way to build power.

Tactics can build power

With any transformative organising initiative you will need to build power. This can involve a process of networking, one-to-one conversations, and a mapping of interests. But sometimes, a well-chosen campaign, with appropriate tactics, can demonstrate to your people that it's possible to win. The process of engaging people in a well-chosen tactic can help them to see themselves as agents of change. People are justifiably proud of occasions when they win and are often keen to ask: 'What next?' Time and again, communities can find novel responses to new challenges, and the key is to build active participation and find a tactic that exploits the targets' point of weakness, where organisers can focus energy in the most effective way to disrupt the existing power balance. Among Saul Alinsky's purported 'rules' were four that are relevant to the choice of tactics. They are worth revisiting.

- **'Never go outside the expertise of your people.'** In other words, your people should feel comfortable with the tactics you are using. They should understand the tactics and strategy, and they should feel that they are an extension of their lived experience. This is a good starting point for discussing potential tactics, but perhaps should not be seen as a rule. Sometimes doing something different and novel will be more powerful, so long as your community feel comfortable with it.
- **'Whenever possible go outside the expertise of the enemy.'** This makes a lot of sense. Too often we rely on tactics that are tried and tested, and our opponents have experienced them before. The consumer boycott, the picket, the strike, the petition … but what if we hit them with something they have never been hit with before? We would hope they will have no idea how to respond. There is nothing more fun than knowing that your opponent has no idea what to do next, and if your people can sense it, then it makes them feel powerful.
- **'A good tactic is one your people enjoy.'** Too often it seems that being involved in progressive social causes is designed to be boring. Who really wants to stand in the rain handing out soggy leaflets to people who are keen to hurry past? But there is no reason why it should be. Tactics like the chicken costume, street theatre generally, or chatting with your newsagent about how 'we' can stop the far-right advert, can be fun.
- **'A tactic that drags on too long becomes a drag.'** Almost by definition a tactic is a small step in a longer-term strategy. While community or workplace organising is a long-

term process, individual campaigns will come and go. It is a mistake to get locked into a long-term battle that you cannot win. If you don't have or can't build the power to win, then find a way to withdraw, rebuild and in your own time, pick another battle. Strikes that go on for too long – the UK's 1984–85 miners' strike or the industrial dispute at Grunwick in North London in 1974–75 being famous examples – rarely win. And a tactic that requires long-term commitment that doesn't show results can become demoralising for some of your people.

As we have seen, power comes in many forms and a good strategy, or even a good tactic, can move a community from feeling helpless to feeling powerful. Given that we generally start off with less power than our target, if we want to win, then we need to be alert to all our potential sources of power, and to learn how to accumulate them and use them effectively. While winning is always our objective, there are times when the process of organising creates a newfound sense of identity and strength within a community, even if the intended outcome is not achieved. That said, we should be very careful about pretending that our defeats are some form of 'partial victory'. Lying to ourselves may be comforting at times, but it is no substitute for an honest analysis of why we lost and what we need to do differently to win on the next issue.

Identifying the locus of power in your campaign

Think of a campaign objective you are seeking to achieve.

Identify the overall decision maker(s) who will need to change their decision for you to be successful.

What do they care about? (Hint: this might be money, it might be electoral support, it might even be 'anything for an easy life'.)

What do you have, if anything, that they want?

What can you do that impacts on them, either by starving them of something they care about, or by rewarding them for moving to support your initiative?

Who are your people, and how can you organise them around this issue?

4

Organising and mobilising: why understanding the difference matters to your campaign strategy

The questions we will deal with in this chapter are threefold: what is organising; how does it differ from mobilising; and why does this matter? We define mobilising as the process of activating existing supporters, for example by calling a protest march, while organising is a process that seeks to build power within a defined population (for example, a workplace, an estate or an electoral district) where the aim is to win over the majority of the population to a particular cause. The distinction matters because, while both are important, it's impossible to organise without some mobilisation of existing supporters; they serve different functions in campaigns. The evolving emphasis placed on the two approaches at different stages in a campaign will relate, explicitly or implicitly, to the theory of change that we talked about in Chapter 2, which is dependent on issues such as the power resources at your disposal, your ability to build capacity, and the strategies you choose to adopt.

Perhaps it might be best to illustrate the difference through a real-life example in a large UK public sector union. The branch was in a local authority in East London. This was a large branch of around 2,000 members and in the year 2000 the local authority (the borough council) announced that it was in financial crisis and to solve the problem it planned to cut wages, close some services including libraries and nurseries, and outsource others such as estate cleaning and refuse collection. The union branch had, for a long time, been weak and ineffective. Yet the employer's financial crisis was the type of external threat that could transform a union branch because it demanded an urgent and strategic response. In line with the recognition agreement between the employer and the union, a mass union meeting was called in the town hall, and employees were allowed to attend during their working hours. Several hundred people attended what was an angry meeting that was determined that the council wouldn't solve its financial crisis by cutting pay and the services to the local communities. The union branch was faced with an important question of what needed to be done to prevent the cuts to wages and services.

One proposal put forward by a small grouping was an immediate walkout – a strike – in defiance of the anti-union laws. Superficially there was some support for this militant activity as it would have attracted headlines in the local paper. There was no doubt that such an action would have spoken to the emotions of those at the union's meeting, many of whom were feeling a sense not just of anger, but also that they were being treated with contempt. This would, however, have been a *mobilising* response, which only spoke to the most committed and angry of the workforce and would only be calling on a minority of members to undertake a symbolic protest action. Let's explore the downside to this approach from an organising perspective.

While this was the biggest trade union meeting at this workplace for a very long time, it was still the case that only around ten per cent of the union branch membership was present and, given that only about half the council's employees were union members, the number at the meeting probably only amounted to around five per cent of the total workforce. As such, few believed that a couple of hours' protest strike following the union meeting would convince the council to change its mind. In short, while this action may have mobilised some of the workforce it wasn't going to generate sufficient power to force the employer to say 'yes', when they wanted to say 'no'.

The union branch's leadership argued for a different approach. They reasoned against an immediate walkout, and instead to vote for a branch-wide ballot for strike action. Their argument was that if the branch couldn't convince most of the workforce to support a strike, then it wouldn't generate sufficient power to reverse the council's cuts. It was argued – and agreed – that the task of the most committed and angriest union members at the meeting was to go back to their workplace and tell everyone about what had been discussed at the meeting, why the meeting had voted to initiate a strike ballot, why everyone in the union needed to vote 'yes' to save jobs and services and to protect wages, and that the workforce could only win if they all stood together. Equally, part of the agreed strategy was that existing members needed to ensure that those who were not yet in the union were told that the union had a strategy to defeat these cuts, and that they were needed to join the struggle if the union was going to win. Finally, and crucially, union members, many of whom both lived and worked in the borough, were asked to reach out to the community groups and organisations in the borough to help build a union–community coalition to defend the services that the council was aiming to cut.

The meeting rejected the proposal for a token walkout and voted instead to organise. This decision was fundamental to what would happen in the council over the next 18 months in a dispute that would eventually save three libraries and stop savage wage cuts to the lowest-paid workers. Mobilising, then, is often about turning your supporters out for a protest, whereas organising is about building the power within a defined structure that means you can move towards forcing your target to change their position.

The nature of mobilising and organising means that the level of commitment of your supporters who are mobilised compared with those who are organised will often be starkly different. With mobilising, even if people feel strongly, the level of commitment required may be fleeting and shallow, a response to an invitation to turn up to a couple of hours of protest, for example, whereas people who are organised are more likely to understand that to win they will need to commit to sustained ongoing activity. That activity won't always be directed at protesting against the target but will almost always involve building relationships within your community, however defined, to increase the power necessary to effect the change you desire. As was said at the start of this chapter, mobilising simply isn't a shortcut or alternative to organising. While there is often some overlap between the two, making this distinction between organising and mobilising is not simply an academic exercise, being reflective about what you are doing and being explicit about the extent to which you are mobilising or organising can lift the fog that conceals the differences between the two.

It matters because a focus on mobilisation alone leaves most of the population in your community – whether that be a workplace, a geographical area or even a cause – as spectators while the 'heavy lifting' is attempted by a militant minority. The myth that a militant minority can substitute for a well-organised community is a damaging and destructive one. It's a shallow approach to seeking to advance towards social change, and often leads to a level of elitism and resentment by those involved against those 'passive', unorganised masses, an issue we touched on in Chapter 1. While mobilising is an important part of social movement activity, it is seldom sufficient in creating a wider context within which to challenge the power and interests of those who stand in the way of social justice. It's not that mobilisation of supporters is unimportant – especially in moments of crisis, and there are examples where mobilisations have pressured employers and governments to shift position on important issues. But, for what Jane McAlevey (2016) refers to as 'the big fights' – where there is a significant cost in terms of money, power or prestige to the targeted decision maker, and in circumstances where the decision maker has not been suddenly weakened by external events that provide an opportunity for an easy win – then we need something more transformative, and that requires organising.

Organising and mobilising: the distinctions

Regrettably the terms 'mobilising' and 'organising' are often used interchangeably, which is problematic and has led to confusion not only in organising practice, but also in reflection upon it. One way to think of the distinction between organising and mobilising is that mobilising is the utilisation of power resources *already available*, whereas organising begins by asking where the latent power is that *needs to be activated* to effect change. Strategic organisers then figure out a plan to systematically build that power and develop the resources needed to win. Put another way:

> mobilizing is most often limited to activating an existing base of support – those who already agree with you – whereas deep organizing involves engaging and activating people who may not initially agree but who, through a process of collective organizing and the development of grassroots leaders, begin to self-identify as part of a community with a shared objective in seeking to challenge injustice. (Holgate, Simms and Tapia 2018: 600)

Hahrie Han (2014), in her book *How Organizations Develop Activists*, defines the difference between organising and mobilising slightly differently. For her, organising involves 'transformational activism' and mobilising is 'transactional activism' and this is a good way of thinking about how the two differ. By this she means that in a mobilising approach, participation is conceptualised as a transactional exchange between an activist and the other party to the exchange, where tasks requested are 'strictly limited in their time commitment and require minimal effort on the part of the activist' (p. 95). The campaign group 38 Degrees might be a good example of this 'minimum ask' approach. In an organising approach, 'the goal is not only to get work out of the activist in the short-term but also to invest in developing the activist's capacity to act' (p. 96), and this is done through an on-going leadership identification process, by having one-to-one conversations, and through the teaching of power by working collectively with others in and beyond the organisation. Han describes the tension many organisations or campaign groups face when engaging people in activity – whether to ask a little of supporters and to make participation quick and easy so as not to overburden volunteers, or to ask for more time and effort in building more relationships to increase long-term capacity for sustained activism. The first approach is tempting as it involves less work, but it's seldom transformational. Instead, it's a transactional approach whereby mobilising organisations provide material resources for their members (leaflets, petitions, template letters or the opportunity to turn up to a protest), and the supporters provide the time, money or effort that the organisation is looking for. In this case, Hahrie Han says:

> support is limited to the information and skills activists need to complete a given task [whereas] transformational outcomes focus on the ways that collective action changes the affects, outlooks and other orientations of individuals and groups. Examples include the increasing ability of people to see beyond their own self-interest, shifts in the belief about their own agency, or changes in public opinion. (Han 2014: 96)

As with all the distinctions we have made in this book, it's easy to contrast mobilising and organising as if they were binary, even contradictory, concepts. However, most campaigns and campaign organisations will deploy a mix of mobilising *and* organising, and some tactics will involve elements of both. That doesn't take away from the importance of the distinction and being aware of the extent to which we are choosing to mobilise, or organise, at any given moment.

Let's return to the real-life example of a mobilising approach, where those who attended the union meeting were being asked to stage a walkout with the 'already committed' minority. In effect, the members were being asked to 'follow'. By contrast, in the organising approach, members were tasked with building greater capacity. Their responsibility was to lead; to go back to their workplace and speak directly to their work colleagues, many of whom would not automatically have been convinced of the value of a strike ballot – particularly at the early stage of the dispute where people needed to be convinced there was widespread support and a chance of winning. The organising approach required that the meeting participants become the *agents of change*, taking responsibility for transforming the views of their colleagues and the dominant narrative in their workplaces about what was possible if the workforce stood together.

Jane McAlevey (2016) has persuasively argued in her book *No Shortcuts* that deep organising is the way that big change is created. By this she means that it's only by winning the hearts, minds and active participation of a 'super majority' (upwards of 70 per cent) of any defined constituency that it's possible to force through progressive changes against the wishes of powerful decision makers. While it is true that there will be times when a mobilising approach might get some concessions from a weak, or even a benevolent decision maker, and conversely an organising approach does not carry an automatic guarantee of victory, what is indisputable is that building a high level of active support increases your power and your potential to win. McAlevey is arguing in the context of workforce organising, where achieving 70 per cent support for industrial action amongst a workforce is a strong sign to an employer that they need to compromise or suffer the consequences. However, the same principles are at work in community organising. While acknowledging the need to mobilise your members in the process of organising, McAlevey dismisses a mobilising-only approach because, as we already implicitly know but seldom explicitly acknowledge, if our existing supporters already had enough power to effect the change we want, then they would have done so by now.

By focussing on occasional moments of protest where an organisation's staff undertake most of the on-going day-to-day work of mobilising activists, a campaign organisation asks relatively little from its members or supporters. Although a lot of effort is put into engaging activists towards occasional mobilisations, the focus of activity is led by staff who direct and inform supporters when and where to turn up, or when to send off letters of protest. In contrast, supporters play a secondary role, if any, in building the base of the movement or being involved in strategy. While an organisation's staff can mobilise members or supporters, when they do this it's most often the already committed 'dedicated activists who show up over and over at every meeting and rally for all good causes, but without the full mass of their co-workers or community behind them' (McAlevey 2016: 10). Jane McAlevey contrasts this with a 'deep organising' approach which is characterised by high levels of participation by union members (in her example) who decide for themselves the issues around which they will organise: 'organizing places the agency for success with a continually expanding base of ordinary people, a mass of people never previously involved' (p. 10). It is worth repeating that: organising leads to a continually expanding base; in other words, it creates rather than drains resources. But as always there is a qualification: a campaign group seeking to develop an organising approach must first find a few supporters willing to start organising. One way to do that might be to mobilise for a day of action around an issue, for example a leafleting campaign on local high streets, and then follow up with those people who participated. Those who responded can now be identified as activists; the question is: can you convert them into organisers?

Often when we mobilise in response to an immediate threat or concern, we may not have a theory of change: reaction is an instinctive emotional response to something that hurts or angers, and often we don't initially stop to analyse the power dynamics or identify where the opportunities are to create change. We might bring our supporters onto the street in what we think of as 'mass' numbers, but there's no direction for the anger and we return home without a plan for further action. People might feel comforted by the sight and the emotion of many people demonstrating alongside them, but if nothing changes, the process can soon become demobilising. Promoting the illusion that a show of opposition will in itself effect change can leave participants later facing the grim reality that they have been ignored. An example of this happened with the protests in the UK against the second Iraq War in 2003. Estimates of up to two million people attended a central London protest, many believing that such a large show of opposition would influence the UK government to step back from the brink of what was anticipated to be, and proved to be, a disastrous and unjust war. Yet the government ignored the protests and went on to wage what the UN Secretary-General, Kofi Annan, condemned as an illegal war (MacAskill and Borger 2004). This was without a doubt the largest protest mobilisation in British history, but it unfortunately didn't generate the power necessary to succeed. Reflecting on this example today we might ask: what was the theory of change in this protest movement? Did it have one? Was there a power analysis prior to calling action, if so, what was it and what would need to have happened to force the government to change its course? There is clearly a place for mass mobilisations, and we looked at the example of the 'Poll

Tax rebellion' in Chapter 3, but if we want mobilisations to be effective, as organisers we will need to plan the next steps in advance: what is it that supporters will be asked to do next to take things to the next level?

The threat is usually more terrifying than the thing itself

'The threat is usually more terrifying than the thing itself' is one of Saul Alinsky's most insightful observations. Imagine how it felt in the British government when that massive demonstration was approaching. Months in the planning, and with all the intelligence coming in saying it was going to be huge, it is simply impossible to know what impact this might have, particularly on your supporters: how many of them might break ranks and speak out against the war? How many of your MPs might pledge to vote against the war? Imagine the day after the protest. Everyone has gone home, the organisers of the protest are exhausted, they have played their best card, and yet your coalition for war is unscathed and intact. There is no credible threat left. Imagine if the organisers of that protest had had a plan for what happened next. For example, if they had called on their supporters to build a commitment in their communities to occupy public buildings, council offices, police stations, courts and so on en masse, and to bring administration of the country to a standstill. Then, rather than the protest being the peak of the government's headaches, it would merely have been a starting point. One of the ways that we win is when we effectively disorganise our opponents. In other words, they can't think straight because they don't know what we are going to do next, but they fear it is going to be more imaginative, and more powerful, than our previous action.

As we touched upon in Chapter 2, John Kelly, industrial relations academic and union activist, has written articulately about what he refers to as 'mobilisation theory' in his book *Rethinking Industrial Relations*. Writing nearly 25 years ago, he means something different from more recent writers when he uses the term 'mobilisation'. The distinction between mobilising and organising has evolved over that quarter of a century, and Kelly's work on 'mobilisation theory' is closer to organising practice than the title might suggest. His concern was with understanding how people move from passive endurance of a wrong to active opposition. He explored how individuals acquire a sense of injustice, how a move from self-interest to collective identity occurs, and the factors that encourage or discourage a move to collective action to challenge that injustice. Kelly's mobilisation theory is not merely concerned with one stage in the organising process, he sees mobilisation as one in a 'set of interconnected concepts that focuses our attention on particular social processes and helps us think analytically about them' (Kelly 1998: 38). These interconnected concepts include how interests are formed collectively – how people come to believe their interests are similar (or in opposition) to another group, and whether their interests are defined in individual or collective terms. It also includes organisation or structure, which provides the framework or capacity for the group to act collectively. Only when these interconnected processes are in place is 'mobilisation' likely to be effective. So, this way of thinking about mobilisation is much more tied into an organising approach. To understand how the mobilising and organising approaches play out in practice, let's look at some examples with which we are familiar.

How a community became organised to win

In 2010 the London Borough of Hackney was in the process of rapid gentrification. The borough, which 25 years earlier had been viewed as undesirable, had suddenly become desirable and house prices were spiralling to dizzy heights. The council was working with a large developer in the process of agreeing a massive development of 'luxury' flats in the centre of Dalston, an area of the borough which, at one time, rivalled Brixton and Notting Hill as a centre for the Black Caribbean community in London. Gentrification had already made the area largely unaffordable for the local, disproportionately Black, working–class, and there was a sense that the council was actively promoting a process that was seeing a rapid demographic change in the area. The emotional term 'ethnic cleansing' was used to describe the change taking place (despite there being no comparison with the forced expulsions of the Muslim and Croatian minorities in Bosnia in the 1990s).

This was a community that feared for its continued existence. The existing public library in Dalston – a prefabricated building opened in the mid-1980s – was named in honour of the Trinidadian Marxist, C.L.R. James. There's a long story about how his name came to be associated with the library but suffice to say that Black teachers in the area had waged a successful campaign to get the council's libraries to carry more culturally sensitive materials, including those that didn't just celebrate Britain's imperial past but recognised the validity and value of other cultures. These teachers had been inspired by C.L.R. James, who at the time was resident in Brixton in South London. C.L.R. James is one of the giant intellectuals of the African diaspora, an unorthodox Marxist who also wrote about his second passion, cricket (see his excellent book *Beyond a Boundary*). He was a leading pan-African, a union organiser among sharecroppers in the American South during the 1930s depression years, an advisor to numerous post-colonial leaders, and a literary critic, as well as a theorist on organising.

When the council approved the luxury flats the developer was required to redevelop the CLR James Library as part of a 'planning gain' agreement. However, the council announced that the newly rebuilt library would, henceforth, be renamed the 'Dalston Library'. There was a real sense in sections of the local Black community that this decision was part of a process of seeking to make the area more attractive to White middle-class City workers, and to erase Dalston's Black working-class community and its history.

A campaign group was soon formed by existing local cultural and community groups. The aim was to keep the name of the library as the CLR James Library. What happened next was a masterclass in community organising. Local churches – whose congregations were often overwhelmingly Black – were approached to lend their support and soon got on-board with the campaign. Meanwhile a local DJ helped to get the message out to a very different demographic, and campaigners spent time speaking to people in the bustling Ridley Road Market in the very heart of Dalston. A petition was launched, more to measure the success of the organising and as a way of having a conversation than to serve any other purpose. The group also found a few high-profile Black intellectuals who were encouraged to write directly to Hackney's Mayor to express why they opposed this erasure of Black culture.

There can be little doubt that the campaign rapidly built a 'super majority' – considerable support within the community – and that the issue was both widely and deeply felt, such that when the campaign group convened a meeting with the council it not only agreed to retain the original name of the library, but also to host an annual C.L.R. James memorial lecture, and to have a permanent memorial to C.L.R. James in the library. At the first memorial lecture later that year, the councillor responsible for the original proposal stood up and opened the session and, with over 300 people in attendance, he said: 'I was always in support of the campaign to keep the library named after C.L.R. James.' Everyone there knew it was not true, but no one really cared: the council had been forced to change its position by the power of community action and that was enough to make him welcome at the ceremony.

Spontaneity and organisation

In drawing this chapter to a close it is useful to reflect upon the words of Aaron Schutz and Mike Miller in their book *People Power* as they neatly draw out the importance of organising and not just mobilising:

> To build a lasting political force on any issue requires not spontaneity, but organisation. It requires a slow process of leadership development. It requires the multiplication of leaders with a long-term perspective, with the ability to plan strategy and the scale of marshalling forces at the right time in the right place. The people who painstakingly create these organisations and leaders at a time when most people attend to the problems of everyday life – these are the organisers without whom no movement can win. (Schutz and Miller 2015: 48)

Of course, they are right, but perhaps they underestimate the power of the 'moment of the whirlwind' when tens of thousands of people decide 'enough is enough'. Spontaneity and organising are not in conflict; in fact, the real magic happens when they coincide.

Despite all that important and necessary work in infrastructure building, real change is very seldom created by a long-established, well-resourced body. Think of the phases of the African American freedom movement. The anachronistically named National Association for the Advancement of Colored People (the NAACP), under the guidance of formidable intellectual W.E.B. De Bois, often combined legal advocacy with building a network of groups across the country in the face of murderous opposition, particularly in the Deep South of the USA. Yet despite its level of heroism and organisation, it couldn't respond to exploit the emerging post-Second-World-War opportunities (many of which had been, at least in part, created by their legal challenges). It took the Montgomery bus boycott, and the subsequent formation of the Southern Christian Leadership Conference (SCLC) in 1957, under the leadership of E.D. Nixon and a young Martin Luther King, to take the struggle to the next phase. The new organisation not only made use of the networks painstakingly built by the NAACP over the previous two decades, but it also employed the legendary organiser Ella Baker who had been national field officer for the NAACP. The SCLC created a massive shift in the pace of the struggle for race equality, as King said repeatedly when asked to tone down the pace of the movement: 'The fact is, we can't afford to slow up. We have our self-respect to maintain, but even more than that, because of our love for democracy and because of our love for America, we can't afford to slow up' (King 1962).

But even the rocket that was the SCLC couldn't keep up with the pace of creativity of the movement. On Monday, 1 February 1960, four Black college students in Greensboro, North Carolina, sought and were refused service at a segregated lunch counter. In a well-planned response, they refused to leave and sat in until the store closed; the police were called but couldn't think of a law that was being broken and left. The students returned the next day in larger numbers, and repeated their sit-in. By the Friday, there were 300 students involved in what was now an occupation. Within days students across the

South were mobilising to desegregate libraries, beaches, hotels and lunch counters. Within two months, the movement was active in 55 cities in 13 states. The young people had heard Martin Luther King urge them: 'if you cannot fly, run, if you cannot run, walk, and if you cannot walk, crawl, but by all means keep this movement moving', and in the process of sitting down they had outrun the SCLC. Fortunately for the movement, Ella Baker both respected the power of spontaneity *and* understood the need for organisation, and in April 1960 convened a meeting of over 200 student activists that led to the formation of the Student Nonviolent Coordinating Committee (SNCC). This organisation was to transform the movement through its tactics of freedom rides (desegregating interstate transportation) and voter registration campaigns – both of which met murderous, but ultimately ineffective opposition from White supremacists.

This relationship between spontaneity and organisation, between mobilising and organising, is therefore a complex one. Established organisations that can't relate to new waves of activity outside of their plans, will ossify, while new agency that can't create organisational infrastructure may burn brightly for a while, but will inevitably fade. Black Lives Matter, Momentum, #MeToo and the Mutual Aid movement during the pandemic are just some examples of moments when vast numbers have become involved in activity, but where there has not been a successful strategy to incorporate those numbers into a long-term organising plan. As campaigners for social justice, we're in a constant battle to hold on to the gains we have made (and to win more) as opposing forces push against us and seek to reassert their power. To succeed we need more than fleeting mobilisation responses to moments of crisis or opportunity. We need stable and sustainable, but also nimble, organisations, and building them involves strategy, power and a theory of change to get us to the place we want to be.

People are often happy to give up their free time to join a protest, with all the attendant sense of excitement that comes from seeing others taking part and hearing speeches that express the passions people are feeling. But the real potential for change takes place when those mobilised in those moments go on to dedicate their time to creating the infrastructure – the meetings, committees, mailing lists, newsletters and campaign research – that can harness the anger over an issue and turn it into positive energy.

We need structures that can absorb people into our movements, those people mobilised during the inevitable, but often fleeting, 'moments of the whirlwind', where hundreds of thousands feel moved to act. Relying on staff of national organisations to do this is counter-productive for two reasons: firstly, they seldom have the time or resources to do it well, and secondly, those people who build a movement from the grassroots upwards create the laboratories within which brand new tactics emerge. It may be that for every successful tactic generated by spontaneity, there will be many examples of less effective ones, but it is the sheer volume of experimentation that is possible during an upswell of support that guarantees that something new and unpredicted is likely to be created. The next chapter will explore in more detail how we build the power we need to effect the changes we want.

Developing the skills of your supporters

Think of a campaign or movement in which you are involved.

Imagine your ideal 'super-activist': someone who has all the necessary skills, knowledge and experience to help transform your dream into reality.

Make a list of those attributes.

Think of your average supporter – which of these attributes do they largely lack, or need to develop?

How is your campaign or movement developing these attributes within your supporters?

What more could be done?

5

Equality as central organising practice

The traditional image of the working-class in the UK is White, and male – digging coal, smelting steel, working on a building site or on a production line. This, of course, has never been a fully accurate depiction of the working-class, as it ignores the long history of multiculturalism around our docks, and the garment workers, the retail, hospitality and food processing workers and the care workers, all of whom were disproportionately women. Today's workplaces may be less strictly gendered and segregated than those that gave rise to this mistaken image of a 'traditional' working-class, and in wider society traditionally oppressed, excluded and marginalised groups have made significant, if insufficient, progress towards equality, but too often our organisations fail to be inclusive. This is not just a matter of ensuring 'fair representation' and 'equal voices', important as those things are, it is a matter of winning and losing, and in the context of the climate emergency, it is about the life or death of the struggle. As Audre Lorde, civil rights activist and writer, explained:

> Any future vision which can encompass all of us, by definition, must be complex and expanding, not easy to achieve. The answer to cold is heat, the answer to hunger is food. But there is no simple monolithic solution to racism, to sexism, to homophobia. There is only the conscious focusing within each of my days to move against them, wherever I come up against these particular manifestations of the same disease. By seeing who the 'we' is, we learn to use our energies

> with greater precision against our enemies rather than against ourselves. (Lorde 1982)

Most organisers will identify themselves and the change they seek to effect as being part of a social justice movement. They may be acting against racism, sexism, climate change, the housing crisis, exploitation at work, or a range of other manifestations of what Audre Lorde refers to as 'the same disease'. Yet, too often, within organisational structures and practices there are examples of the very same patterns of oppression that people are seeking to end. Some people mistakenly believe they are part of a 'single-issue' campaign and try to isolate their movement from the 'distractions' of addressing 'other issues'. Given the complexity of the forms of oppression that are manifest within our society, and the extent to which we are all socialised to find them normal – even those oppressions that directly impact upon us – it's no surprise that social justice organisations struggle with what has come to be known as the intersection of oppressions.

For some people, so long as the key focus of the organisation is not undermined by the toleration of other forms of oppression then those oppressions tend to go largely unchallenged. There are too many examples to list, but at times trade unions have been not just institutionally racist and sexist, but on too many occasions overtly so. Race equality organisations have at times been notoriously sexist and the environmental movement far too slow to recognise that the climate crisis is racialised. Trade unions have been struggling, some with more determination than others, to address under-representation within their structures. Women, racialised minorities and disabled members are often absent or under-represented, while LGBTQ+ members are, to varying degrees, invisible.

Tony Benn, former UK Member of Parliament and socialist, used to recount a parable. He would tell how a young child fell down a deep well in a village, and that the people from the village came to help. They tied a rope to the top of the well and dropped the rope down towards the child, but it wasn't long enough, so another rope was dropped down, and again it wasn't long enough. This went on until the village had used every rope at their disposal. Finally, as they were close to despair, they heard the child call out: 'tie the ropes together'. For Benn, the interconnectedness of our struggles was the key to how they could be won. If only we could just tie our struggles together, we would find the strength needed to win on multiple issues.

Meanwhile, Marshall Ganz, organiser and gifted educator, argues persuasively that leadership is a collective process, and that good leadership is always diverse – not just in terms of viewpoints – but also in terms of lived experience. Good leaders use their own experiences and those of those close to them as a resource to judge potential interventions in new, uncertain and evolving situations. Collective leadership benefits from any form of diversity because the group then has a wider and deeper pool of lived experience on which to draw. So how do we move our organisations forward to be more inclusive?

Inclusive organising: liberal or radical approaches?

Perhaps we should start by recognising that it takes some effort to organise in an inclusive way. It's an effort that can be repaid many times over by the increase in power that you are able to generate, but it does require commitment. Before going on to discuss some real-life examples of where inclusivity has made a difference and where it's been missed, it might be useful to explore the difference between 'equality, diversity and inclusion' (EDI) approaches, traditional liberal approaches, and more radical liberation approaches. In EDI, the reason for inclusion is that it is in the interest of businesses or organisations to be *seen* to be diverse and inclusive. The limitation of this model is that it tends to be satisfied with tokenistic 'representation', perhaps in 'customer-facing' roles, but seldom is it reflected in the boardroom. Sometimes this diversity exists more in annual reports or promotional literature than in reality. A few well-placed photos of staff showcase the organisation's commitment to diversity, while the decision making remains firmly in traditional hands.

An alternative 'liberal' approach is to think that those with 'privilege', arising from their 'insider' status, should use their position to create space for a few people from traditionally excluded communities to make 'the first steps' upwards. It's an approach that, despite its best intentions, at times exhibits elements of 'saviour syndrome' and can lead to notions of 'good' and 'bad' minorities. The 'good' are those who gratefully accept the gift of access to the privileged club, while doing nothing to upset the system that created that privilege and its accompanying systematic exclusion in the first place. The 'bad' are those who show no gratitude for being allowed into the club and continue to seek to tear down the processes that give rise to exclusion. Both approaches, while arguably much better than doing nothing, fail to see the core role of the *agency* of the oppressed.

A liberation approach starts from a different perspective. Liberation, according to Paulo Freire (2005), radical educator and philosopher, is the opposite of oppression: a situation in which the oppressed group challenge the power of their oppressors and by doing so change their conditions. A liberation approach to inclusion and diversity starts by recognising, as Audre Lorde (1982) puts it: 'there is no such thing as a single-issue struggle because we do not live single-issue lives.' If we are to 'tie our struggles together', then our organisations must strive, however imperfectly, to be models of the vision of a society we wish to win. This is not merely a tactical choice, but a definitional restatement of who we are. Let's revisit some past campaigns to see how these issues have played out in practice.

Building alliances through intersectional approaches to organising

In the early 1980s the animal rights movement was predominantly White, even though numerous racialised minority communities were culturally sympathetic to the ideas of vegetarianism and not harming animals. In the late 1980s, we became the joint organisers for animal advocacy group, Animal Aid, responsible for expanding its networks and the activity of its local groups. Much of this involved mobilising members to undertake high street protests against particular firms involved in animal exploitation – in particular, companies that used animals in experiments for cosmetics. We also encouraged uninvited inspections of frozen food counters to identify 'hock burns' – also known as 'ammonia burns' – on poultry. This was a painful and unhealthy condition caused by birds being raised in broiler houses where they were forced to sit in their own effluents. Other activities included the usual collecting of signatures on petitions to ban the seal cull, or pro-vegetarian leafleting outside of McDonald's and other meat-based food outlets.

Animal Aid was invited to join a discussion convened by the Young Indian Vegetarians about hosting a vegetarian picnic. For some in the organisation it appeared a side issue and quite distant from the concept of 'activism', or the 'lobbying' that members were used to. Yet we decided to explore how we might work together. At the time, far-right groups were seeking to infiltrate the animal rights movement, opportunistically using concerns about faith-based (Halal and Kosher) slaughter methods as an 'in' to build support for their racist politics. While most animal rights campaigners are reluctant to see the meagre humanitarian step of pre-stunning an animal before slaughter waived, few if any were impressed by right-wing political opportunists seeking to exploit this issue when they showed no compassion for their fellow humans, let alone animals. Nonetheless, far-right groups were, at this time, gaining support, and their presence was unsettling.

We met with the Young Indian Vegetarians organiser and liked his idea, which was very simple; the group wanted to organise an annual vegetarian picnic to bring together people from the Asian community – where vegetarianism was motivated by a range of faiths (principally, Buddhist, Sikh and Hindu) – with the wider vegetarian movement to begin to build alliances and understanding between different sections of society. This approach allowed Animal Aid to work with people who hadn't been in the organisation's orbit before and to broaden the base of its activity. Animal Aid organisers were used to speaking at meetings where people wanted to organise information stalls and protests but were now part of a planning committee that was meeting in a range of Gurdwaras, and Hindu temples across London, with the ambition of organising a picnic, which at first sight seemed quite limited. However, at meeting after meeting, Animal Aid organisers met new groups of people, discussing the idea of a mass vegetarian picnic and at the same time building relationships by sharing food. People from each group were learning from each other and had the opportunity to speak about their social justice organising approaches.

At one temple, Animal Aid organisers spoke to a group of young people, many of whom were soon to leave home to attend university. We talked about the range of concerns Animal Aid had, about not just meat *per se*, but about factory farming, the fur trade, animal experiments and the hunting of animals for sport. At the end of this meeting, several of those present said they would be joining Animal Aid's student network once they got to university. We had, in the language of organising, gone to where people were, and created a bridge between their community and our organisation. As to the picnic, it was great fun. A bit like a trade union festival, but without the alcohol. People were encouraged to bring and share food, there was traditional Indian dancing, and a few speeches, but in general, as at all great festivals, people just sat around, eating, chatting, and occasionally cheering a performance. The festival ran every year while we worked at Animal Aid. The relationship deepened and provided a small bridge between communities. Sometimes we are too focussed on winning a campaign and we forget to take the time to build the alliances necessary to build the power we need to win, yet simple activities like this can broaden the base of our social justice movements and encourage us to explore new approaches. A picnic, like any food-sharing event is a great way to create a sense of community, and the slow pace of the day provides the opportunity to create new connections.

The intersection of oppressions

One example of how it's easy to excuse the absence of marginalised or oppressed groups within decision-making structures, and how this impacts on who is invited in or left out in terms of our organisational structures, is the case of a union branch that unconsciously accepted the under-representation of racialised minority members. This was a branch of an education union who were about to go into dispute with their employer – a further education college. The branch committee were determined to win against their employer and brought together a core of activists who were familiar with working together. The college was in the heart of east London, where most of the students were from racialised minority communities. Yet there wasn't an ethnic minority union member on their committee. The committee agreed a negotiating position, including the 'ask', the 'target' and a bottom line for the negotiations. The negotiations went well, and the employer made sufficient concessions for an agreement to be reached. Later the branch secretary was asked why there were no Black members on the committee, and his response was that teaching in further education colleges was a tough job. He thought that Black people probably had enough problems without 'sticking their head above the parapet' and becoming a trade union rep. While clearly showing concern for the discrimination faced by ethnic minority members, the consequence of this viewpoint was that the branch was unconsciously rationalising, and *accepting*, the absence of important voices on their committee. Within the branch committee were militant anti-fascists, who were always present on anti-racist mobilisations, and very happy to put themselves at some risk when attending street confrontations with the far-right, yet they seemed to have meekly accepted the under-representation of racialised minority members in their branch. The Reverend Desmond Tutu, from South Africa's anti-apartheid movement, is reported to have said, that to be neutral in the face of oppression is to side with the oppressor; in the same way, to be ambivalent in the face of under-representation is to acquiesce to the forces that create that exclusion.

A union example of inclusive organising

Another example is of a local government union branch that was in a poor state, with low levels of membership, many vacant reps' positions and many workers and even union members viewing the union as an external third party, rather than the sum of their own efforts. One section of the union was particularly badly organised and was seemingly unwilling to change – but change it did, at least temporarily, after adopting an inclusive organising approach. Initially, there was simply an acceptance that there was low representation, but there wasn't a concern to rectify this and, for some, it was even believed to be beneficial as it suited their individual interests. Comfortable with a limited amount of facility time some had little concern about organising new members or widening the reps' base to increase representation of the diverse workforce. The section committee was run by a monoculture of White self-declared 'radicals', who operated to keep other potential reps away by consciously alienating them: 'we have driven the right-wing out' was their proud boast. Their definition of 'right-wing', however, was anyone who disagreed with them. This residual group had only tangential connections to the workers they nominally represented but despite this, or maybe even because of it, they viewed themselves as the most radical section committee across the council. Inevitably, given their approach, they were the least effective at organising members when the union entered a year-long series of disputes with the employer. In fact, they were an obstacle.

During this period of industrial turmoil, whole sections of the workforce who had never previously been reached by the union began to organise themselves. The so-called 'hard to reach' groups were those working in small sites with round-the-clock rotas, they were a predominantly 'low-skilled', female workforce with high levels of racialised minority workers, and between them they were holding workplace meetings and electing new reps and instinctively reaching out to other associated workplaces to help them organise. Soon this new grouping was becoming central to the renewal of the branch until they encountered their 'radical' stewards' committee.

The newly organised members were told by the stewards' committee that they needed to seek their permission before organising any more workplace meetings. The newly organised reps had little time for what the rule book allegedly said about whether or not they could organise their work colleagues, and so decided that they needed a committee that was enabling rather than restricting the whirlwind of organising that was taking place. When the opportunity arose, they elected some of their number to be the officers of the committee and used their newly acquired positions to continue to build from the base up. This began to have an impact on the old guard. The 'dinosaurs', many of whom had not turned up to meetings, began to organise – not the workforce – but a rearguard action against the new officers. They packed small meetings, passed motions of no confidence against the new officers, criticised them and demanded that they perform any number of irrelevant bureaucratic tasks, rather than focus on workplace organising.

Within a year, the new energetic and diverse reps had been worn down by the tactics of the old guard and, like their predecessors, were driven out. The 'dinosaurs' back in control of the committee settled down to their posturing and comfortable irrelevance, secure in the knowledge that they could pass any left-wing motion they wanted. This is an extreme example of how some union branches are run, but it is not an isolated problem.

A generation previously, Arthur Scargill had decried the gap between left-wing aspirations and industrial effectiveness, at a time when 'the Irish Question' was central to the left in the UK:

> If you've got a revolutionary leadership that can't even win wage increases, but can go on platforms all over Britain on the Irish question and a thousand and one other things, the workers won't have any faith in that leadership. That's been one of the problems in the past in this union and one of the problems in the past in many other unions, progressive leaders who do not know how to fight properly for their members. (Scargill 1975)

Scargill could also have said that there are staunch anti-racists, who make great speeches, and attend large mobilisations, who have little notion of how to make their own branch inclusive. But making the necessary change is not particularly hard, it just requires some thought and a genuine commitment.

An example we can draw upon with regard to organising women, is a UK rail union, which had national committees to reflect different employers. Network Rail was one of the largest employers with which the union negotiated and there were three individual negotiating committees reflecting the company's structure, and then a national committee which was responsible for company-wide issues (principally pay). At the time the national committee was 100 per cent male. The railways in the UK are disproportionately male workplaces, and women were less likely than male colleagues to be union reps, and those that were, didn't seem to progress through the union structure. At national committee level, women were simply not represented. This was a real failure by the union, that at the time had no programme to actively encourage women to step forward, and to support them on the journey to becoming more senior reps.

The committee was asked by the organiser to consider why women were absent and what could be done about it. The chair of this committee was a track worker, a blunt-speaking rep, who was used to getting his way in negotiations. He was, however, considered a bit of a relic by many in the union. He worked in an all-male environment, where it was accepted to laugh along at sexist 'jokes', and yet, perhaps paternalistically, he would never tolerate such 'jokes' being told in front of women. True to form, at one point in the discussion about what could be done to get more women involved he said: 'I don't mind you getting women involved, so long as you are not trying to get rid of old dinosaurs like me'. It was meant as a joke, and when in reply he was told that that was exactly the plan, he laughed along, indicating that despite his gruff exterior, he was going to support this initiative.

The discussion itself could have infuriated those more familiar with discussions on inclusivity, and it showed that the committee had not discussed, or even thought about the issue seriously before. While the committee was clear that the under-representation wasn't the fault of women – it was said that 'women prioritise the home, and caring, and you can't criticise them for that' – there was little consideration of what barriers the union itself, or the employer, might have placed in the way of women coming forward, or progressing in reps' roles. After a sincere, but perhaps not particularly insightful discussion, it was decided to ask women members what obstacles restricted them from stepping forward. On the face of it, perhaps not exactly a radical move – but a move, agreed unanimously, that would prove transformative.

Following an approach from the union, Network Rail management agreed to release women union members to attend a reps 'taster' session for women who might be interested in going on to become shop stewards. The employer was sympathetic to the idea, not only because they were at least nominally supportive of diversity, but also perhaps because they assumed (wrongly) that women reps may be less challenging than those men who saw the current chair as a role model.

The national committee sent a survey to all women members working in Network Rail, explaining that the union was concerned that women were under-represented in its structures, and it wanted to find out what more it could do to remove barriers to women's participation in their union. The final question was: 'Would you be interested in attending a taster course to learn more about what being a union rep requires?' Forty women said 'yes', of whom 20 attended the taster session, and all the women who attended the reps taster went on to become reps. Within a couple of years, the chair of the committee was a woman, and it was within this context, that the union went on to launch an equal pay campaign.

While the former committee chair was, on the surface, the antithesis of politically correct he was nevertheless a trade unionist who believed in justice and fair treatment. He was proud of the simplicity of the solution that his committee had developed. Following the involvement of new women reps, he became a powerful advocate of taking action to involve more women in the union. This was all the more persuasive because of other people's perceptions of him as a self-declared dinosaur, and the (mostly wrong) assumptions they made about him and his politics.

As to the women reps and whether they were more accommodating to management, C.L.R. James famously asserted that Henry Ford, in the 1940s, had employed African Americans in his car plants in the belief that in a racist labour market, they would be grateful for the work, and consequently less militant than the White autoworkers. However, by 1948 the African American workers at the Ford plant in Detroit were among the best organised workers in the industry. C.L.R. James claimed that Henry Ford had recognised this and therefore decided he wouldn't employ any more African Americans. James concluded: 'He thinks he will do better with women. But they will disappoint him too' (a prescient statement given the subsequent role of women workers at the Dagenham Ford plant in winning equal pay). And so it was with Network Rail. The presumption that an increase in women reps would make life easier for the employer was mistaken. The increase in women reps at the union coincided with an unprecedented, and largely successful, campaign for gender pay equality – something the union had not actively campaigned around previously.

Transforming the profile of an organisation: an example

Another example we can draw upon from personal experience occurred when working for the then UK anti-fascist organisation HOPE not hate. While it was primarily concerned with opposing the exploitation of racism for electoral advantage by the far-right, it was a largely White-led and staffed organisation, and its network of volunteers were predominantly White. This was something that needed to change if the organisation was to be more effective. Yet it posed a number of challenges: How should HOPE not hate lead an effective response to provocative far-right electoral and street mobilisations, and how was it going to address the representation deficit where the communities most affected were under-represented?

When staging provocative marches, the far-right seek to intimidate a whole community. They're not concerned about making friends, and the wider community tend to be bystanders to their actions. Their aim is to provoke a conflict, normally with radical sections of the local youth and, if possible, leave with the local youth fighting with the police. They come to create fear, spread division, to exploit pre-existing tensions, to make people feel isolated and to generate headlines. Taking Saul Alinsky's 'rule' that 'the action is the reaction', HOPE not hate became determined to ensure that after such provocations, the affected community would feel more confident, united and strong, and that the only headlines the far-right achieved were headlines about community unity.

When standing candidates in elections, the far-right generally seek to manipulate a community's sense of loss, of anger and of betrayal, and hitch it to their racist agenda. This can be a particularly hard act to defeat because the messaging is, 'we share your anger and pain' and 'we will do something about it'. In communities that have felt abandoned as a result of deindustrialisation, where once proud, unionised and relatively affluent working-class communities have seen jobs disappear, young people having to move away, and too many of those left behind drawn into addiction or other destructive behaviour, this can be a seductive lie. Such communities have seldom heard answers to their concerns from the political mainstream, and it's in these circumstances the violence and racism of the far-right can appear a small price to pay in exchange for some form of hope – even if it's a totally false hope.

Meanwhile, despite the acute violence of the far-right, it was seldom the biggest or most urgent threat to people from racialised minority communities. People were more likely to experience racism from their boss, from the police or from a group of drunks after pub closing time, than they were to meet racist thugs looking to beat up a random stranger. The far-right have always symbolised the poison of racism, but however acute their contribution is to spreading it, the overall cumulative effect is probably less than that of the drip, drip, drip of institutional and structural racism that racialised minority communities face on a daily basis. While the far-right are undoubtedly the most virulent racists, their relatively small numbers meant they are seldom a priority for people from the communities they target.

HOPE not hate had a dedicated crew of people who were either infiltrating far-right circles, or were recording the actions of the thugs, whether that be campaigning in elections, running 'blood and honour' gigs, or marching intimidatingly through communities. These infiltrators, and the inside information they passed out, was central to a campaign of destabilisation within their organisations. With the rise in confidence of the racist British National Party (BNP) – which for a period of time managed to combine election successes with street mobilisations – and the use of racist rhetoric by UKIP, racism was poisoning public discourse. The eruption of another group, the English Defence League (EDL), created a new force, one that was virulently racist but which tried to hide this behind a veneer of being opposed to 'Muslim extremism'. It was also at least nominally anti-Nazi – although this may have been a ploy for their founder to avoid a leadership challenge from pre-existing Nazi street-fighting gangs.

A challenge for HOPE not hate arose when an incompetent and vile racist planned to march against the 'Jewification' of Stamford Hill, an area of North London that has been home to a large

Jewish community for decades. At the time, the Nazi elements of the far-right had been eclipsed by the street thugs of the EDL. This individual wanted to rally hardcore, street-fighting Nazis on the basis of obscene antisemitism. The virulence of his hatred was such that even hardcore anti-fascists were shocked by the level of incitement to racial hatred involved in this mobilisation. He had certainly found a target in this area of London. The Charedi Orthodox Jewish community wear distinctive clothing and on the sabbath are very visible as they travel on foot to the synagogues in the area. The protest was certainly provocative; there hadn't been a Nazi mobilisation in this part of London for a generation, but he managed to catch the imagination of the diehard, embittered Hitler worshippers, who had been marginalised by the rise of the EDL. What he wanted more than anything was a reaction – preferably a violent confrontation in front of the world's cameras.

The local community in Stamford Hill – and not just the Jewish community – was obviously scared and there were some pre-existing tensions between the various communities in the area that the far-right might be able to capitalise upon. The challenge for HOPE not hate was to ensure that intercommunity tensions were not exploited and to make sure that Stamford Hill didn't become a battleground on which a Nazi resurgence was built. HOPE not hate recognised the dangers of the situation, but also the possibilities. Firstly, the far-right had no base in the area and while there were some low-level tensions between communities, these had been largely managed, if not resolved, by years of hard work by community activists and leaders. The Charedi Jewish community was largely insular, many of the community elders were direct descendants of victims of the Nazi Holocaust and viewed any community tensions through that lens. They knew how ordinary people could be moved to do, or to condone, unimaginably terrible things as a result of antisemitism. Understandably it was difficult to trust outsiders.

The campaign's starting point was that the far-right was aiming to spread division, fear and hatred, so the test of any strategic response would be whether the community was more united, confident and positive once their mobilisation was over. It helped that the Charedi community had good relationships with the local police, and it was evident that on this occasion, the police had no sympathy for the Nazi menace. It was decided to arrange a series of community meetings, and at these it was agreed that the community would downplay the event and, given the police commitment to contain the demonstration, it would be better for it to be a 'damp squib' rather than a scene of conflict.

In the run-up to the event, people from visibly different communities in the area were asked to take a photograph together and share with a hashtag #WeChooseHope, using the provocation of the far-right as an excuse to promote unity. A bilingual leaflet in English and Yiddish was produced and distributed to every house in the area celebrating the community and encouraging people to join the #WeChooseHope online campaign.

When it came to the time and date of the event only 20 far-right activists turned up and marched about a hundred yards surrounded by over a hundred police. A small counter-protest did take place, but the majority of the community kept well away. It was the ultimate 'damp squib', and threats to return regularly were abandoned.

But what was left behind? Was the community more united, less fearful and more positive? The response suggested the approach had a positive effect on community relations. Three local rabbis wrote public letters of thanks to the wider community. One, who was perhaps the most community-engaged of the Charedi rabbis, sent a note of thanks to HOPE not hate (in addition to the public letter of thanks just mentioned). Another, who was known for his deep empathy and roguish charm in sometimes challenging intercommunity meetings, said that the response had made him feel proud to be a 'Charedi, British, Cockney'. But perhaps the most important response was from a rabbi who traditionally was among the least engaged with the wider community and indeed had, in the past, urged his followers not to attend intercommunity meetings. He wrote, publicly, on behalf of the Union of Orthodox Hebrew Congregations, to thank 'the whole of the community' for their support.

The Nazis abandoned their attempt to stir up racial hatred in Stamford Hill, and their leader was jailed for the inflammatory leaflets and social media content. Despite this, the idea of re-centring British Nazism back onto its roots of antisemitism had taken hold in some of the far-right groups, and a few months later, the same group decided to descend on Golders Green, the heart of the North London British Jewish community. This time the group planned a static demonstration – with no sense of irony – at the local war memorial, in the very centre of the community. But they picked the wrong place.

Golders Green's Jewish community is far more diverse than Stamford Hill's, with an eclectic mix of Charedi, orthodox, liberal and reform congregations. The area is also home to a wide range of other communities. It is also the spiritual home of the Community Security Trust, a British charity providing safety, security and advice to the Jewish community in the UK, and which evolved out of the legendary anti-fascist activities of the 43 Group and its successor, the 62 Group. This was a community with Holocaust survivors, so the idea of Nazi advocates coming into the area was horrific. A series of meetings were arranged with Jewish organisations in the area and from that a leaflet was produced and an online petition launched, calling on the police to relocate the 'protest' out of the area. A team from HOPE not hate visited faith and community groups to highlight what was happening. A majority Black church was just yards from the far-right's planned static demonstration, and it immediately offered enthusiastic support from its congregation. This turned out to be the same elsewhere as it was a multi-faith, multi-ethnic community truly comfortable in its diversity. The whole area was leafleted with a flyer that doubled as a poster in gold and green, proclaiming 'we choose hope'. People were asked to display it in their window and within a short time these posters could be widely seen across the community.

A local businessman with a number of the shops on the high street told HOPE not hate that he would take the leaflets, and that all his shops would display one. In the weeks before the planned provocation we were overjoyed to see that every shop – including estate agents, and chain coffee shops – was proudly displaying the poster. Two days before the provocation the campaign heard from the police that it had instructed the Nazi group to move their proposed rally to central London, well away from the community they wished to intimidate. On the day itself, organisers and the community took hundreds of yards of gold and green ribbons and used them to decorate the planned assembly point. Local MPs, councillors and an array of faith leaders joined in. There were so many volunteers that the lamp posts were decorated for about a mile in each direction.

The community chose hope – not hate

It is hard to describe how much fun it was just being in Golders Green that day. Hundreds of people came down to help decorate the street furniture, and to celebrate that the community had come together and created an environment in which the police were persuaded to use their powers to keep the area safe. Two weeks later, *The Jewish Chronicle* carried a supplement – an eight-page HOPE not hate insert with articles from across the community celebrating the success of the mobilisation. One article was written by residents of a care home, some of whom were survivors of the Holocaust. There was a picture of them, some in wheelchairs, each holding a sign saying: 'we choose HOPE'. The far-right had been defeated in their attempt to spread fear, division and mistrust. This particular Nazi mobilisation was the last organised by that group, and the refocussing of racism by the organised far-right onto the Jewish community was abandoned.

Birmingham unites by community organising

A few weeks later, another far-right activist announced plans for regular monthly provocative marches through Birmingham, this time targeting the Muslim community. Inspired by the far-right across Europe, the person planned to create a mass street movement against the Muslim community. For HOPE not hate it was back to the drawing board. How could it ensure that rather than gaining momentum, this initiative fizzled out? This time it had an additional advantage because there were strong trade union contacts across the region. Unison, Unite the union and the Communication Workers Union (CWU) in particular were very supportive and provided space to host meetings. Contacts at Birmingham Central Mosque also helped reach deep into the community. After much discussion, it was decided to host an event the day before the far-right's action. This was held in the

Birmingham Central Mosque and rather than being a traditional rally, it was a community organising event.

Over 500 people attended the event, including representatives from across the faith sector, with local MPs, community groups and regional secretaries from major trade unions – a true cross-section of Birmingham society. People were grouped at tables and were asked to think about issues that were causing frictions between communities in the city, and what could be done about it. Diverse groups worked together to find solutions. Each table selected a person to report back to the wider group, and in the mosque, rabbis, vicars, Quakers, alongside politicians and trade union leaders, shared the proposals created on their table. Together we were literally building community connections in response to the far-right's attempt to divide. A city centre rally the next day turned into a mini carnival. In addition to this, a major online petition was launched to call on the police to relocate the far-right out of the city, which achieved its aim. The end result was that 200 far-right activists marched around an industrial estate near the airport where few could see them. They made their usual shocking and inflammatory speeches, but they were effectively talking to themselves, and even they must have been left wondering what the point of their action was. This was the first and last of their 'monthly' protests.

Origami swans against the Nazis

HOPE not hate began to crystallise these approaches to involving communities in marginalising those who were intent on spreading division into a community-organising strategy. It trained organisers and supporters in how to respond to such provocation by developing a 'when hate comes to town' training module. The starting point was firstly to find allies in the community. Inevitably, many of these allies were from racialised minority groups and organisations. But by engaging with them, the organisation became increasingly diverse not only in its personnel, but also in its thinking – drawing as it did from different lived experiences. This strategy found its most clear expression in the small town of Aylesbury in south-east England. It had been the focus of numerous far-right mobilisations over the years, and local traders hated the days when the far-right and counter-protesters would face off in the market square. Invariably when this happened, the police rapidly told stallholders to pack up and leave as they closed off the area, hitting the traders in their pockets.

On this occasion a local group, in association with a HOPE not hate organiser, devised an innovative and fun approach. The town's symbol was a swan, so the group produced an anti-fascist leaflet with instructions on the back, of how to fold it into an origami swan. Something so simple and innocuous had a real impact. When people got the flyer, they folded it along the relevant lines and created a swan. The 'ask' was that people should place this in their window as a sign of solidarity with their neighbours. A group of committed locals set to work distributing the leaflets, and soon house after house had an origami swan in the window. This may not – at first sight – seem a particularly powerful act, but a group of local Muslim teenagers thanked campaigners for the efforts and expressed their surprise at just how many of their White neighbours had displayed the swans. This simple act had made the support for the local Muslim community very public. On the night before the proposed far-right rally, a team of community activists came together to make hundreds of origami swans and decorate the local trees and lamp posts across the town square. On the day the provocative march was due to take place, traders proudly displayed swans on their stalls. The end result was that only a handful of far-right supporters turned up and they were completely marginalised.

Reflecting the communities most affected by racism?

But what impact did these initiatives have on moving HOPE not hate to be more representative of the communities who were most under threat from the far-right? The first obstacle the organisation faced was that prior to 2015 it had not employed anyone from a 'visible minority' background. There was perhaps an assumption that being an organiser for HOPE not hate would mark someone as a target, but being an organiser from a racialised minority community was likely to be worse. There was a fear that someone from a racialised minority community sent out to organise in a racist area may be at greater risk. Yet this mindset changed when funding was secured to bring a US organiser to the UK for a training project that recruited five young HOPE not hate organisers, one of whom was Sikh.

Funding was later secured to crystallise some of the community-building into a training event called HOPEcamp. The new organising team wrote and delivered a four-day training programme designed to equip supporters to organise in their communities over the longer term. In particular, the learning from the 'when hate comes to town' events – mapping your community, strategic planning, as well as community-bridging and -building techniques, were all explained in the programme. The clear purpose of the training was to equip supporters with the skills they needed to deliver community-building and, in particular, resilience in the face of far-right activity in their communities. Many not only used the skills they developed to progress the work of HOPE not hate but also realised that the method and techniques were transferable into politics, the third sector and trade unions. Crucially, HOPE not hate now began to activate their supporters in a proactive way. Rather than wait for a far-right provocation, local groups were encouraged to build alliances locally around periodic 'days of action'. These included a banner drop for 'Build Bridges Not Walls' after the election of Trump in America in 2016 and events like Refugee Week, as well as specific foci on voter registration drives as racialised minorities tend to be disproportionately absent from the voting register. Local groups working in collaboration with organisations in their area run by and for those from racialised minority communities soon saw the profile of their base shift to one that was more representative.

By the time of the 2017 UK general election – just two years later – HOPE not hate's organising team was diverse, including organisers of Colombian, Asian, Lebanese, Hawaiian, Caribbean and Portuguese heritage, and the supporter base was also increasingly diverse, particularly in communities which were the target of the far-right. As with so much of organising, the key to building a diverse base is to go to where the people are, find the natural organic leaders and engage with them. In a society rife with structural inequality and exclusion, simply expecting a diverse group to reach out to your campaign is a flawed strategy. It takes a conscious effort to organise inclusively. It's not hard or rocket science, and the benefits repay the effort, but like anything else, it doesn't happen automatically.

Developing a diverse leadership within your organisation

This is an exercise you can undertake in your organisation/community

Firstly, think of a group, organisation, or movement with which you are involved.

• Consider who the 'leaders' are, and their profiles – ethnicity, gender, age, disability, class, sexuality, and so on.
• Next, consider your base of activists and supporters, again thinking about their profile.
• What groups are unrepresented, either at leadership or grassroots level?
• What do you think the reasons are for that under-representation?

Make two lists of the factors that are barriers to wider involvement, headed 'external or societal factors' and 'internal factors'.

Consider firstly what you could do to address the internal factors.

Now consider the steps you could take to mitigate the external societal factors.

Choose one under-represented group. Think about the issues your group is concerned about and score them from one to ten according to the extent to which those particular issues are likely to find a resonance within the under-represented group.

Then score those issues on the basis of how much prominence they have in your campaigning.

If you find that the issues that are most relevant to this group are ones you give least prominence to, then maybe you should consider reprioritising.

Finally, think about where you would reach members of this under-represented group. For example, if you are thinking that you want to reach more young Muslims, you might think about the mosque, but you might also think about the local college, or campaigning in a particular area of town. Do you have anyone involved from this group, and if so, can they help you devise a strategy for engagement?

6

Leadership and the development of leaders

This chapter explores different approaches to leaders and leadership development, because without leadership and a strategic direction for your cause, organising will be unfocussed and unproductive. However, as we will explore, there is a wealth of difference between the traditional 'managerial' concept of leadership and the role of leadership within social justice movements. Finding people who will work with you rather than against you is the first step to building power and leverage as you increasingly involve people beyond those who are initially committed. The chapter will also reflect on the concept of 'organic leaders' and explore who these people are and how to create the circumstances where they not only feel involved but have ownership of their actions. The chapter will use the experience of the authors in direct-action groups, and particularly the hunt saboteurs, where everyone is expected to plan and deliver actions, as well as from more traditional groups such as trade unions, where people are often required to respond to a call to action from their 'leaders'. We will draw upon Marshall Ganz's theory of 'collective capacity' to explore how we find, and then develop, effective changemakers.

We will consider how organisations can best build the capacity of their membership, and thereby their ability to win, and explore the importance of disagreement, and disagreeing well, which is a process that allows for the organisation both to respond to changing external factors and to develop the critical faculties of the next generation of leadership. The conflict between Ella Baker and Martin Luther King – both leaders, but in quite different ways – will be explored, and the relevance of these different approaches will be looked at through the modern concept of 'distributed leadership' in the context of the Barack Obama, Jeremy Corbyn and Bernie Sanders grassroots uprisings.

We focus on leadership as it's central to any organising practice – leadership is about enabling others to achieve results, rather than directing, managing and expecting people to follow blindly. It's about building relationships that enable groups to grow and increase their influence, while drawing upon the diverse lived experiences of supporters to find appropriate strategies to win. In business studies, there is a distinction between the role of leadership and that of management. The primary responsibility of a manager is to ensure smooth delivery of a predetermined plan, for example delivering a product to market. This may involve complex processes, including resource allocation, people management, and managing external partnerships. No one is suggesting that managing is necessarily easy, but it's a world of difference between this 'steady state' management process and the process of leadership, which Marshall Ganz defines as: 'accepting responsibility for creating the conditions that enable others to achieve shared purpose in the face of uncertainty' (Ganz 2010: 1)

While every one of these words is important, the phrase 'in the face of uncertainty' is particularly so. In social justice movements we are not interested in managing the status quo; on the contrary, our ambition is to overturn the current state of affairs.

According to Ganz, this requires:

> leadership from the perspective of a 'learner' – one who has learned to ask the right questions – rather than that of a 'knower' – one who thinks he or she knows all the answers. This kind of leadership is a form of practice – not a position or a person – and it can be exercised from any location within or without a structure of authority. (Ganz nd: 2)

To achieve our purpose, we often create organisations to gather support, marshal resources and focus the efforts of those who share our ambitions for change. These organisations need some level of management – even small groups need to have some understanding of their financial income and expenditure – and if events are organised, then some responsibility needs to be taken for the safety and welfare of those participating. If staff are employed, and there are very few examples of systemic change that have not involved organisations with staff, then a whole range of responsibilities, including wages, pension provisions and tax kick in. Such organisations require managers: someone responsible for administration and ensuring that the organisation meets its legal requirements (for example, financial returns to Companies House, payment of wages, obtaining appropriate insurances, raising finances and so on). However, this role is fundamentally different from the leadership that is required to effect change in a complex system. Unfortunately, too many organisations fail to distinguish between the role of leadership and management. There's no reason to expect that a highly effective manager/administrator will necessarily have appropriate leadership skills and be able to support a movement to navigate the levels of uncertainty that exist in facilitating a process of change. Equally, a visionary leader may not have advanced administration skills.

Let's think a little about leadership and the role it has in organising. Throughout social justice movements there are very different leadership models, sometimes within the same movement – and even within the same organisation – which can result in conflict. Think of trade unions which at times have overly bureaucratic formal leadership, where some of those leaders may be resigned implicitly or explicitly to managing decline and therefore have little focus on leadership development, and contrast this with the dynamic workplace/grassroots activism of groups like the UK's Blacklist Support Group – a rank-and-file justice campaign and support network for anyone caught up in the UK construction industry blacklisting scandal. In the African American freedom movement, there were also contrasts between what its arch-enemy J. Edgar Hoover described as 'messianic leadership' (referring to Martin Luther King or Malcolm X, for example) and what has come to be described as distributed leadership – Ella Baker being perhaps the most obvious example – in which leaders develop the leadership and strategic capacity of everyone around them. Marshall Ganz believes that leadership includes taking on the responsibility of creating conditions that enable others. Unfortunately, in social movements, too often we replicate the hierarchies that we seek to dismantle.

Let's look at some examples of organisations and their approach to leadership. On a personal level, we first became active changemakers through the anti-blood sports movement in the late 1970s/early 1980s. Prior to this involvement we had, along with many others, signed petitions and donated funds to various good causes, but it was the involvement in the hunt saboteurs that took us from passive opponents of injustice to active changemakers. It's likely that sabotage of the hunting of wild animals is as old as the blood sport itself – with people taking covert steps to reduce the risk of animals getting killed. We are aware that organised resistance stems from around the time of the Second World War, when US servicemen, stationed in rural England, were aware that they would soon be risking their lives going into battle while the landed gentry would be killing animals for fun. A few servicemen took matters into their own hands and began to disrupt local hunts. Later, a group of fishermen began to systematically disrupt hunts, and in 1963 the Hunt Saboteurs Association (HSA) was formed. At that time the advocacy group, the League Against Cruel Sports, had been active for nearly 40 years. Hare coursing, stag hunting, otter hunting and, of course, fox and hare hunting were all legal, and indeed it wasn't unusual for high profile figures, including members of the royal family, to participate in these blood sports. At the annual Waterloo Cup hare coursing event it was common for hares to be ripped apart by two competing dogs; sometimes this barbarism was caught on camera and broadcast on television. Meanwhile, at fox and stag hunts, young children would have their faces smeared with the blood of slaughtered animals as 'blooding' was a rite of passage. Yet after 40 years of anti-blood sports campaigning there was little to show for the efforts of oppositionists. The establishment of the HSA, however, both helped to raise the public debate and understanding about animal cruelty and, for those opposed to blood sports, created an option to save lives rather than waiting for Parliament to act. There can be little doubt that the sabotage of fox and other hunts was both a form of direct action and a form of 'propaganda by the deed'.

HSA activists (the 'sabs') would get between the quarry and the hunter, obscure the scent of the quarry and disrupt the hounds. Fox hunts go out in the morning and 'block up' fox earths (their dens) so the hunted fox will have nowhere to go to ground. Consequently, the sabs went out prior to the hunt and unblocked the earths, taking the opportunity to spray the area liberally with harmless scents to obscure the scent of the fox, or to lay a false trail that would later lead the hounds off on a harmless waste of time. Sabs would also use a hunting horn to compete with the hunt master for control of the hounds. If successful, they would take the hounds off for miles in the wrong direction. Not surprisingly, the hunts and their supporters were far from impressed and routinely used the threat and actuality of significant violence to deter the sabs. Most 'hits' would involve two or three carloads of sabs coordinating together to minimise the risk of the hunt actually killing. Sometimes things got violent, with hunt supporters physically attacking the sabs, who also had to contend with the police who routinely saw the sabs as 'the problem' and creatively used their legal powers to harass and criminalise sabs.

How did leadership emerge in a direct action context?

In hunt saboteur groups the structure was loose and based upon activity. Leadership wasn't something on which members voted. To be effective, groups had to know where the hunt was going to be – not always an easy thing as they became very secretive. Sabs needed to be able to arrange transport to where they needed to be and have sufficient understanding of the hunt's strategy to be able to deploy tactics effectively. Additionally, it was helpful to be able to navigate the hunt 'heavies', either by avoiding them or by ensuring that any interaction didn't result in violence. Following the emergence of the HSA, hunts tended to go through phases: initially ignoring the sabs, then moving on to organised violence against individuals and sabotage of sabs' vehicles designed to deter them from returning. If that did not work, it was followed by the hunt going underground and no longer publicising their meets in the hope they wouldn't be found and disrupted.

In the loose grassroots operating model of the HSA, leadership involved demonstrating an ability to find the hunt, and the talent to find and train new recruits in the culture and tactics of the organisation. It required the competency to raise finance, particularly if the hunt was routinely sabotaging vehicles, and the skill to support anyone who had been arrested, which often meant finding solicitors with a commitment to social justice and civil liberties. It was seldom that all these attributes resided in one person, so shared leadership emerged. Leadership was tested, week in, week out, in the field and there was no hiding from the results; either you prevented a kill, or you didn't. This wasn't the form of leadership where one person was telling others what to do. Individuals had to know and act instinctively when confronted with a situation. For example, if a hunted animal crossed your path, and the hunt was not far behind, what you did in that instant mattered and everyone in the field needed to know how to make judgements about what was the most effective intervention.

Over time, new approaches evolved. Once portable video cameras became available there was the ability to record the hunt and the kill as a means of influencing public opinion and the political parties. Some groups faced with violent hunts went invisible, preferring to get into the field long before the hunt arrived, soaking the ground with scent, unblocking earths and then from a distance disrupting with the use of the hunting horn. Others responded to the same issue by flooding a hunt with dozens of sabs, seeking to outnumber the heavies, so that they couldn't prevent the sabs from operating. If there was a leadership disagreement about which approach to take, most often the group would simply amicably split, agreeing to disrupt different hunts, and both approaches would then be tested in practice.

What was unique among direct-action groups similar to the HSA was that within local groups no one voted to decide what others would do – this just wasn't the way groups operated. Ultimately, the HSA was a leadership training ground where each group – collectively – took responsibility for creating the conditions that enabled one another to achieve the shared purpose of saving lives in the face of uncertainty.

The formal bureaucratic leadership structure of trade unions

It's useful to contrast this approach to leadership with that adopted by trade unions and perhaps the 'left' more generally. Often in such organisations people can be judged on what they think rather than what they do. In these groups factions tend to form whereby people advocate for a particular 'platform' and then these competing platforms contest elections. People are asked to vote for candidates – often whom they don't know – on the basis of a few paragraphs in a manifesto designed to outline their vision. When this happens, individuals are not necessarily being judged by their ability to effect results, but on how positive their vision sounds. Sometimes in union elections, challengers will appeal to people's frustrations, often blaming the existing 'leadership' for any dissatisfaction. Unfortunately, this can lead to a cycle where members' votes are cast for those who speak well, rather than those who act well. In such cases, members can come to believe that all that is necessary is for these newly elected eloquent 'leaders' to be left to get on with the task of winning on behalf of members. There is a danger that this type of election does nothing to activate the wider membership, which is the only source of the necessary power to effect change in the workplace.

There's another trade union tradition, one that sometimes sits alongside the one just described. In the 1930s, the concept of rank-and-file trade unionism emerged. This was based on the belief that workers could organise and win – irrespective of the bureaucracy. It emerged in the engineering industry, where regular changes in working patterns were taking place and where changes were negotiated locally – with effective reps negotiating a 'plus payment' for accepting the new process or working practice. With new products, came the opportunity to negotiate a renewed rate for the job. At the time, employers were keen to increase production and open to negotiating what was referred to as a 'piece rate' – in effect, payment based on output. The level of the piece rate was determined by the negotiating skill of the local rep and the level of support they had within their department. Soon a significant part of workers' wages was made up of these plus payments, or piece rates. Reps were judged by the outcomes of what they were doing – the pay in their members' pockets. This rank-and-file leadership at plant level involved developing a network of reps who could press management at every turn and maximise the rates of pay for every job. Winning meant having a well-organised workplace, because power and leverage came from being organised, and the boss knowing that work would come to halt unless workers' demands were met. Like the local hunt saboteurs, this day-to-day localised bargaining was a training school for trade union leadership based on developing organised support from those working alongside the rep, and there was no hiding from the results.

In the late 1960s, the government convened the Donovan Commission, with the aim of reducing conflict in the workplace, intending to replace it with consensus. The Donovan Report called for a 'professionalisation' of unions and a recognition of the value of employee voice (but not power). As a result, legislation was passed that allowed union reps paid time off for trade union duties and training. Instead of local workplace reps negotiating on behalf of themselves and their fellow workers, a paid union official, or a worker released from their normal duties, would do so. This, perhaps more than all the other changes in industrial relations over the last 50 years, has done most to neuter trade unions and limit the development of workplace leaders. Arguably, it is a more significant shift than the whole raft of anti-union laws that followed; at the time the vast majority of strikes were unofficial, whereas today there are virtually none of these 'wildcat' strikes. This professionalisation has led to a situation where outcomes of negotiations are seen to be dependent upon the skills of the union negotiator rather than the level of workplace organisation. Accompanying this change, for most members, the union is now perceived as a form of insurance policy. Workers believe that they are buying a service from a union, rather than working together with fellow members to create the power that will limit the ability of their management to make arbitrary decisions that will adversely affect them.

Today, most union reps spend most of their time on things like casework, recruitment – which is not the same as organising – and passing resolutions to be debated at a higher-level committee. Often this leaves little time for negotiations with management which have a direct impact on their working lives. There are of course exceptions, and this is not the way things operated in the past. For example, in local government there used to be an elaborate structure of negotiations. In each department there were regular management/union consultation meetings, each directorate would have a committee to which any unresolved issues at department level could be referred, and at local authority level there was a joint consultative committee that was chaired by councillors. Here, big issues were discussed, such as the almost inevitable annual round of cuts, but also issues unresolved at directorate level. Big issues and regular reports were then debated at full council meetings, with trade unionists invited to speak in front of elected councillors.

Today, many unions, including the lay leadership, are opposed to local bargaining. While there are arguments for national bargaining in preference to local bargaining – there can be benefits to both – there are implications from an organising perspective. Perhaps this is best illustrated by the UK further education sector, where employers refuse to bargain nationally; instead, there is a series of national 'framework agreements', none of which are binding on individual colleges. The union negotiates hard for a national agreement on 'recommended pay', which is then often ignored by local employers. Yet there is so much scope, not just for winning and building at a local level, but also for the development of a new generation of union leaders. Much like the hunt saboteurs, local union reps involved in local negotiations have to make decisions in complex and changing circumstances, and this requires building the support of members at the local level. Equally, there are some issues that can only realistically be dealt with at a local level: issues like failures in building maintenance, bullying managers or disproportionate use of formal procedures against minority staff. These issues can only be dealt with effectively when local management understand there are consequences if the issues are not addressed. These local negotiations and the contest for power and control over the workplace is a training ground for practical leadership. It's here that reps learn how to judge what is possible, and how best to achieve it.

One example is from a local authority's environmental health division, where union reps raised an issue about casualisation of staff. With uncertainty about long-term finances, departments were tending to recruit people on fixed-term contracts or to resort to using agency staff. Annually, these contracts would be extended for another year, leaving employees in an endless employment-status limbo. The local union researched the issue and built a campaign through reps, and then made a convincing case to local management to undertake an audit of all fixed-term contract and agency roles. While some temporary roles, for example fixed-term contracts to cover maternity leave, or extended sickness, were seen as entirely appropriate, others that had been renewed annually for seven or eight years clearly needed to be converted to permanent roles. Some agency workers had been working indirectly for the council for years; individually they were being paid significantly less than their colleagues while, at the same time, it cost the employer significantly more to employ them through the agency. Converting these agency roles to permanent in-house employees not only created job security for the staff but also saved the council money. It wasn't a hard argument to win, but it was only possible because the union, at a local level, was taken seriously and had the reach and capacity to undertake an audit of all casual jobs and make a case for why they should be converted to permanent positions.

The following year, the environmental services department was facing serious cuts, which would inevitably mean job losses. A large part of the department's work involved administering housing renewal grants either to elderly and/or disabled residents or to landlords to bring their properties up to modern standards. The funding for these grants came directly from central government, and was ring-fenced, and so formed no part of the council's cuts agenda. Discussions in a workplace union meeting were fairly despondent until someone remembered that many years previously the council had used some of this 'capital renewal grant', to fund the roles necessary to administer it. In other words, a small amount of capital expenditure (long-term investment in the borough's housing stock) could be used to fund roles which ordinarily would have been seen as 'revenue' expenditure (wages). The cost of administering the grants was a tiny percentage of the overall budget, and without staff, it would be impossible to deliver the grants, and the ring-fenced money would be lost.

The union position was that the work of grant administration should be funded from the grant pot. When this was presented to management, they initially were sceptical that it would work, but after enquiring with the finance department, they responded positively, and as a result no posts were lost and no one was made redundant. This 'fix' was only possible because local union members were involved in the discussions and one of them had a memory of how things had been done differently.

At about the same time, the council had decided to go through what it described as a transformation process. The council definitely needed some transformation, but not this particular version. A process was begun which was designed to make everyone feel insecure whereby all council employees were to be forced to reapply for their own jobs. Report after report went to committee in which existing jobs were 'deleted', existing staff were identified as redundant, and new, near-identical jobs created for which the existing staff had to apply. This process was almost certainly not compliant with employment law and had serious equality implications, including a systematic refusal to acknowledge the right of women on maternity leave to return to work. This transformation process began at the top of the organisation and was cascading down through the structure.

In one department, proposals came forward for team leader posts to be deleted, and then exactly the same roles were being recreated at a slightly higher grade, which meant none of the existing postholders would have assimilation rights. Their manager took the opportunity to update their job description to include all the tasks that they had absorbed over the years but which had not previously been updated on their job descriptions. The local reps saw this process as a war of attrition and were determined to fight against these unfair practices at lower management levels, as they understood that if this abuse was not stopped, the next step would be that this process of 'reorganisation' would be cascaded down to front-line union members. The local union reps recommended to the team leaders that before their jobs were formally deleted they should apply to have them regraded, on the basis they were already doing all the tasks described in the new role. In a delicious twist of fate, their manager, who had just been through the unpleasant process of reapplying for his own job, was asked to comment on the validity of their regrading appeal. He simply agreed with their/the union's assertion, that they were already doing all the new items on the new job description. They eventually retained their positions and pocketed a pay rise; in this department, the so-called 'transformation agenda' stalled before it even reached the front-line staff.

All of these little negotiations, battles and manoeuvres taught the local reps how to play the system, how to argue convincingly that their proposals were 'in everyone's best interest', how to compromise when they had no power, and how to push when they did. This is how trade unionists used to be trained and local leadership developed. Of course, reps need to understand how to run a disciplinary case, or a series of negotiations, and classroom training is an essential element of their development, but the real learning takes place addressing issues creatively in the workplace. Without this, reps become just the mouthpiece for members' complaints largely ignored by the employer; little organising takes place and certainly no leadership development; and the union is viewed as a well-meaning, but largely ineffective advocacy organisation rather than the sum of its members' collective efforts to effect change.

Speechmaking: not always evidence of great leadership

In movements for social justice, either industrial, communal or political, we tend to find ourselves either seeking or being saddled with varying degrees of 'charismatic' leaders. The long list of disappointments, of people who once made rousing speeches, but who over time prove to be self-serving, or simply idiosyncratic and wrong, is long. There is plenty of evidence of people with these traits in both political parties and trade unions. Others, despite good personal credentials, have perhaps inevitably proven incapable of single-handedly resolving all our problems. Incidentally, many of these figures don't reflect the gender or ethnic diversity of the wider movement: such 'leaders' tend to be made up primarily of White men, which perhaps says something additional about the deficiencies of the charismatic-leader model of leadership within social justice movements.

There are, however, exceptions to this tendency to have great speakers who are ineffective, and some unions are a model of good practice for leadership development, for example when traditional paid union 'officer' roles are elected directly from the membership. This happens in the UK's rail union, the National Union of Rail, Maritime and Transport Workers (RMT), and in the Communication Workers Union (CWU), where local lay leaders rise to national leadership positions for a time and then there's an expectation that people will 'return to their tools' after a period of office and, as a consequence, knowledge and experience is shared and collectivised. The RMT has, for historical reasons, created a process by which reps at a local level develop the skills necessary to win disputes and, as a result, the charismatic figures that have come to characterise the organisation in recent years, Bob Crow, former general secretary, and Mick Lynch, current general secretary, can not only 'talk the talk' but, because of the way the union is organised, very often can actually deliver *with* members.

From where do leaders arise?

There are leaders everywhere within our communities, although maybe they (and others) don't necessarily see themselves as leaders. They organise in their communities, ensuring things that need to be done are done, often quietly and without recognition. As organisers we need to learn to spot these organic leaders and nurture them. A person who was excellent at this was Ella Baker. She was a field officer for the National Association for the Advancement of Colored People (NAACP), and in the 1940s she would tour the Deep South trying to put together a network of activists. She was always welcome in the majority Black churches that were later to become the backbone of the emerging civil rights movement. But it was seldom the charismatic preachers by whom she was captivated. The people who impressed her were those who got the jobs done that afforded the preacher their pulpit. These were often women, whose organisational skills were honed doing the mundane voluntary tasks that were necessary to keep the church functioning. It was these women who become central to the success of the African American freedom movement. In what might seem an unlikely place to find activists, another source of leadership was in the networks of the Black women's hairdressers. These hairdressers would visit clients in their own homes, where they were able to talk freely. These women weren't dependent on White patronage for their income and couldn't be blacklisted by the White supremacists. They became a key element in the communications channels that were central to the mobilisations of the civil rights movement, in part because they facilitated two-way communications – the movement had its asks, communicated through trusted voices, but it also heard what the mood of the community was. Similarly in the UK during the 1963 Bristol Bus Boycott, perhaps the first assertion of community power by the Windrush Generation, one of the key networks was through the local DJs. With racism in society excluding the Black community from traditional venues for weddings, birthdays and other celebrations, a network of community DJs came into being who provided the soundtrack to the community. These DJs were networked, in one way or another, to almost every family in the community. The point is that leadership is everywhere, as organisers you just need to find it and tap into it.

Finding leadership in communities

How do you, as an organiser, go about finding leaders? Let's use an example from our own experience to illustrate the point. When a major supermarket decided to build a superstore with a housing development on top adjacent to Abney Park Cemetery in North London, local people were alarmed at the adverse impact on the cemetery, a designated nature reserve. There were concerns about the impact of increased traffic, the lack of affordable housing in the scheme and the demolition of a series of live/work units. The local community felt it was wrong in so many ways that it needed to be challenged.

A public meeting was called, which was packed, and what was powerful was the range of interest groups represented. There were tenants from the live/work units, volunteers at the cemetery, local shopkeepers whose livelihood was threatened, traffic campaigners and many more. Prior to the meeting, when people were leafleting the high street to garner support, a guy approached and said: 'Hello, I am a planning nerd.' We found he was not only self-deprecating but had an encyclopaedic knowledge of local planning rules and regulations. Another offer of help came from one of the people whose live/work unit was going to be demolished. He was a graphic designer with many useful skills for the campaign. A music journalist offered to help with a newsletter. When the protest group organised a 'zombie parade' a group of supporters turned up with a massive PA system that they wheeled around the streets. There was also a fundraising social which volunteers who worked in the catering industry turned into a sit-down meal. A volunteer at the cemetery nature reserve was a former lawyer and amateur botanist who was able to advise on the ecological impact of the proposed development. A local shopkeeper whose business would be threatened if the development went ahead, spoke to every shopkeeper on the street and raised money for the campaign. All of these people were leaders in their own right and they coordinated like-minded people to work alongside them as the campaign developed. The campaign's ethos gave them permission to utilise their leadership skills. This is the networked, distributed leadership that provides campaigns with the potential for greater strength and active involvement beyond an initial small grouping.

All these people found the campaign rather than the campaign finding them, but the campaign was structured to create such opportunities for people to contribute whatever they could do most effectively with their skills and time. The best example of these unsolicited offers of help was when, despite a fabulous campaign, the council granted the development planning permission. After this was reported in the press, an email was received from a local resident who was a barrister specialising in judicial review and environmental law, offering pro bono assistance. Needless to say, this was rapidly taken up and was central to the subsequent success of the campaign.

The campaign had taken an outward-looking perspective, keen to engage with the whole community and to make space for different approaches. It produced a poster with an illustration of how many supermarkets were within one mile of the development. It undertook price checks to illustrate that the new supermarket would not be cheaper than the existing ones. It advised tenants in the live/work units about their legal rights, and ultimately launched a judicial review. Fun was central to the campaign; a zombie parade and a separate bug parade were staged both to gain press coverage and to celebrate the scale of support. The first signified that even the dead were rising up from the cemetery in protest, and the second that the local wildlife wanted to express their opposition to the plans. When a local restaurateur and business leader was quoted in the paper allegedly calling the campaign 'nimbyism' (a term of abuse), campaigners who were regulars at his restaurant spoke to him and he agreed to allow, free of charge, the use of the basement of the restaurant for one of the big public meetings and additionally provided a free cocktail to everyone who attended.

This was a fun campaign to be involved in and there was only one enemy: the developer. It was a unifying campaign with a strong story of us. But none of this was an accident. It was a strategic choice to be open and inviting, and community leaders (official and unofficial) came to us volunteering their skills and experiences. Despite the early perception from some seasoned veterans within the community that 'you can't win planning disputes with supermarkets' the campaign went on to achieve 100 per cent success.

Why organic leaders are important to have on side

Saul Alinsky believed that within every community there were 'native' or 'indigenous' leaders. Jane McAlevey argues that in every social circumstance, whether that be at work, on an estate, or in a club or organisation, informal or 'organic' leaders naturally emerge. No doubt there are complex and different ways in which individual leaders surface that could fill a whole book in itself, but for now let's focus on the fact that within any social group some people are likely to have more influence than others. This might be because of force of personality, through generosity of spirit, or simply because they are the ones who best judge the mood of the group.

Both Alinsky and McAlevey argue convincingly that changemakers need to find and recruit these leaders to our cause. Although, as McAlevey points out, this isn't always easy. Often a workplace leader may not feel they need to be part of a collective; they may even feel that the union is a negative influence, 'defending the indefensible' when representing some members facing disciplinary action. In her argument, she says that those organic leaders who are against you are the key to success. If you can 'flip' them so they start advocating for your cause among their group, then it is a huge step forward. Indeed, it is one of the most powerful ways in which you can shift the balance of power. If they are actively hostile and you cannot change their view, then you need to reduce their influence. For McAlevey, a change process begins by mapping the organic leaders within your community, or in her terminology 'structure', and giving each a score on a scale ranging from fully supportive to hostile and then working out a plan as to how to use them, flip them or reduce their influence. This concept of organic, native or indigenous leaders (we think these terms are all describing the same thing) is a useful insight, but it often relies on a 'leaders are the people who have followers' definition of leadership. This is in contrast to the Ganz-based concept of leadership, in which leaders are not the people with followers, but those developing leadership skills in others.

Another alternative perspective when thinking about leadership is to think of 'leaders' as followers. This model suggests that 'leaders' reflect rather than shape the views of their constituency, and that leaders will follow the crowd – albeit a few paces in front. In this model of change, you need to create a momentum by shifting a few people who then influence others so that the centre of gravity within the group shifts, at which point the 'leaders' will switch.

Distributed leadership is central to organising

In his writings Marshall Ganz talks about 'distributed organising' models, but these could equally well be labelled 'distributed leadership' models. Blueprints for Change – an open library of how-to guides put together by campaign innovators – describe distributed organising as a process that 'activates a network of self-starting supporters/campaigners in multiple locations, which can spread across geographical boundaries, interests, and cultural groups. It draws on the initiative and energy of volunteer organizers to start groups and lead teams with varying degrees of autonomy' (Blueprints for Change 2023).

In comparison, traditional NGO-led campaigning and party-led political organising tends to rely on more command-and-control leadership, and paid staff and organisers to mobilise others to act and raise awareness. However:

> Though more horizontal when compared to traditional command and control leadership, distributed organizing often relies on a central coordination group to launch the network and to drive it towards common goals and milestones. When done properly, it can help a movement or campaign scale rapidly and channel huge amounts of collective power. (Blueprints for Change 2023)

This is surely the embodiment of Ganz's method, and within it can be seen two elements of leadership: the central leadership or coordination group that 'launch the network' and 'drive it towards common goals and milestones', and then the local and regional leadership that builds the power of the movement from the bottom up. Or, as Wilf Sullivan, former head of race equality at the UK's Trades Union Congress (TUC) has argued, people think that in a movement everyone should be doing the same thing, but in reality, people need to be doing a range of different things that take us towards the same goal. An important, if little understood, element of leadership is therefore simply giving people permission to act. This process of giving permission can also be described as ceding control. Marshall Ganz makes this distinction between power and control. For example, in distributed organising, part of the strategy to build power is for the organising centre to cede control to the base. In what might seem counter-intuitive to many people, a reduction in control is a prerequisite for an increase in power. Ceding control is part of the process of creating the conditions that enable others to achieve shared purpose. Perhaps the best-known (but undoubtedly flawed) examples of this approach are the successful first campaign run by Barack Obama for US president, and the later ultimately unsuccessful campaign for Bernie Sanders to become the Democratic candidate for president. What characterised these campaigns was a massive amount of hope that things could be different, vast amounts of small donations to fund the campaigns, and large numbers of people volunteering their time to make it happen.

In terms of leadership development or capacity-building, the campaigns might better be judged not on the short-term objective (important though that was) but on the extent to which they shifted power and agency. The distributed organising machine incredibly created the context in which the surviving veterans of voter registration and desegregation campaigns of the 1960s witnessed the inauguration of a Black president. But tragically that organisation was rapidly demobilised once Obama was elected to office. People were thanked but then stood down when, in reality, the counter-offensive, from the Tea Party to Trump, was just getting started and their activity was needed more than ever. The history of the United States might have been very different if that distributed network had been maintained.

In 2015, a 73-year-old Bernie Sanders announced his candidacy for the Democratic nomination for president of the USA. It was an audacious move for an outsider in the Democratic Party, yet he came close to winning the nomination. What he did was largely unprecedented in Democratic politics. He refused to take campaign sponsorship from big donors, and instead relied on what Alinsky would have referred to as 'the little people' – the masses of people who don't normally have any say or influence in big politics. Sanders raised $73 million from more than a million contributors, with the average donation being less than $28. Jeff Weaver, Sanders' campaign manager, commented, 'What we are showing is that we can run a strong, national campaign without a super PAC and without depending on millionaires and billionaires for their support. We are making history and we are proud of it.' (Politico 2016). Sanders' rallies were also huge, with as many as 28,000 attending in Portland (*Washington Post* 2015). But what happened to this base of support? The answer is that it dissipated because once the selection campaign was over supporters weren't mobilised for another four years.

Four years later Bernie Sanders once more stood for the Democratic nomination, and again he lost. In organising terms, he wasn't developing leaders, he was developing followers. Imagine for a moment if the 2015 campaign had been followed by, say, a conference in which those involved were encouraged to implement a campaign in their community based upon the issues on which Sanders was campaigning. It could have been over poverty, health care, race, or gender equality, for example. If so, the momentum of the Sanders' campaign could have rolled forward into a 'do it yourself' reform movement generating pressure across the country. Yet it didn't, and there was no momentum to move forward. As a consequence, there was no young emerging leader who could have taken on the mantle when Bernie Sanders was too old and too frail to carry it any further. As with the Obama campaign, despite being truly inspirational, it was also a largely wasted opportunity.

Another example of flawed leadership is the campaign around the election of Jeremy Corbyn in the UK as Labour Party leader, and the formation of the Momentum group to support him. While Momentum's campaign scaled very rapidly, and the unprecedented leadership election victory inspired many people, its subsequent focus on internal Labour Party infighting and voting for 'left' candidates in internal elections failed to change the external environment, leaving many in the wider electorate susceptible to lies and smears (as it happens, many emanating from within the Labour Party machine) against Corbyn and the party he led. The often-impressive numerical mobilisations in the election period proved incapable of changing the dominant narrative, and with Corbyn's election defeat, Momentum, as an organisation, largely collapsed, not even leaving behind a convincing 'continuity Corbyn' candidate in the subsequent party leadership election. In the face of internal and external opposition, five years of Corbyn's leadership of the Labour Party failed to deliver electoral success, but it also failed to convert the legions of 'Corbynistas' into local campaigners who could effectively organise their communities. The only protection against lies and slander directed towards a left reformist candidate is a well-organised base, and five years is ample time to turn a significant percentage of 'supporters' into active leaders in their communities, but tragically this didn't happen.

These are all examples of a partial, flawed, distributed organising approach that failed because it was used for a short-term objective rather than as a means to build long-term capacity. The historic achievement of getting Barack Obama elected and the significant shift in US politics around race was followed by the disaster of Trump. What we can perhaps learn from this is reflected in the wise words of Myles Horton, who said that ultimately building the capacity of people to act in the pursuit of sustainable change is arguably more important than winning the short-term objective.

Leadership development

Another question to consider is whether we can develop our own leaders, or is it the case that people are 'born to lead'? In the Marshall Ganz model of leadership, leaders develop the leadership in others and, as we saw in the hunt saboteurs or the traditional model of local union negotiations, the way you organise can 'create the conditions' that are conducive to the development of leadership potential. Yet the reverse can also be true: autocratic leadership can reproduce the very power dynamics within your movement that you want to eradicate from wider society. If you want to lead, these are some traits that are worth developing in yourself and others.

Ask don't tell

A basic curiosity about others is key to leadership. This involves listening to other people's stories, asking how they feel about a situation and what motivates them. It's commonly assumed that leaders have all the answers, but this is wrong, leaders need to have the right questions. The right answers will flow when the community uses its collective knowledge to find them.

Be comfortable with disagreement

It is said that unity is strength, but while it is true that unity in action is strength, unity in thought is a weakness. Group think occurs when people are more comfortable in reaffirming their pre-existing views or reinforcing a particular viewpoint, irrespective of material evidence which contradicts their beliefs. In contrast, dissent and disagreement are essential to innovation. If we go back to Marshall Ganz's definition of leadership, he says this takes place 'in the face of uncertainty'. When we are seeking to create change there will always be a range of things we simply won't know at a particular time in a campaign. For example, what exactly will it take for the target to change their position? How much support do we have in our community? What might change that will create a new opportunity to advance? There will likely be different opinions about all of these, and leadership involves working with these different views. The alternative is a stagnant agreement that too often fails to recognise when any of the above factors are changing.

Diversity

The more diverse your leadership team is, in terms of identity and lived experience, the more likely you will find the answers you are looking for. The more experience in a campaign meeting, the greater the collective resource there is to draw on. This diversity could be in terms of age, gender, ethnicity, disability, and so on, but it could also be in terms of other lived experience. The more difference in the room, the more likely someone will have experience of a solution to your problem. If you want to win more than you are currently capable of, then audit your core group and ask questions such as 'What experience is missing?' or 'Which networks are not represented in our core personnel?'. Finding ways to plug those gaps is a step towards a better, more knowledgeable leadership model.

Actively make space for innovation

Experimentation with tactics is always fun, even if something doesn't work. There's no shame in accepting that a particular approach has proven ineffective and finding an alternative approach. Having a range of tactics running alongside each other can increase your influence, as it draws in different people attracted to different ways of working. So long as everything operates within a broadly defined strategy, then encourage your people to experiment with different approaches: apart from anything else, it puts more pressure on your target as they don't know what your campaign will do next. The zombie parade in the Save Abney Park Cemetery campaign was a lot of fun and didn't feel like people were being asked to reinvent themselves as stereotypical 'activists'. It felt more like a community carnival, and it was almost impossible for the target to confront.

Don't be afraid of compromise

It is a myth that anything short of your aspiration is a defeat or a 'sell-out'. There will be many times when the power you can generate is insufficient to win the full aspiration of your campaign. Meanwhile, there is no such thing as a glorious defeat. The art of compromise is something learned by activity. There will be times when your forces are exhausted, and you will need to settle for little more than a token advance: the alternative is a complete disintegration of your support. If you never compromise, then you will miss numerous opportunities for small advances, and those small wins can be steps towards building the confidence of your people to challenge themselves to build the power necessary so that they can win more. Those voices who demand nothing short of complete victory, whatever the balance of power, are almost inevitably absent from the work of building the power to win anything.

Make democracy real

For some people, democracy starts and ends with an election (for a shop steward, general secretary or committee member). The role of the voters after the election is often simply to follow instructions from the elected 'leader'. Real movement democracy actively involves the supporters – not merely a small group of activists – in making decisions on a day-to-day basis. This democratic practice ensures accountability of the leadership, it acknowledges those who are contributing to the activity of the campaign and invites ownership of the strategy, and it creates the opportunities for developing supporters as leaders, making their knowledge and experience central to the strategising of a campaign.

Learn (collectively) from your mistakes

Part of the art of leadership is to navigate setbacks. No campaign advances in a straight line from a simple start to a resounding success. There are times of swift advance, and times of serious setbacks. Your people need to learn from every phase of the campaign: they need to be part of the decision-making process all the way through. Setbacks can create the determination that 'we need to redouble our efforts and become better organised', or they can lead to bitter, ultimately self-destructive, internal struggles to apportion blame. Learning and reflecting as a movement after a setback, without recrimination, can be the most valuable opportunity to develop leadership.

In society we are taught to think of leadership in terms of either 'great leaders', who are somehow better than the rest of us, or positions of power, elected officials or business leaders. But in organising terms, leadership is a movement practice, and developing the leadership capacity of all our people is the only way we generate the ability to consistently win. If it is true that there are only two sources of power in society – organised money and organised people – then we need to organise a lot of people, and that requires the development of leadership throughout the length and breadth of our movements.

Finding and developing leaders

In a campaign or movement in which you are active, ask yourself:

- Where do we find leaders?
- How do we develop leaders?
- How do we ensure diversity in our leadership?
- To what extent do we give permission to supporters to be creative?
- What processes do we have for collective learning from both success and setbacks?

And then ask yourself, what do we need to change to do all of these things better?

7

Developing a 'story of us'

In 1987, we were told by the prime minister, Margaret Thatcher, that there is 'no such thing as society', yet most people believe that there is, or at least should be, something called society of which we are all part. Without a sense of 'us', how do we, as organisers, build communities of interest – people who come together to effect change for the better? Within society there will be competing communities, including some forces that are detrimental to a progressive social justice agenda. It's important, from an organising perspective, that we have a clear understanding of who is 'us' and who is 'them' when undertaking power analysis. Put simply, it affects our ability to mobilise our forces for change. It's not simply a question of who is with us and who is against us, but who *should* be with us, a question of whose interests converge with the changes we want to see.

Utilising Marx's distinction between a 'class in itself' and a 'class for itself', in this chapter we'll explore how the way we identify 'us' and who is in and who is outside our community can make a difference to whether or not we are likely to win. Whether it is defeating narratives of division, or creating an alliance to effect local change, it matters who makes up, and how we identify, an 'us'. The chapter will draw upon experiences in post-industrial towns where deep divisions between communities have emerged as a consequence of poverty, exclusion and racism, and the false narrative that blames the wrong 'others' for a situation in which people feel they have been left behind. We will explore how, through community organising practice, it's possible to develop new narratives of 'us' that have the potential to bring together divided communities.

The chapter will also explore the synergy between Marshall Ganz's work about developing 'stories of us' and Jane McAlevey's 'super majority' organising approach, which argues that to win big, we need to have majorities of 75–80 per cent within any defined community. Put simply, if organised people are to win against organised money, they have to be organised en masse. A question posed here will be: how do we create a story of 'us' that's both unifying and – to use John Kelly's terminology – attributive, at the same time?

In this chapter we will use a number of examples to illustrate how to create stories of us. One is a dispute in the London Borough of Hackney in 2000, when the council effectively declared itself bankrupt and planned to cut services, jobs and the wages of low-paid council employees. Libraries, nurseries and other services were under threat and the local trade union branch responded with a traditional industrial action strategy, but also undertook a community-based response involving library users and nursery supporters. Another example will be from a training unit the authors delivered in Teesside in 2019, when they asked the group about the story of their town, and then unpacked who was missing from this story, and how people could be written back in. But first let's dig a bit deeper into why this is such an important task for organisers.

How a story of 'us' can lead to building a strong base of support

Effective changemakers instil hope into a community, a belief that their grievances are justified and that together they can build the power necessary to achieve change. This involves being able to articulate those grievances in a way that binds people together such that they *feel* that they are part of a unified collective. Feel is emphasised because movement building for social justice causes is as much about the heart as it is about the head. As Marshall Ganz informs us, this is because it's often emotion that motivates people to act and, equally importantly, to value those who feel similarly. This sense of valuing others is the building block of solidarity, and to create this solidarity in action organisers need to translate both values and concerns into a shared narrative. While we traditionally draw upon logic, evidence and data to persuade, or to win arguments, it's stories that create empathy. Think of how listening to someone tell their story can be much more effective than an expert detailing the scale of a particular problem. People expressing how something affects them personally can evoke an emotional response – you can feel someone's pain when you hear their story, precisely because it's personal and not abstract. It's something to which you can relate.

What we are trying to do as organisers is to translate these 'stories of self' into 'stories of us' – stories that articulate the shared values held by a community and reflect our common concerns. This 'story', along with a vision or strategy for change, is what gives confidence to people to step up and commit to action. The development of these stories of 'us' is a critical leadership function, and an important role of leadership is to help shape the narratives that allow groups to coalesce. Marshall Ganz describes a story of us in this way:

> Public narrative can be used to access the emotional resources needed to respond mindfully by mobilizing hope over fear, empathy over alienation, and self-worth over self-doubt. Leaders learn how to tell a 'story of self' that can communicate the values that explain why they have been called to lead; a 'story of us' that brings alive values their community shares; and a 'story of now' of the urgent challenge to those values that requires action. (Ganz 2016a)

Further it's much easier to win a campaign if you have high participation and widespread support, particularly so when you are operating in a hostile environment. When you demonstrate that you have the majority of a community or a constituency with you, who are willing to act together, then not only do you build the confidence of that constituency, but you are also increasing your power and leverage. By organising what Jane McAlevey calls 'structure tests' (these can be thought of as 'practice runs' designed to demonstrate to your supporters and to your opponents that you have the capacity to mobilise to win), you can both build solidarity and test objectively if you have built sufficient power.

An example of a structure test might be a workplace petition to management where you get a super majority of the workforce to sign it. If you can do this, you will have demonstrated to both your members and the employer that you are not acting as 'just a few malcontents' but an organised workforce. On an estate contemplating a rent strike, getting people to put a poster in their window will visibly show fellow tenants how much support you have.

These visible shows of strength build confidence and determination for the big fight. Without them campaigners are operating in the dark, not sure what forces they have behind the issue and uncertain about the chances of winning. A blind call to action that turns out to be poorly supported will lead to supporters becoming deflated and demoralised when they realise that they are a vocal or 'militant' minority without the power to win. They can feel misled and misused as well as reluctant to take further action in the future. While we can't always guarantee a win, supporters need to believe that there's a realistic chance of success when entering into any dispute, and a structure test provides an objective indication of whether you have built the majority support which is almost always necessary before acting.

Who are your people?

The African American freedom movement organiser Ella Baker would famously ask young activists 'who are your people?' in an attempt to get them to think about their constituency. It's a deceptively simple question, but one that's useful for organisers to ask at the start of campaigns. Too often, social justice campaigners unconsciously create a subculture that unintentionally reinforces how different they are from the majority of their community/ constituency. Having become aware of and mobilised over a particular issue that you're campaigning about, it is perhaps easy to think other people who are not active on the issues are not worth bothering with as they don't have the same sense of urgency or understanding. It is an easy, if disastrous, mistake to make.

Many of us like to spend time with people we feel are similar to us, and who share our values and so on. For example, many animal rights campaigners may prefer not to spend Christmas sharing a table with people consuming a traditional animal-based roast dinner. Feminists and race equality activists probably want some 'down time' away from the weathering that comes from continual exposure to normalised oppressive narratives. We all need such safe spaces to unwind, reflect and recharge, but for changemakers to permanently retreat into these 'safe spaces' is a mistake, because if we want to win, then we need to be building our base and widening the scope of our engagement. Too often organisations that begin as outward-looking can over time become almost cult-like as they exclude, consciously or unconsciously, people who hold a different opinion on a particular subject. When this happens, groups become smaller, more elitist and unable to build the wider support needed to achieve the change they are seeking.

In contrast, Marx famously argued that the emancipation of the working-class must be conquered *by the working-classes themselves*. Contrary to some erroneous views, he wasn't saying that the emancipation of the working-class would be the work of a militant minority acting *on behalf of* the working-class. Marx's answer to Ella Baker's question 'who are your people?' would likely not be 'people who share my vision of a future socialist society'. Far less would it likely be 'the comrades in good standing within my particular variant of a socialist party'. Instead, Marx would more likely answer that 'our people' includes the working-class 'as a whole' – warts and all. It's clearly the case that we will seldom have all 'our people' on side, but as organisers we are aiming to build a sufficient majority that will provide the power we need to win. It would make things easier if everyone had the same view on social justice issues, but we don't all start from the same point. As organisers, one of our roles is persuading people of the issues we care about and that involves developing a 'narrative of us' to widen our scope of influence.

If we accept Marx's view that emancipation of the working-class must be conquered *by the working-classes themselves* it does, however, raise a number of questions, because the working-class is – like most things – riddled with contradictions. As an example, it is well known that during the 1976 Grunwick dispute, involving industrial action in North London by a group of largely Asian women, a delegation of miners, a thousand strong, attended the mass picket to show support. Later, following the 1984–85 miners' strike, because of the support from the organisation Lesbian and Gays Support the Miners, we witnessed the miners promoting LGBTQ+ rights throughout the labour movement. Yet, in both these examples, it's likely that some of these same miners would have engaged in telling racist or homophobic 'jokes' *at the same time* as they were supporting these two groups within the working-class. This is not to castigate them, but to highlight and recognise that we are all influenced by what Gramsci would refer to as the dominant narratives in society. What he means by this is that many of the ideas and beliefs that people hold are shaped by what he refers to as 'hegemony' or ideological control. Often winning change is very much about a contest over ideas and beliefs. Many conservative or reactionary beliefs don't necessarily arise from individuals' own thinking but from the dominant ideas of what is considered 'normal' and legitimate. These ideas are actively promoted in society through the media, education and other institutions, and provide legitimacy for the way things are and consequently induce consent in the face of oppression. Gramsci's understanding of narrative reminds us that civil society can be, and often is, a sphere of conflict over ideas and norms. The goal of strengthening 'civil society' can be pursued either by building civic institutions to complement (or hold to account) states and markets, or in a Gramscian sense of building our communities' capacities to think differently, to challenge assumptions and norms and to articulate new ideas and visions.

This conflict of narratives is illustrated when, within three years of the National Union of Mineworkers delegates winning a vote at the Labour Party calling for full equality for the LGBTQ+ community, Thatcher's government fired the first shots in what has become known as the culture wars by prohibiting the teaching in schools of the 'acceptability of homosexuality' without any significant backlash. So-called 'British values' at the time were deeply homophobic – not to mention sexist, ableist and racist.

Marx, influenced by the German philosopher Hegel, talks about class in a contradictory way. Indeed, his whole philosophy is based on the notion of contradictions and the way these are resolved. Marx talks about the difference between a class 'in itself' and a class 'for itself'. While his writing on this is far from clear, it is easiest to think of a class 'in itself' as merely a group of people with a similar relationship to the means of production (that is people who have to work for a living). Objectively from a sociologist's perspective they constitute a class. However, without an understanding of their position, status and potential (class consciousness) then they have no agency *as a class*. We can recognise this in the way people feel that 'things just happen' and there's little that can be done to effect change. However, once class consciousness begins to develop – once people begin to recognise their shared experience and common needs – once they begin to have a shared story of us, then they are able to develop agency: the ability to act collectively in their own interests. Then and only then, they become a class *for itself*. While it is useful to distinguish this terminology as if these two states were mutually exclusive and *class in itself* and *class for itself* are binary opposites, in reality, the level of class consciousness and the sense and acts of solidarity that accompanies it is often in flux, sometimes increasing and sometimes retreating.

The working-class, is notoriously susceptible to narratives of division. Time and again, working-class communities have been divided by anti-immigrant or anti-minority rhetoric, narratives about a 'woman's place' and hostility to the LGBTQ+ community. Yet, it also retains an intrinsic sense of solidarity and empathy. These two tendencies are regularly in contradiction, and often people can believe two seemingly incompatible things at once: for example, someone may believe that we should do everything we can to provide support for refugees from the horrors of war zones, but also accept that we need to 'stop the boats' bringing those self-same refugees to our shores. One reason for this contradiction is that people often think emotionally and not always rationally. For most of us it feels terrible to see the devastation of a war zone and it *feels* like something should be done to help. Yet at the same time, when fears of 'invasions' or 'hurricanes' of refugees are perpetuated by the press and even government ministers, it *feels* like something should be done to stop this flow. There is a conflict between genuine empathy, and artificially manufactured fear, but our emotional responses lead us to 'believe' two incompatible things.

One reason that incompetent conservative politicians in the midst of a climate crisis, a cost–of–greed crisis and a housing crisis spend so much of their time creating fear around asylum seekers, critical race theory and the rights of the trans community is that they want us, the working-class, to remain fractured, afraid of 'the other' within our community, rather than organising to challenge their policies that are making us all poorer.

Britain is sometimes asked to tap into its inherent 'Dunkirk Spirit', or reminded how plucky pilots won the Battle of Britain as the population withstood the Blitz. More recently, David Cameron, former UK prime minister, asked us to believe that 'we are all in it together', implying that they are suffering just as much as we are. At other times, the ruling elite seek to divide us, evidenced during the 1980s, when the National Union of Mineworkers were depicted as 'the enemy within'. Similarly, the women at the Greenham Common peace camp were said to be a threat to our very existence. Stories, even contrived ones like these, have power, which is why we need to work so hard to establish a positive counter-narrative that builds unity and self-confidence among our people. The next section gives an example of how a group of trade unions managed to do that in regard to advancing gender pay equality.

Redirecting the narrative on gender pay

When organising the gender pay equality campaign we talked about in Chapter 2, the union organisers knew that the employer's first response would be denial that there was a gender pay problem, and the second response would be to say: 'We don't have any more money, so if you want us to increase women's pay, then you will have to accept that we will reduce the pay of men'. Given that the industry was male-dominated, and the majority of the union's members were men, if this narrative – equality for women meant a loss for men – had gone unchallenged it could have had a potentially disastrous impact on the union's campaign. The union organisers knew they had to find a way forward by challenging the company's narrative. The reason why women were systematically underpaid was not predominantly because of individual prejudice, or misogyny, but because of a deeply flawed pay structure with arbitrary pay rates. While arbitrary pay structures almost always disproportionately impact on women, it doesn't mean they are fair to men, merely that they are even more unfair to women.

The employer had used what they termed a 'forced ranking' system. Forced ranking is a controversial management tool that measures the work performance of employees based on how they compare with each other instead of against fixed criteria. It's a management framework for awarding bonuses and promotions. Performance-related pay is often flawed, inaccurate and subjective, as it relies on subjective perceptions of employees' work quality. But in a forced ranking system, irrespective of what a manager thinks about the performance of their team, only a small number can be ranked as 'outstanding'. In the case we are referring to this forced ranking meant that a certain percentage of workers within each department had to be ranked as 'poor' in terms of their performance, even if they objectively were not poor performers. Only a small percentage could be ranked as outstanding, even if everyone was delivering way beyond expectations. It was not uncommon for people to receive their annual appraisal from their manager with a note apologising for the fact it did not reflect their true performance, but despite this apology, with a performance-related pay structure, the ranking impacted on their take-home pay. The system was held in contempt by the workforce – widely and derisively referred to as 'false ranking' even by the managers who were required to implement it.

The union undertook a pay survey that revealed just how big the difference in wages was between the highest- and lowest-paid workers doing the same job – there were clear inequalities which provided the union with the knowledge base to challenge the employer. The union's campaign was framed not solely on the moral high ground of gender pay equality, but also on the basis that the pay structure rewarded you for *who* you were, not for *what* you did. The union suggested that if you were friendly with the boss and went for after-work drinks, you were more likely to get paid higher than the colleague who did just as good a job but didn't socialise after work. The arbitrary pay structure was impacting on everyone's right to be paid fairly for the work they did, and equal pay legislation was the tool that would dismantle this dysfunctional and unfair pay structure. The strategic use of equality legislation was essential to winning this campaign, but the union's story, or narrative about arbitrary pay being unfair across the board, including to men, was essential to disarm the company's suggestion that equal pay for women meant lower pay for men. Without a counter-narrative, a unifying 'story of us', the union could not have as easily sustained the support of a predominantly male workforce in its campaign for gender pay equality.

Bringing us together

We have established that the aim of an organiser is to build an inclusive 'story of us' – a story that brings people together rather than divides. But how do we practically do this? In his wonderful book, *Fractured* (2021), Jon Yates explores our sense of identity using the concept of 'people like me'. He says there's a natural tendency to identify people as being either 'like me' or 'not like me', or more colloquially, there are the 'us' and the 'them'. Crucially, he demonstrates that these categories are dynamic and changing. Think of the examples mentioned earlier of the miners who supported the Asian women of Grunwick, or the LGBTQ+ community who supported the miners.

There is an example in *Fractured* of a psychology experiment where volunteers – all football fans – were registered to participate in a psychology experiment in a university building, and then told to cross the campus to another building where the experiment would be conducted. In fact, unbeknown to them, the experiment would take place as they crossed the campus. Before the volunteers left the registration building the person registering them struck up a conversation that either reinforced their identity as a football fan in *general*, or as a fan of a *particular football team*. As they crossed the campus, someone wearing a football jersey from a rival team would trip and fall to the ground – this was part of the experiment. Those volunteers who had had the element of their identity as a supporter of a *particular* football team reinforced were more likely to walk on by and not offer any help to the person in need, who was 'not one of us'. Those who had had their sense of being a fan of *football* rather than a particular team reinforced were more likely to stop for the supporter of the different team who, despite that, was still 'one of us'. The experiment therefore emphasised how people's sense of identity was pliable. The 'us' could be supporters of my team, or it could equally be football fans in general. In other words, as Marx had perhaps less eloquently expressed, the way we see and define ourselves can impact on our empathy and actions. Those of us who want to win need to weave together stories that speak to our audience and encourage them to think of themselves as part of a bigger 'us'. In fact, as organisers, we need to co-create those stories. But a separate and equally important part of public narrative is our ability to tell our own story. Because allowing people to see a little of who we are helps them to understand what it is we believe in and why we are seeking the change for which we are advocating.

A story of self: who are you and why does it matter?

We each have multiple elements of our core identity. It might be that you are defined by your work – traditional work roles such as 'docker' or 'mineworker' were once hugely defining. Today few of us are defined by our industry, but the work we do and the relationships that stem from it are important elements of our identity. Maybe you are a 'united' fan, part of a huge number of people who each season suspend reality to believe your team will (this year) prove they are indeed the greatest, sharing emotional moments, when your dreams 'fly' and then watch as those dreams, as they say in East London, so often 'fade and die'. Perhaps you are defined, or partly define yourself, by your family role, as a partner, carer or parent? Or perhaps you have a strong sense of your regional identity: a Scouser, a Cockney or a Geordie? Maybe your migration status defines you, either in your eyes or those of others? Your faith might be a significant part of your sense of who you are, or you might be passionate about a particular type of music. What is interesting is that all of these are points of reference for you as an individual, but they are also points of connection with others who share that characteristic. The magic comes when we weave a story of us which touches on all these multifaceted elements of our individual and collective story.

A great example of weaving these individual stories into a story of us is the poem 'This is the place'. Written by Tony Walsh (aka

'Longfella') originally to raise funds for a Manchester charity, it took on an added poignancy after the Manchester Arena atrocity, where 22 people were killed by a terrorist suicide bomber, 10 of the victims teenagers or younger, and the youngest an eight-year-old. There was a sense of outrage, anger and fear as people defiantly attended a mass vigil the next day. The poet read his poem to the crowd. It told a story of Manchester, and throughout it built on a 'story of us', referring to it as 'ace' and 'the best' with its well-known music scene. On its industrial past it referred to its cotton mills and steel works. It talked about Manchester's diversity where some are born there, some drawn there, but how they all call it home. It touched on the city's humour in making people laugh, and 'taking the mick'. It covered politics, including how its suffragettes created a pride in sisterhood. The poem concludes about how Manchester people have seen hard times, but they keep fighting back with Northern grit and wit. The poem finished with an obvious reference to the murders the day before, calling on people to stand strong together with a smile on their faces – a greater Manchester forever.

It is hard to imagine a circumstance in which people needed a story of us quite as much as they did that day, and hard to imagine that need being more effectively met than by this celebration of everything the city stood for. A few days later the far-right called an anti-Muslim protest seeking to exploit the sense of anger and sacrilege at the murders, which had been claimed in the name of Islamist extremism. A Muslim woman turned up to challenge the narrative that Islam was a religion of violence and hatred. As she arrived a group of men who had come to this anti-Muslim rally approached her and advised her it was not safe for her to be there. She told them that Islam was a religion of peace, and that she was staying to talk to anyone who was prepared to listen. They decided to stay close to her to protect her from any violence. While the thugs of the far-right entered into a pitched battle with the police, the woman continued to simply tell her story of her faith and its values. She exchanged email addresses and received a thank you from one of the men. He said he was grateful for her taking the time to talk and was inspired by her strength. They went on to collaborate on bringing communities together.

Remember this was a man who had attended an anti-Muslim rally, who came away from that encounter committed to working for cross-community understanding. Such is the power of our story.

Building an inclusive story of 'smoggies'

We delivered some community organising training to a group of Labour supporters in Teesside, and as part of this we showed the group the Longfella poem recital we have just described, and asked them, in small groups, to gather the elements of their town's story. Teessiders refer to themselves as 'smoggies'. The term arose from the smog that was produced as a result of pollution from the local chemical and steel plants. Visiting football teams would taunt the locals by calling them smog monsters, or smoggies. Yet Teessiders became fond of the name – proud as they were of the area's industrial past – so they were happy to adopt the term 'smoggies'. Using this identity of smoggies as a starting point, the group explored the extensive industrial heritage of the area, revealing as it did many partial views of the historical working-class – men working in chemical plants or tending furnaces – hard work undertaken by proud men who perhaps went straight from work to quench their thirst at the local pub. This collective memory is a huge asset to community organising: we have a past, and often it is a past with much to be proud of, even if it needs to be challenged and at times recast. In the Teesside group's initial story of 'us', women were almost entirely absent and there was no mention of asylum seekers, despite Middlesbrough at the time having the highest concentration of asylum seekers in the country, and despite women and asylum seekers making up a significant part of the group with whom we were working. After surfacing these 'missing stories', the group were asked to revisit their story of us and make it more inclusive, something that they did with enthusiasm. This example illustrates just how invisible we can be in our own stories and how with a little thought we can retell those stories in a way which paints us back in.

Hackney, East London, a story of us

In 2000, faced with a financial crisis, the local council in Hackney, East London, effectively declared itself insolvent and planned to shut libraries, close nurseries, privatise more services and cut staff wages. The union representing workers at the council immediately agreed to ballot for strike action, but rather than focussing the dispute solely on jobs and pay, the union fought this dispute on the issue of the state of council services and the need to protect them for the community. There already existed a series of 'friends of' various services in Hackney, particularly for the area's parks and open spaces, which had suffered seriously as a result of previous cuts. Residents could already see the deterioration of their open spaces as the council workforce had been squeezed and were concerned to ensure it didn't get worse. However, the two areas which were particularly targeted for cuts were nurseries and libraries.

Some of the local trade unionists had children in the nurseries, and they began speaking to other parents making the connections between job cuts and cuts to services. It wasn't long before a plan was hatched for parents to occupy the two nurseries due for closure. This was dramatic in terms of publicity, and the local TV news cameras were soon inside the nursery, filming the kids playing and the parents strategising. Meanwhile, the union branch delivered regular provisions of food and nappies.

What had begun as a council cuts initiative rapidly became a community issue with the union and its members at the heart of coordinating the resistance. Friends of Hackney Libraries groups sprang up immediately, initiated by library staff. Library users were invited to a meeting, and they took over the campaign to save the libraries. Soon there were whole ranges of different groups and communities mobilising, in advance of a day of strike action. A local samba band, the 'Rhythms of Resistance', became a mainstay of the regular demonstrations and rallies outside the town hall. On one particular occasion, while the council was meeting to agree further cuts, the band paraded into the meeting playing their samba drums so loud that the council meeting had to be suspended. Meanwhile, environmental groups joined in, and hundreds of cyclists in the south of the borough effectively caused traffic gridlock.

One of the least politically engaged demographics in the borough were women from the Charedi Orthodox Jewish community. The Charedi community has a high birthrate, and the community has a significant number of nurseries across the borough. The long-established community group Friends of Hackney Nurseries was a cross-community organisation. When it took a position of opposition to the closure of nurseries in the borough, it was informed by the council it would no longer be allowed to meet on council property, so the union arranged a space for them. The union was invited to speak to Friends of Hackney Nurseries about the campaign and the scale of the proposed cuts. When the group heard about the resistance to the cuts from community groups, women from the Charedi community were keen to offer their support. They arranged to take their children out of the nurseries and blockade a major crossroads in the borough. The Charedi community had a well-deserved reputation and a self-image of being a very law-abiding community. The idea of them mirroring the actions of the anarcho-cyclists seemed an unlikely scenario, but as it turned out, the day of action was an incredible success. Council offices and depots were shut across the borough, the main trunk road through the borough blockaded by anarcho-cyclists in the south and observant Jews in the north, library users, friends of the parks and open spaces, tenants and residents' associations were all coming together in a movement demanding the cuts be halted.

A 'story of us' was emerging, which was 'we the people' of Hackney – whether workers, residents or service users – against a council which had lost any vision of delivering for the community. It would take two years before the dispute was finally over, and ultimately, as so often is the case, it was a mixed bag. Partial victory though it was, none of it would have been possible without the sense of 'us'. As Marshall Ganz says, movements have narratives. People in Hackney had a sense of pride in their collective unity. It was a story of us that would continue to serve the community well.

We are not the same

A unifying story of us is not about pretending we are all the same; instead, it is about finding the resonances and harmonies that arise despite our differences. It's about being comfortable with our diversity and seeing it as a strength while recognising that we have a common history, common needs, and a common humanity. How then do you create a common story of us? By definition, a story of us has to be inclusive, so when campaigning against the far-right, for example, we don't start from a narrow story of militant anti-fascists (although that story does deserve to be celebrated, it's not necessarily the story that will move the centre ground in a community). A good way to start is to think about what experiences and feelings people share. For example, if you were to tell a story about a particular town you might celebrate the local football team (even if they are not very good), or there might be a nightclub where generations of teenagers have celebrated their 18th birthday – somewhere where everyone has a memory, or at least knows a common story. There might be a particular schoolteacher who everyone liked, there might be a local workplace where there was always some work – albeit low-skilled and low-paid – available and where lots of people would have worked, even if it was just a summer job. There may be a particular landmark where everyone meets in town; there are memories and connections everywhere in communities. Telling these stories evokes something about what it means to live in this town, it's the shared experience that makes those stories at the same time familiar, personal and unifying. But your stories need to add something else: to be organising stories, they need to be a morality tale. Marshall Ganz puts it like this:

> A plot begins when a protagonist moving toward a desired goal runs into an unexpected event, creating a crisis that engages our curiosity, choices he or she makes in response, and an outcome. Our ability to empathetically identify with a protagonist allows us to enter into the story, feel what s/he feels, see things through his or her eyes. The moral, revealed through

the resolution, brings understanding of the head and of the heart. (Ganz 2009a: 3)

Perhaps the textbook story of us is Barack Obama's speech to the Democratic Convention in 2004, four years before he was the Democratic candidate for president. He began: '... let's face it, my presence on this stage is pretty unlikely. My father was a foreign student, born and raised in a small ... village in Kenya. He grew up herding goats, went to school in a tin-roof shack. His father, my grandfather, was a cook, a domestic servant' (Obama 2004). Obama spoke of how his parents gave him an African name:

> ... believing in a tolerant America your name is no barrier to success. They imagined me going to the best schools in the land, even though they weren't rich, because in a generous America you don't have to be rich to achieve your potential ... in no other country on earth is my story even possible.

What's interesting about this speech is that in one sense it's true in that it describes Barack Obama's life story and that of his parents, but it's not typical of the experience of the children of migrants in America. When he quoted the Declaration of Independence, 'We hold these truths to be self-evident, that all men are created equal', he didn't mention that it would be nearly a hundred years after that declaration and would require a civil war before America abolished slavery. People who heard him speak knew of the gap between the aspiration and the reality, but he was stood in front of them declaring that sometimes the American Dream delivers and maybe, just maybe, they could make it deliver a little more often. It was inspiring imagery, and an audacious hope that was to carry him all the way to the White House and would mobilise millions to believe in him, and the dream of America. Stories can reconnect us with our values, even if the story we tell is more aspirational than documentary.

In terms of developing your story of us you might want to think about what distinguishes your group from your target. In the Hackney example we used in the previous chapter there were community tensions before the far-right sought to mobilise, but people responded to a narrative that said — to borrow from the murdered UK MP Jo Cox — 'we have more in common than that which divides us'. People may have had any number of reasons to be irritated by their neighbour, but they came together because they were convinced by a narrative that said that 'this is Hackney, we get along despite our disagreements, and occasional fall-outs; we don't need 'outsiders' coming here stirring trouble'.

A story of us is a powerful organising tool. It can bring people together, believing that they can become a better version of themselves. It can tap into the deeply felt values that people aspire to, but don't always live by, and it can defuse the narratives of division that we too often absorb.

What's your story of us?

Here is an exercise you can do with your group in developing a story of us.

What is the 'story of us' of the place where you live?

Consider the giants of your town, the people who have made a mark by doing something good, as a politician, a trade union leader, an environmentalist, or business leader?

Consider whether there is anything special about the humour, the entertainment, the parks, the architecture, the sports or faith groups. What are people in your town proud of?

What challenges has the town been through? How did it respond?

Try telling this story in a way that shows the common values of the town. Once you have drafted your story, ask yourself who is missing, which groups' contributions to the town have not been reflected. Then go back and retell the story, writing these groups back in.

8

Communication and the changing of dominant narratives

This chapter will explore the importance of narrative and how it can be used to change minds – an important skill in organising practice. You may have heard of the phrase 'controlling the narrative'. This is where people and organisations want to prevent people from forming their own opinion. Instead, they want us to interpret 'facts' in accordance with their own messaging. To shape the narrative is to create a particular version of events that presents your view and weakens the narrative power of your opponents. Many campaigners can resist this ideological power control by developing their own counter-narratives, but often our adversaries have more powerful media outlets behind them that influence what the wider community believe and think.

Toxic narratives can spread like a virus over social media. Simplistic assertions that blame 'the other' for all our fears and sorrows can feel comforting, whereas evaluating why our communities are suffering can feel dangerous. Unfortunately, right-wing authoritarian populists have learned this well, and deliberately feed narratives of hatred, most topically, directed towards asylum seekers and refugees. It's a calculated strategy designed to divide and disorientate our communities, and get us voting for, or accepting, policies that impoverish us all.

The power ideology has over us is often in inverse relation to the level of organisation of our campaign groups – the more organised we are, the more likely we are to be able to maintain a persuasive counter-narrative. The less organised communities are, the more likely people are to absorb the narratives controlled by powerful individuals, organisations and the media. This has become more complicated with the rise of social media and artificial intelligence, where it's increasingly difficult to separate fiction from fact. The control of information therefore provides adversaries with a means of power to minimise or nullify dissent – our job as organisers is to counter this, taking us back to the earlier point about creating a story of us. When people come together to organise, they will need to generate alternative narratives and through their struggles create a powerful challenge to the erstwhile 'dominant' narratives. This is part of our role as organisers.

What are narratives and how are they used?

Sometimes dominant narratives are conscious ideological intentions. For example, 'fox hunting is a form of pest control' was first muted as an excuse to allow fox hunting to continue during the First World War when horses were requisitioned for fighting at the front. 'Public ownership leads to inefficiency' was consciously generated as a narrative that would reduce opposition to the privatisation of public utilities. But some narratives may just be assumed rather than consciously peddled. A common one levelled at vegetarians was that 'if you don't eat meat, you will become ill because you won't have any protein'. Organisers have been rewriting the dominant narrative through campaigns, whether about animal welfare, contributing to turning the tide of public opinion against battery cages, or about countering claims against public ownership of the rail industry, or in relation to immigration debates. Often our starting point is with facts trying to destroy our opponent's arguments – but facts, as we've already discussed, don't always touch people's emotions and it is feelings that often cause people to act or become involved in campaigns.

Another area we need to consider is social media. Every progressive organisation is now struggling with navigating the link between digital and real-world campaigning. The objective is to use information technology to find and inspire the largest supporter base into effective action. But what can happen is that resources are diverted into feeding the 'echo chamber', where existing supporters simply repost or retweet, but no one new is influenced. This chapter will review some of the literature on 'big organising' and reflect on the difference between using social media 'in a crisis' and as a long-term tool. It will also explore the use of 'online communities' and their relationship with community organising theory. We will draw upon three particular campaigns, one around fighting a supermarket development and another around the closure of a women's gym – both of which successfully mobilised a local community to defeat unwelcome planning developments. The third used a social media as part of a campaign to out-mobilise provocative far-right initiatives targeting minority ethnic communities.

Many people may feel that they aren't influenced by advertising, that they are able to make their own mind up, or that they are unaffected by the noise on social media. Yet we are all influenced, to varying degrees, by advertising and messaging, much of it subliminal. Companies spend billions of pounds on advertising and marketing, and they wouldn't do this if it wasn't effective. Social media is primarily a series of advertising platforms – its primary function is to find a large and lucrative audience for marketing. An impact connected to this is the amplification of biases. In advertising and social media, we see bias when stories are selected or slanted to please advertisers, our news feeds are also designed to feed us the stories we are most comfortable with. Of course, in mainstream media reporters or publishers often choose to report one-sided interpretations of events and sometimes deliberately misrepresent political parties, union or campaign leaders, or even whole communities. We all have biases, and one of the most common is 'bias blind spot' – a belief that we are not biased. In one experiment, a tiny fraction of one per cent of participants thought they might be more biased than average, everyone else believed they were less biased than average, which of course cannot be true. GPs, when asked if they are more likely to prescribe a drug if they have received a promotional gift from the manufacturer assert 'no', but when asked if colleagues might, they overwhelmingly say 'yes'. We all think we are largely unaffected by propaganda, advertising and dominant narratives, but the opposite is often the case.

The power of narrative is such that we even tend to believe the lies that are told about ourselves. Sometimes narratives reflect and act to normalise, explain and 'justify' deep injustices in our society:

the relative social and economic disadvantage experienced by women compared with men, by racialised minority communities compared with the White majority, and so on. Sometimes these narratives are deliberately deployed to demonise a section of our community with the aim of further marginalising them within our society, refugees and asylum seekers being the most obvious example, although the demonisation of the transgender community is not far behind.

We are bombarded by such narratives every day. The communication of these narratives may be explicit, as in the government talk of 'invasion' by 'bogus' asylum seekers, or it can be implicit in the stories that the media view as newsworthy, which means some 'un-newsworthy' stories simply don't get heard. The narrative of men as business leaders is reinforced every time that we see a FTSE 100 CEO who is male and, on the odd occasion that a women CEO is interviewed, it feels like the exception that proves the rule. When we read stories of how a Black female barrister is mistaken for the defendant by the court clerk, or the Black woman MP is mistaken for the cleaner, we are shocked, but not surprised.

In an Ella Baker School of Organising training session on challenging racism (Ella Baker School of Organising 2023), Black people in the room are asked 'Has anyone ever repeated a racist stereotype about your community in front of you, claiming "they are all like that" but then corrected themselves by pointing out that they didn't include you in their comment, as you are "one of the good ones"?'. The reaction during the session is always a deep sense of recognition of this experience from participants. The point of this question is that it illustrates the hold of a dominant – in this case, racist – narrative, even when it doesn't accord with people's own lived experience. And this is the key for organisers challenging racist, and other, narratives of division. Rather than shouting at someone, 'You are really stupid', or worse still, 'You can't say that, it's racist [or sexist/homophobic/transphobic, etc]', if you want to successfully challenge the narrative of division, then you need to ask, 'Is that something you have seen or experienced yourself?', to which the answer may come back, 'No, but everyone knows it's true'. If you discuss vegetarianism with people who have not thought about vegetarianism before, they may suddenly become an expert on nutrition informing you that 'you can't live healthily without meat, you won't get all the necessary protein, vitamins, and minerals' even when they are speaking to someone who is vegetarian and healthy.

Many of us have grown up absorbing dominant narratives, some of them are so ubiquitous, we don't even view them as contested. Marxists have long considered this idea of dominant narratives. Marx himself asserted that 'The ideas of the ruling class are in every epoch the ruling ideas. ... The class which has the means of material production at its disposal, has control at the same time over the means of mental production' (Marx and Engels 1987). As so often with Marx, he has made an insightful observation, but has perhaps overstated it. In effect, he is saying that the wealthy in our society control the means of production (they own the factories in which we work) and they own the newspapers and have control over the content of school curriculums. We might, of course, ponder whether Marx over-simplifies the question, yet this doesn't challenge the broad brush of Marx's assertion that dominant ideas tend to reflect the ideology of the ruling class.

The Italian Marxist Antonio Gramsci enriched Marxist thinking about ideology and consciousness in his prison notebooks. From 1926 he spent 11 years in Mussolini's fascist prisons and wrote extensively on politics and philosophy. Whereas Marx's writing implied a rigid determinist view of dominant narratives or ideology, arising directly from the control of the means of production, Gramsci suggested that the issue of ideology (the battle for ideas) is simply another field of class struggle. In fact, Gramsci elevates the issue of ideology to a more dominant role in Marxist theory. He says, as all Marxists do, that the ruling class, or bourgeoisie, have historically appropriated wealth and control of the means of production through brutal force – think of the trans-Atlantic slave trade, or the Highland Clearances in Scotland. But Gramsci asserts that the ruling class maintain that control *primarily* through their control of the dominant narratives. Yes, they have prisons, riot squads and even the military at their disposal, but these are only used in times of crisis, the day-to-day business of control is to convince us either that there is no better way to organise society, or that there is no way to achieve an alternative vision. He described this narrative control as 'hegemonic', meaning that it can appear incontestable, it becomes what he refers to as 'common sense', something which he contrasts with 'good sense'.

Gramsci and others who have followed him assert that the field of ideology is contested, either expressly through campaigns, trade union or political organisations, or through the friction between people's lived experience and the dominant narratives that misrepresent them. While Gramsci recognises that for most of the time, as Marx asserted, the dominant ideas are the ideas of the dominant class – this can change. This is true, particularly in times when the ruling elite are in a time of crisis or disorganisation, or when the oppressed get organised. The oppressed can and do create their own counter-narratives that better explain the world as it is and the world as it could be. These ideas, that are perhaps always present, if dormant, can suddenly gain popular support. There is, therefore, a constant conflict between the dominant narrative, and what has been referred to as the subordinate narratives. Our job as changemakers, if we want to see real change, is to weaken the grip of the dominant narrative, and to encourage engagement with a narrative of change.

More recent social movement theory, particularly those scholars who have focussed on the African American freedom movement, suggest that social justice advances arise through a combination of opportunity, organisation and 'cognitive liberation' a freeing of our minds to see the potential for the world to be different. According to sociologists Frances Fox Piven and Richard Cloward, this process of cognitive liberation consists of three elements. Firstly, there is a loss of legitimacy of the current settlement: 'large numbers of men and women who ordinarily accept the authority of their rulers and the legitimacy of the institutional arrangements come to believe in some measure that these rulers and these arrangements are unjust and wrong' (Fox Piven and Cloward 1977: 4).

Secondly, there is a loss of fatalism, people who traditionally felt that the current arrangements are inevitable and unchanging, begin to assert rights. They come to believe that they are entitled to something more, and break from the internalised oppression that says they are to blame for their disadvantage, or that they are not worthy of the full rights of citizenship that others enjoy.

Thirdly, they also come to believe that what they do matters, in effect they discover their agency: 'people who ordinarily consider themselves helpless come to believe that they have some capacity to alter their lot' (Fox Piven and Cloward 1977: 4). It's important to stress that in social movement theory, this is not an individual process, but a collective one. A community, however defined, begins – as a group – to lose faith in the existing power structure, begins to correct 'the fundamental attribution error – the tendency of people to explain their situation as a function of individual rather than situational factors' (McAdam 1982: 50), and comes to believe that, in the words of the African American freedom song, 'we are the ones we have been waiting for'. As such, a subordinate, insurgent or challenger narrative needs to assist in moving people to three key conclusions – it is unjust, it is not inevitable, and we can change it.

It was the passage of very limited civil rights legislation in 1950s America that shattered the dominant narrative in the Deep South that Jim Crow apartheid was unstoppable. But it was the eloquence of Martin Luther King Jr that created a powerful and unifying counter-narrative that said that a people were on the move. In his 'I Have a Dream' speech, delivered 28 August 1963, at the Lincoln Memorial during the March on Washington, he said:

> When the architects of our republic wrote the magnificent words of the Constitution and the Declaration of Independence, they were signing a promissory note to which every American was to fall heir. This note was a promise that all men, yes, black men as well as white men, would be guaranteed the 'unalienable Rights' of 'Life, Liberty and the pursuit of Happiness'.

These words were sufficient to mobilise large numbers of people who would be prepared to face the threat of jail and even death for asserting their rights. Such is the power of a counter-narrative, and its ability to move people.

Marshall Ganz, as we have discussed previously, believes in the power of narrative. In his theory, there are three elements to a public narrative. A story of self, a story of us and a story of now

– a comprehensive counter-narrative has to reveal something about your values, about your shared identity and about why it is necessary to act now. But a powerful counter-narrative has to link directly to the lived experience of those who it seeks to mobilise. It has to be crafted such that it reveals, through the emotional response that people have to the narrative, that which they already know, but have not previously surfaced. To do that requires a full analysis of the context of the problem.

How do you develop a counter-narrative?

A good place to start is with a mapping exercise. While this can involve producing a geographical or physical map, for example in a workplace where you can map who is working in each department, it's more than this. While the former is important – essential even – the questions you need to be asking in the exercise relate to the power dynamics of the structure in which you are organising. For example, who has the power within a particular situation, and who has an interest in changing it? The fact that natural allies might not agree with you at this moment is not necessarily important. Changing that is part of the job of delivery, but for now, the issue is who is affected and in what way. Part of this involves also asking who is invisible, or not even mentioned in the dominant narrative. Giving visibility to all groups in a counter-narrative is a powerful way to build allyship. Also, who are the players who are denigrated, intentionally or otherwise, by the current dominant narrative? These people will warm to a retelling of the narrative that is inclusive or even uplifts them. But who are your people, and what story do they need to hear to move them from passively accepting the status quo? Let's look at some examples.

Public ownership of the railways

Perhaps one of the enduring ideological narratives in the UK is the one that suggests that the public sector is inefficient, bloated with bureaucracy and slow to change. This narrative emerged as part of a deliberate decision to privatise much of the public sector – telecoms, electricity, gas and water utilities are classic examples – and the first step was to underfund these services. Then, when people were fed up with the inefficiency of public services, the government blamed those failures on the fact that they were in the public sector (rather than that they were underfunded). Since the governments of Margaret Thatcher in the UK in the 1980s and 1990s, there had been a binary narrative that amounted to 'private sector good, public sector bad'. The wholesale asset stripping of housing, energy, rail, water and the telecoms sectors was achieved in large part because of the power of this deceptive narrative.

Today we are living with the consequences of treating monopolies like water and sewage as if they were subject to the 'discipline' of the markets in the private sector. Untreated sewage is pumped directly into our rivers and seas until there is an outrage, and then we are told that the water companies haven't the funds to pay for the remedial work to stop the discharges, and we will have to pay more to remedy their failings – because they gave their surpluses away as dividends to their shareholders.

The rail sector was among the last of the big industrial privatisations and was driven largely by ideology – an ideology of profits to shareholders at the expense of investment, and a reduced wage share for workers. Unlike the UK, no other European state has privatised its rail services, and the privatisation in the UK has been a catastrophe for the travelling public. Rail users in the UK pay higher fares than in Europe, and the government subsidy goes towards swelling the coffers of private companies. Meanwhile, franchises routinely fail and are temporarily brought back into public control where public money is used to sort out the mess – only to be re-privatised at the first opportunity. It is not surprising that this dominant narrative, of private sector efficiency, was subject to challenge.

In 2012, the Transport Salaried Staffs' Association (TSSA) – a transport union representing mainly management grades, but also ticket office and platform staff (the train 'dispatchers') – was concerned about plans to cut ticket office and station staff across the network. The union had a long-standing commitment to returning the railways to public ownership. However, at the time, the Labour Party, while nominally committed to public ownership of rail, consciously avoided speaking about this issue because it believed it to be a vote loser. The union needed to up its game and get organised. Rail fare increases tend to be announced in late August each year, and the union decided it was possible to use the inevitable dismay at above-inflation price increases to question why trains are so expensive, and so often late or cancelled. The TSSA established the first community organising department in a UK union, and the organising team were tasked with generating a groundswell of opinion for public ownership of rail.

There was a Conservative government at the time, so there was a particular focus on identifying Conservative marginal constituencies so as to put pressure on local politicians. Fortunately for the campaign, a lot of commuter towns are disproportionately Conservative-voting. The union's organising staff joined commuter trains coming into London where they leafleted every commuter. The travelling public were a captive audience, and by linking high fares, low service levels and huge profits for the private companies – including cross-subsidiaries of European national rail operators – it was possible to challenge the ideology that public ownership of rail was an inherently bad idea.

Union-called days of action in communities saw staff recruiting volunteers to get involved leafleting commuters across the country. WhatsApp groups were set up, local passenger groups met and began to press for changes and more accountability. Conservative MPs found themselves in front of packed rooms where rail unions were treated as champions of the railways rather than mischief-makers. Local campaigns against 'rip-off' car parking charges at railway stations were springing up everywhere. Soon the *Daily Telegraph* newspaper, normally seen as an advocate for privatisation, was reporting that commuters – including in Conservative marginal seats – were in favour of public ownership of the railways. It is worthy of note that, while the term 'nationalisation' remained contentious, 'public ownership' which means the same thing, was not. At the time of writing, according to the *Daily Telegraph*, and in spite of the last government's ideological commitment to rail privatisation, over 43 per cent of the rail passenger industry, based on passenger miles, is now in public ownership (Gill 2023). One of the first acts of the 2024 Labour Government was to introduce a Bill to bring railways back into public ownership.

This campaign was effective in challenging the dominant narrative because it tapped into the lived experience of commuters, people who paid among the highest rail fares in Europe, for some of the worst service, with regular cancellations and over-crowded trains. To them, the train operating companies did feel like carpetbaggers, particularly the European companies, who were repatriating profits to subsidise their own national railways. It's significant that although up until the TSSA campaign no one was articulating these concerns, importantly, passengers already *felt* something was wrong, even before they heard any arguments or saw any graphs about comparative costs. The union's counter-narrative felt right; it provided an alternative frame for thinking about the way train services should be delivered. This counter-narrative did not start from high principles, about transport being an essential public service that should be under public ownership, but rather from people's lived experience – their feelings – with what was wrong with the current system, and suggesting there was a credible alternative. It followed the old adage: start from where people are.

A short-term victory over Farage

In 2016, the Nazi-based far-right electoral challenge had all but disappeared, but the mantle of exploiting voters' fears of immigration had been passed to the United Kingdom Independent Party (UKIP), a party that was using all the racist imagery of 'a foreign invasion' to campaign for the UK to leave the European Union. In early 2015, it looked on course to win two or more general election seats. The party's leader, Nigel Farage, was reportedly ten points ahead in South Thanet, and its candidate in Thurrock also looked almost certain to win. An assessment of its strategy was clear, it was seeking to exploit discontent across society.

UKIP's aim was to motivate Labour voters to buy into its racist narrative of blaming immigration – particularly those Labour voters living in deindustrialised communities who felt that society had moved on and left them behind. But it was also campaigning for votes from those in working-class communities who were doing OK but who resented the tax they contributed to pay for essential public services that they did not use but they believed to be disproportionately used by 'wasters' who chose poverty rather than hard work. UKIP also wanted to win disaffected middle-class Conservative voters. In short, it wanted to be all things to all discontents.

A little analysis of the seats where the party was doing well suggested it had some genuine support in the community, often with a range of local councillors. HOPE not hate, the anti-racist and anti-fascist organisation, sent its organisers into UKIP's target communities to steer counter-campaigns, and the first thing the organisers did was speak to the other parties in the election. The aim was to get some intelligence on exactly where the UKIP vote was and the issues it was mining for support. Labour would advise the organisers not to even bother campaigning in certain wards, as they were 'lost to UKIP'. These 'lost wards' were always where the organisers started. They worked to change the narrative in these areas, working with locals who had signed up to help the campaign. It was often an education to HOPE not hate supporters to see a part of their town – which they may not have visited before – where all the signs of entrenched intergenerational poverty were very evident. These are the areas where strongly held resentment from people that feel left behind can provide fuel for divisive parties like UKIP. But an alternative narrative was set out in the leaflets produced by the organisers. As one said:

> Not so long-ago Thurrock was a prosperous working-class community. There were plenty of good, well-paid jobs: on the docks, in the quarry and chalk pits and at the Ford's car plant. This contrasts with the opportunities our young people have today, where work is often low paid and seldom permanent.

People were reminded that 'the old jobs were only good jobs because our communities organised to make them that way'.

What the HOPE not hate campaign was doing was tapping into a 'story of us' and this proved powerful. While people in the towns were nostalgic for the 'good old days' before their community was visited by deindustrialisation, the framing of the 'good old days' story as a product of trade union organising was something to be proud of, and many people remembered with pride the way they, or their parents, were trade unionists. The call to working-class pride even went so far as to evoke a well-known local former dockers' leader, whose daughter wrote on a HOPE not hate campaign leaflet in Thurrock:

> my dad died in 1996, but if his beloved Tilbury was to be represented in parliament by UKIP, he would turn in his grave. Please use your vote on 8 June, and please do not vote for UKIP, a party that does not represent our values or care about our needs.

The chameleon that was UKIP was not just influencing traditional Labour voters but was also appealing to traditional Conservative voters. Here the HOPE not hate organisers resorted to good old-fashioned snobbery. They opportunistically encouraged voters from the pockets of middle-class, middle-England that exist in these communities to look down their nose at the upstarts of UKIP. One example was a leaflet used in coastal South Thanet that outlined that Farage, far from campaigning for the British fishing industry, had not attended a single meeting of the EU fisheries group of which he was a member.

There were also a group of impoverished people who had long ago given up voting, but whose resentment was being mined by UKIP. For these, HOPE not hate produced a 'fat cat' leaflet that explained that UKIP wanted even more tax cuts for the rich than were being proposed by the Tory government. The counter-narrative was that UKIP was no friend to the disadvantaged in post-industrial communities where many were forced to rely on benefits and desperately needed public services. Finally, organisers used the catch-all rallying cry 'defend our NHS'. UKIP leaders were on record as advocating the abandonment of a health service free at the point of delivery, and in favour of insurance-based 'pay when you are sick' schemes. It didn't need to be outlined that such schemes would lead to a two-tier health service.

Armed with these leaflets, campaigners went out into UKIP heartlands. The systematic leafleting exposed UKIP as a one-trick pony, their support did not hold up over the election campaign. In South Thanet, organisers produced a four-page 'wraparound' advert for the local newspaper. They could have written copy to reflect HOPE not hate's anti-racist values and advocated for a more compassionate, inclusive Britain, but the people who felt like that were not going to be voting for UKIP anyway. Instead, organisers chose to focus on a narrative that was likely to connect with disaffected voters. This included the failure of UKIP's councillors to deliver when in office in Thanet Council, its leader's absence from fisheries committee meetings, and its tax, health and other plans. The counter-narrative also recognised the importance of women's votes, explaining that UKIP wanted to get rid of the 'red tape' of equal pay legislation.

The campaign purposefully chose not to use the narrative of UKIP is a racist party. Organisers knew from experience that people – particularly those that we defined as the 'I'm not racist but...' group – who are tempted to vote UKIP don't change their voting patterns because they are labelled racist. Instead, this approach can foster a victim mentality, whereby people adopt the view that 'you can't say anything these days, otherwise they will call you racist'. Instead, community organisers chose to go in hard on the issues that exposed that UKIP's policies would hurt the communities they were courting.

The weekend these papers with the 'don't vote UKIP' message were delivered to every door in Thanet, local anti-racist groups were euphoric. Every door, every family, every voter received a counter-narrative that said that UKIP was incompetent, supported tax cuts for the rich and viewed the NHS as a 'waste of money'. The following weekend, UKIP tried to hit back, booking a similar wraparound, and this time, the mask slipped – the party exposed itself. Rather than responding to concerns about the party's tax policies, the NHS or its record in local government, or on EU committees, it resorted to the basest of dog-whistle racism. UKIP explicitly accused Labour and the Conservatives of being soft on issues of race. The impact for UKIP was counter-productive. The 'I'm not racist but...' voter may tolerate implicit racism and be comfortable with 'mild' racist policies but doesn't feel comfortable with explicit racism. UKIP had played the race card and it backfired: its candidates didn't win the elections. UKIP's narrative of division was weaker than a narrative of hope and did not stand up to scrutiny when challenged.

Transformative conversations

While it may be easy to construct a narrative, it's quite another to get that narrative taken up and owned by people. How do you spread a narrative, and how do you move people from what Gramsci would have called the mistaken narrative of 'common sense' towards one of 'good sense'? From a belief that nothing will change, 'that's just the way things are', and that no one is ever going to listen, to one where people think it is wrong, it doesn't have to be this way and crucially, if we work together, we can change this.

There are many ways to spread your organising narrative; you could, for example, pay for an advert in the local paper, create a clever meme for social media, or fly-post your message. The more ways that someone receives a message the more likely they are to hear it, but the most important way to communicate with people is through good old-fashioned face-to-face conversations. This is the way you are more likely to transform someone's views. By definition a transformative conversation is going to be one in which you want to change the mind of the other person. A common, but perhaps flawed approach is to tell someone they are wrong and attempt to impress them with your command of facts. Or you might engage with some form of discourse that proves conclusively that every premise on which they have reached their conclusion is logically flawed, demonstrating that you are a far more logical person than they are. In truth these – some might say, elitist – approaches seldom work.

If we are serious about changing someone's mind, then we need to engage with, rather than dismiss, what they have to say. If someone says, for example, that there are too many immigrants, rather than quoting to them the contested facts about the economic benefits of immigration, you might want to ask them what harm they think immigration does. They might respond by arguing that immigrants take 'our jobs', add to the shortage of housing or take up public health resources, or that if migrant children can't speak English, they will hold back the local kids at school. We might be uncomfortable hearing these responses, but at least the person is speaking to us, and this provides us with the opportunity to move them from repeating the dominant narratives endlessly repeated by the media and politicians, to exploring their own lived experience. Adopting an approach of *interested enquirer*, asking people broader questions about what factors they think have contributed to the loss of decent jobs, the causes of the housing shortage, the crisis in the NHS and the failings of our local schools, is a more fruitful approach. Putting people on the defensive is unlikely to be a transformative conversation. We are not looking for an argument, we are looking to unlock the humanity within the person we are speaking to, even if they are currently convinced of a toxic narrative.

What is a transformative response to a person saying that the children of immigrants are undermining learning in our schools? Well, it wouldn't be to challenge the assertion directly. After all, it could be a credible argument – especially in an under-resourced school – that a pupil with low English skills is going to be one more challenge to an overworked teacher. However, taking a Socratic questioning approach, you might ask, 'What do you think is the cause of school underfunding?'. This shows that you are engaging with the person's concerns, and it gives you the opportunity to probe the real issues that are at the heart of why so many pupils are failed by their schools. It may well lead to the realisation that there really is no convincing argument that migration is the cause of long-term chronic under-investment in schools. What an organiser will have done here is to start by engaging with the specific area of concern raised by the person and asked them to look at it from a different angle. Looking at it in this different way may well give rise to a very different answer, not one imposed by the force of their argument, but one discovered by engaging with their questions. A similar approach could be taken to the issue of the absence of good quality working-class jobs, the crisis in the NHS (which of course benefits massively from migrant labour) or the housing market.

The more we deal with the issues that people raise in a non-confrontational way, the more we 'ask' rather than 'tell', and the more we strive to create 'non-violent communication', the more we create the space for the other person to review and reflect on their ideas.

Creating space for unwelcome opinions?

If we accept that changemakers are unlikely to change people's views without discussing them, then we have to find ways to get people to speak. A trade union rep encouraging people to vote in an industrial action ballot campaign will find it difficult to change someone's view by simply telling them the union is calling for a 'yes' vote, and that the person is expected to support the union's position. Instead, a transformative conversation might start by asking: 'Can you think of one good reason to vote yes, and one good reason to vote no?', or, 'On a scale of one to five, how supportive are you of the proposed strike?'. Both questions acknowledge explicitly that there's a range of opinions and factors to consider, and invite the individual to share their thoughts. Once people are sharing, even if their thoughts are 'I can't afford to lose money by supporting the strike', they can be encouraged to reconsider their analysis and conclusions. Perhaps by asking, 'Why is it that you are so short of money?', to which the answer might well be: 'Because I am not paid enough!', suddenly we are on our territory, and a question begs to be asked: 'How can we get the boss to increase wages?'. Rather than seeking to create a climate in which we morally coerce someone into saying what we want to hear, an effective organiser, having a transformative conversation, will ask how the person feels about the wages they get, and the challenges of living on them. This of course is the perfect starting point for a discussion of why people should be supporting the strike.

Key to transformational conversations is an understanding that people use emotional reasoning. They often form an opinion based on how they *feel* about an issue, not because they have thought about it very deeply. This brings us back to Gramsci's concept of common sense and good sense. Those who try to manipulate people seek to exploit their feelings, in particular their fears. Yet if we don't engage with how people feel about an issue, and merely explain the facts as we see them, we are unlikely to connect. If we want transformative change, then we need to also focus on their hopes and aspirations, but we cannot do that effectively if we negate their fears.

Part of our job as changemakers in any transformative conversation is to relate to how people feel. The person who tells you they are frightened for their children's future is surely someone we can relate to, whether their concerns are climate change, unaffordable housing, or a jobs market that looks set to value humans less than machines. A discussion on how we feel about an issue is one way to surface the drivers for a particular conclusion; 'we don't want immigrants round here' is an emotive response that almost never has anything to do with migration. Another great technique for transformative conversation is called the unfreezing question, which is helpful if you are discussing an issue with someone, and they constantly repeat a particular phrase. They might, for example, say: 'We just need a cap on immigration, and once that's reached, that's it'. You could ask them what level of cap they might think was appropriate but, more importantly, perhaps ask them, 'If the national cap had been reached, and if there was a shortage of teachers at your children's school, or trained nursing staff at your local hospital, would you want to make an exception to fill those vacancies?'. You may be surprised how many 'absolutes' become flexible once they are tested in this way against real-world issues. Once someone has accepted that there will be exceptions, you have shattered the 'broken record' and there is now room for a wider conversation.

Another useful technique in a transformative conversation is using a 'difficult question' at the right time. If you were organising on a rundown housing estate, where the landlord was failing to do repairs, and the community is fractured and fails to speak with one voice, you may be speaking to someone who cares deeply about getting the repairs done but doesn't want to work with 'them lot' – whoever they are. Once you have built a level of trust in the conversation, you have listened and engaged with their fears and shared a little of your story, and have agreed that the repairs will only get done if the tenants exert power over the landlord to make them do it, then you can ask the 'difficult question': one that gets to the heart of their concern about working with people they don't like. You might ask: 'So what you need to decide is, what do you care most about: getting the repairs done, or not working with the other group of tenants? You are not going to win if you are divided, so which means more to you?'.

This difficult question needs to be followed by a long silence to allow the person time to consider your question. Too often in conversations, we feel the need to fill the silence. But on this occasion, the silence is a sign that the person you have been talking to is thinking, in fact they may be thinking frantically, because they really want the repairs done, and they really don't want to work with 'the other lot'. You have to give them time to consider if you are right, that there really is only one way to build the power necessary to win the repairs, and that is by a united group of tenants demanding they are done – and organising to pressurise the landlord to do them. You have to give them the respect that allows them to explore any possibility that you are wrong, and then to decide which, indeed, is more important to them. As we have said, this is a powerful technique, but it can only be used after you have built trust, otherwise, it will feel like a trick question (which it is not).

In this chapter, we have explored the concept of narratives and how to change them; in the next chapter, we will look at negotiations, a process that is always deeply influenced by both dominant and subaltern narratives.

Thinking about narratives and counter-narratives in campaigns

Consider a social justice campaign in which you are involved.

See if you can identify a dominant narrative that impedes progress on this campaign.

Ask yourself why this narrative has such power. To what extent does it speak to people's fears? Perhaps list the fears and concerns that it provides a 'simple', if mistaken, answer to.

Consider your counter-narrative. To what extent does your counter-narrative engage with the fears that the dominant narrative exploits?

Does it need to be retold in a way that more clearly acknowledges and seeks to address those fears?

Where is the hope in your story, and how will you convey it to people who are currently influenced by the dominant narrative?

How will you avoid simply telling people they are wrong, and instead ask questions that encourage them to activate their curiosity and re-examine the question?

9

The art of negotiation

This chapter will explore the art of negotiation, and how important this is to all aspects of organising from negotiating with your adversary to negotiating with allies, and even within your own organisation. Classic negotiating theory argues that there are 'bottom lines' beyond which people will not go and the scope for agreement is in the overlap between the two parties' opposing bottom lines. But often, whether this is when negotiating with an 'opposition' or with a potential ally, there is no clarity about where such an overlap sits. Being a good negotiator may get you closer to the maximum your opponent will give: their bottom line. However, transformative change can happen if you can move their bottom line towards you, and this can be done in two ways – adding value to the benefit of working with you or adding costs to the price of working against you.

This chapter will draw upon Walton and McKersie's (1965) theory of labour negotiations, where they argue it's important to understand the sub-processes of negotiation – integrative and distributive bargaining, and the importance of attitudinal structuring as well as inter-organisational bargaining – all of which we will consider in relation to specific negotiating situations. Key to any form of bargaining is how to combine effective negotiation with actions outside the negotiations that may materially affect the other side's 'bottom line'. It's perhaps surprising that few campaigners are great negotiators, and indeed there is, at times, an unhealthy suspicion of negotiation. Yet if we want to be changemakers, rather than permanent protesters bearing witness to some injustice or another, we will need to know when to and how to negotiate.

Types of bargaining

Before moving on, we should perhaps define some terms that are widely used when analysing negotiations and negotiating theory.

Intra-organisational bargaining

This is about the negotiation that takes place *within* an organisation. A one-dimensional approach to negotiations assumes that there are only two viewpoints representing the competing interests in the negotiations, with each side supporting its negotiating position uniformly. However, almost every negotiating position is a compromise. Each of the parties to the negotiations will be a coalition of interests. Within a workplace setting there will be a range of opinions from the management side as to how to progress an issue, and an equally diverse range of opinions on the employee side. Before a negotiation can begin between the employer and employee representatives, there will need to be an agreement as to what will be put forward by each side, and this is what we call intra-organisational bargaining.

Inter-organisational bargaining

This is about the negotiation that takes place *between* organisations – in this sense, it's what we generally understand as bargaining, when we, as campaigners, reach a certain stage in a campaign where we are sitting down with our opponents and are looking for concessions. The types of negotiations can be many and varied: between representatives of employers and employees; between two political parties considering working in coalition; between the organisers of a boycott and the subject of that boycott. Such negotiations *always* end in a compromise, as each side shifts position and trades in exchange for concessions.

Attitudinal structuring

Attitudinal structuring is a long-term process that takes place when two parties have an ongoing relationship that involves multiple negotiations. It tries to foster cooperation and trust and a shared approach even to difficult questions. For example, by suggesting that some principles are assumed, for example, an employer might want to assert that they have a 'right to manage' and, if successful, this would reduce the union's willingness to challenge management decisions that their members did not like. In effect, in attitudinal bargaining, you are seeking to manage the frames through which the other side negotiates.

Integrative bargaining

Sometimes called 'interest-based bargaining', integrative bargaining describes a negotiation in which both sides are seeking to find mutual benefit based on their shared interests. In essence, it happens where both sides have a shared objective and are looking for a 'win-win'. In industrial relations this might include a negotiation over health and safety, where both the employer and the trade union would 'win' if they could reduce the incidence of workplace injuries.

Distributive bargaining

In distributive bargaining, it is acknowledged that for one side to 'win' then the other side must, to some degree, 'lose'. It is about distributing the benefits of the bargain. A classic example might be if you were to buy a second-hand car from a dealership. Your interest will be to get the car at the lowest price, while the salesperson will be seeking to get the maximum price possible.

Trading: the art of give and take in negotiations

Now we have this framework for understanding negotiating practice we can look at some specific examples of successful and unsuccessful negotiations. One great example, which has already been mentioned in Chapter 3, was when the council refuse workers had been on unofficial strike. After a day of standoff and disruption, a meeting was held and the issues resolved. Legally, the council could have sacked the whole workforce for taking unofficial action, but realistically that was not going to happen as it would cause greater disruption and would likely escalate the dispute across the employer. The negotiations were successful, and the matters resolved, at which point the union rep wanted to clarify that there would be no deductions from wages for the day's stoppage. When the employer looked unwilling to make that commitment in writing, another union rep said, 'I don't have time for this, if you take a penny off their wages, the members will be back out on strike next week,' and simply left the room – the employer didn't deduct anyone's wages. A classic example of a negotiator using their power position to get what they want. However, even when you don't have the level of power like those workers did, it is still possible to get great results because of skilful trading.

In this aspect of negotiations – trading – you can figure out with a bit of research what the other side have that you want, and you can trade for it with something that you have, and are happy to share, that they want. A good example is where a rail company wanted to introduce something called matrix management to their data management department. Essentially in a matrix management model you have two managers, one who is responsible for your long-term career – booking your leave, arranging training, annual appraisals and so on – while the second is responsible for supervising your work on a day-to-day basis for a particular project. The idea is that you can be working on a project, for a week or a month, or whatever, and will be managed by the project manager. You will change your projects regularly: as one comes to an end, you are allocated to another, swapping one project manager for another. In effect, in matrix management each employee will have two managers at any one time, managing different aspects of their role. This is a model adopted across many IT departments, and is perhaps neither better nor worse than more traditional management structures. However, union members working in the department were horrified at the thought: they considered one manager was bad enough, but two sounded like double trouble. An additional factor was the proposal that this new management structure would be brought in as part of a wider restructure, and there were fears that there would be redundancies. Traditionally such reorganisations had been seen as an opportunity for the employer to weed out people whose faces didn't fit.

The union, however, had seen matrix management introduced elsewhere, and while there had been a great deal of resistance to its introduction, union members later became quite happy with it. The resistance tended to result in people feeling miserable for six to twelve months, before accepting it actually wasn't as bad as they had anticipated. The reps saw this as an opportunity to trade. They knew that the company had, as a matter of principle, never before conceded a no-compulsory redundancy agreement, but here was an ideal opportunity to win one. In negotiations the union reps asked for a no-compulsory redundancy/no loss agreement for the reorganisation and in return the union would support the introduction of the matrix management system, helping to dispel some of the myths while explaining to its members how it had worked elsewhere.

In the negotiating meeting the reps message was: we know there is nothing wrong with matrix management, it makes a great deal of sense, and is an efficient use of resources, making staff more agile, while protecting their long-term future. We don't have any problem with it, but our members do. They are also fearful of a reorganisation that might see them out of work, or offered a lower-grade role, so if you give the union a no compulsory redundancy/no detriment agreement, and a commitment to review matrix management in six months' time, we will explain to our members they have nothing to worry about with matrix management, and because they trust their union more than they trust you, we can save you a great deal of time and anxiety trying to address our members' concerns.

After taking some time to consider, the employer agreed and the union met with their members and explained that where it had been introduced elsewhere matrix management had come to be accepted, that there was an agreed review process and, most importantly, an agreement which would guarantee no job losses. The members overwhelmingly voted to accept the proposal, and everyone, including the local management were happy. It was a classic 'trade off' because in the terminology it was not a 'nil-sum gain' and everyone was a winner.

Nil-sum gain: where one side loses

A 'nil-sum gain' is where for me to win, you have to lose. Here the negotiation is about who gets the best deal rather than finding how both sides can be better off. An example of a nil-sum gain was the negotiations at the end of an industrial dispute in 2005 at London's Heathrow Airport between Gate Gourmet and the union representing their workers. The workforce was predominantly Asian women who prepared ready meals for long-haul flights. The workers had previously been directly employed by British Airways (BA) and had recently been outsourced to Gate Gourmet. The new employer wanted to make changes to conditions of employment to increase competitiveness with other low-wage, low-cost suppliers. Several meetings had broken down as the union was not willing to accept reductions to their members' wages. In a pre-prepared provocation, the employer brought in lower-paid agency workers, allegedly to replace existing workers. This provocation caused the workforce to walk off the job and into a union meeting (technically a form of unofficial industrial action). The employer, however, had anticipated this and had pre-prepared dismissal notices for the 700 workers.

And so began a long, and ultimately disastrous, dispute. The employer bussed in a replacement workforce, on lower wages, and refused to allow the pre-existing workers back. After months of dispute, and a London-wide leverage campaign, part of which was coordinated by the authors of this book, the company eventually agreed to meet with the workers' union. They were prepared to allow some of the workforce to return, but only on new reduced terms and conditions. For others, the employer offered small sums of compensation (between £5,000 and £8,000) to those who didn't come back, and it had a 'blacklist' of staff it would not take back – some allegedly because of their trade union roles, others because of their previous sick records. The majority of workers accepted the 'deal', which was – at the same time – both deeply unfair *and* a remarkable achievement by the union negotiators given their almost complete lack of leverage in the power relationship. Fifty-six women refused the deal, encouraged by a vocal left-wing sect who claimed they had been 'sold out' by their union and should continue their fight. The women recognised that what had happened to them was unjust and an abuse of their rights and decided to 'fight on', taking their case to an employment tribunal, where they lost. In effect, the employer had set a trap, and the women had taken part in what, by the legal definition, was unofficial industrial action, and the tribunal ruled that the workers couldn't therefore claim unfair dismissal. These women ended up with nothing. A hard lesson in the risks of confusing what is morally right with what you have the power to achieve in negotiations.

Learning from losses

What we can learn from losing is an important lesson taught by Arnie Graff, a leading organiser in the Industrial Areas Foundation (IAF) – the group established by Saul Alinsky. In a training session Arnie used a scenario in which an elderly owner of a small factory was keen to retire. His business had been struggling financially for a number of years. It was based in a small town with high levels of unemployment and was the main employer in the community. The owner had a choice of two buyers, one intended to close the factory and to build housing on the site, while a second potential buyer had made an offer that was conditional on the workforce taking a 5 per cent pay cut, in exchange for which he would guarantee all jobs at the factory for five years. The task for people in the training session was to act as union reps and to negotiate with the new potential buyer. He had set a deadline for an agreement that day, otherwise the offer was off the table, there would be no investment in the company and all workers would lose their jobs.

Arnie had set aside time for teams to formulate a negotiating strategy. One after another each of the teams entered into negotiations with Arnie, who played the role of the potential buyer. No one wanted to accept the pay cut, and each team had numerous options to put to the prospective owner – all of which were rejected. At the end of the exercise, every single group had reached an impasse, the buyer pulled out, the factory closed, and the workforce were out of work in the small town where the factory had been the major employer.

The scenario was designed such that there were only two possible outcomes, either the workforce accepts the pay cut, or the jobs go. There were two choices – one was bad and the other worse. It was based on a training module within the IAF that was first utilised by Saul Alinsky, which involved a role play of an incident in the Peloponnesian Wars, in which a city is offered a choice, either surrender and give up your wealth, or face the city being sacked and the population executed. The defenders refused the first option, and so, by default, chose the second. This is what participants had done in Arnie's industrial version; they all rejected the unpalatable option, and, by default, chose an even worse one. Arnie's point was to show that negotiations are not primarily about what you want, but what's possible to achieve. There will be times when action outside of the negotiating room can create new possibilities, but that does not negate the truth, that a negotiator who rejects something that is unpalatable despite the fact that the alternative is worse is, in effect, choosing the worse option. This is exactly what happened with the women at Gate Gourmet who chose to 'fight on'.

While negotiations tend to take place at a specific moment in a campaign or struggle, they are a crucial part of that process, therefore choosing the point at which you negotiate is important. If you attempt to negotiate before you have built up a head of steam behind your campaign, then your adversary will likely be aware that you have limited leverage. A better time to negotiate is when your campaign is gathering momentum, but before this momentum dissipates.

Organising is different from negotiating, but both are important for organisers

Myles Horton from the Highlander Folk School contrasted organising with negotiating, both of which are important to any campaign but involve different skills and approaches. He said that if a negotiator wants five of something, she will start by asking for ten and hope the negotiations will eventually lead to an agreement on five. In contrast, for Horton, organising was a process by which you started out demanding five, because that was all you could achieve at that time, and then, as your power increased, you increased your demands, because your vision of what is possible expands as your power grows.

The starting point in negotiating theory is an assumption that each side is likely to be better off with an agreement than without one. There is, therefore, an objective value to each side in reaching an agreement to avoid the otherwise negative consequences. Negotiations are really about the way you divide up the benefits of that agreement. A good question for a negotiator to ask themselves is: what is it that *we* have that *they* want? Sometimes, it's simple: what they want is for us to be quiet and stop agitating. Saul Alinsky learned early on that he had the capacity to rile up his target, and time and again he would make his people laugh while infuriating the opposition. He publicly threatened all sort of outrageous stunts, many of these he never actually delivered. He once threatened to close down Chicago's international airport by getting thousands of the inner-city dwellers to queue up to use the bathrooms, taking plenty of time to do so. He told the authorities, that their city would be a laughingstock, as international travellers would not be able to access any bathroom facilities as they arrived off their flights. Perhaps Alinsky was aware of the situationists, because he certainly enjoyed issuing these empty threats that caused widespread outrage. While Alinsky is known as a great organiser he was also a skilled negotiator who wanted to get a seat at the table. He ensured his opponents knew he would be more trouble locked out of the room than he would be if he was admitted.

It was this principle of the employer wanting a quiet life and avoiding disruption that forced Gate Gourmet back to the negotiating table. The dispute was causing embarrassment to BA, and particularly so when baggage handlers walked out on unofficial action to support the Gate Gourmet workers. International headlines in the media linked BA – a company very protective of its brand – to the seemingly shoddy treatment of its former employees by Gate Gourmet. The solidarity campaign had seen numerous public and inter-union rallies at Heathrow Airport where a 24-hour continuous protest was being staged. These events were supported by local communities, for example with food and refreshments provided by the local Sikh gurdwara, fundraising events at local West London venues and a delegation to the Labour Party conference. As the employer wanted wage cuts and a quiet life, the offer to take back the majority of the sacked workers, on lower wages, and to compensate the others was the price they were prepared to pay to see the winding down of the community campaign.

Changing culture to facilitate negotiated outcomes

In a complex series of negotiations between rail unions and London Underground in 2007 there had been a slow breakdown in industrial relations over a number of issues, some of which should have been resolved relatively easily. But the employer had begun responding negatively to anything the union wanted. A series of strike ballots by two unions, the TSSA and the RMT, led to three days of negotiations in a hotel in central London. Day one didn't start well. The employer's representative described one of the RMT's leading reps as 'insane'. In their opening remarks, the TSSA representative said:

> we have a mandate for strike action, but we have come here to resolve a number of issues. If these issues can be resolved through negotiations, then we won't need to strike. What we won't do is sit here while trade union negotiators are abused and insulted. We have come to do a job of work, and we won't succeed if we are merely trading insults.

There were 13 separate items on the agenda, some of which were more important than others. The meeting agreed to discuss the full 13 items as a package so, that way, if a satisfactory resolution could not be found on one item, it didn't necessarily mean that agreement couldn't be reached. Over three days a great deal of 'horse trading' took place, with each side making relatively minor concessions in an attempt to encourage movement on the other side. In the end, despite the earlier confrontational tone, progress was made, and an agreement reached.

This is illustrative of the 'attitudinal structuring' mentioned at the start of this chapter. At the start of the three days, each side wanted to 'win' at the expense of the other, in part because of a history of confrontational interactions between the unions and the employer. Changing the culture of the discussions was an important part of creating the possibility of movement on both sides. The alternative would most likely have seen the strikes go ahead, followed by further talks, which, once people's minds were more focussed, ended with an agreement not dissimilar to the one that had been reached in advance.

This is also illustrative of one of Saul Alinsky's 'rules': the threat is usually more terrifying than the thing itself. Strike action, when used appropriately – and well-supported by the workforce – is an incredibly powerful tool, but a standard piece of advice from trade union negotiators is that you have more power the day *before* a strike than you do the day after. This is because the employer doesn't want the disruption and expense of a strike, but once you have acted, the employer has suffered the disruption and expense, and no concessions by them the day after will reverse the action that has already taken place. Without a credible follow-up from the union, the employer may choose to simply await the union's next move, knowing that union members will be losing money on each strike day. However, the day before a strike the cost of settling the dispute might seem more attractive than the disruption and costs associated should the strike go ahead. It's also illustrative of Alinsky's first rule: 'power is not only what you have, but what the enemy thinks you have'.

The day before a strike the employer – and too often the union – has no certainty how successful it is going to be. An employer may guess that between 30 per cent and 60 per cent of the workforce might back the strike, but they are, most often, not certain. Yet the day following a strike, an employer will know exactly how many workers stayed away from work. Proposing a deal the day before the strike not only means the employer has an incentive to reach a deal, but it also means that they don't know for sure how much power you have. There may well be times when you are confident of mass support and when you want to show the employer just how powerful you are, and how much cost and disruption you can inflict if they won't reach an agreement, but for most trade unionists, most of the time, they are more likely – unless very well organised – to be closer to the Gate Gourmet end, rather than the bin workers' end, of the spectrum of power. This can be the same with any form of community action. For example, if a community is concerned that a proposed development is not meeting the needs of their community, they may consider a campaign of disruption, of legal challenge and lobbies of the planning department, but once again, negotiating in advance is often when you have the most power.

When entering into difficult negotiations it's important to think about long-term relationships. As a trade union, you will still want to have regular productive meetings to discuss issues relevant to your members' concerns. As such, however difficult a struggle the dispute becomes, you will want to ensure that your relationship is not irreparably damaged. A leading negotiator for London Underground used to have a saying – he would characterise negotiations as 'dancing' and industrial action as 'boxing' and say: 'let's see how far we get dancing, and if we end up boxing, we will deal with that when it comes'. In other words, the negotiators, while representing different positions, were well aware of the potential for the negotiations to fail, and the consequences if they did, but this was defused by recognising these were all part of industrial relations practice.

An important aspect of good negotiations is that you are clear what you want and what you are prepared to give, and can demonstrate that you are able to deliver what you promise in the negotiations. Questions for organisers are:

- Who do you represent? In a trade union this may be the whole workforce or just part of the workplace.
- How much support do you have from your constituency?
- Do you have the confidence of your members when you go into negotiations and what are the decision-making processes?
- Do you have a mandate to reach agreement with the employer?

Developing a bargaining position: the importance of having a mandate

Many years ago, a group of people were involved in squatting a disused council building in Sheffield and they declared it a peace centre. The local council took legal action against the squatters, but at the same time offered to negotiate. A handful of squatters went to a meeting with council officers and came back with great news. The council had no immediate plans for the building and were prepared to suspend possession proceedings in exchange for a guarantee that the squatters would leave the building with six months' notice when the council required the building. The negotiators returned jubilant to the squat. Unfortunately, the anarchists in the squat were furious that the group had negotiated an agreement with the council, which they saw as part of 'the oppressive state', and as a result there were no further negotiations with the council. This is why negotiators need a clear mandate when going into talks. With trade unions it is fairly simple – the workforce has joined a trade union that's recognised for negotiations. The employer and the trade union will have mechanisms for endorsing or rejecting any prospective agreement (normally for unions, through a process of ballot).

But in other circumstances it may be less straightforward. You might be part of a community campaign negotiating with a local council where there are many 'players' on their side, such as the councillors (both those in the majority party and those in opposition), senior managers within the authority, perhaps a developer who is seeking to influence them, and maybe a local residents' group that's being offered inducements to support a particular proposal. On your side, there may be a range of groups who have only one thing in common – a desire to stop this proposal. Before you can enter into meaningful negotiations with any reasonable chance of success you need to do two things. First you need to 'map' the forces against you. Who are they, how powerful are they, and what are the reasons they want to progress this plan? Then you need to map your side. Imagine the issue is a development such as the one adjacent to Abney Park Cemetery we discussed in Chapter 6. Among those opposed to this development were environmentalists concerned about the nature reserve at the cemetery, residents of the live/work units that would be knocked down, local independent shopkeepers who feared their livelihoods would be threatened, park users and those concerned about traffic management. In this particular case there were no direct negotiations with the council, but if there had been, then there would have needed to be some internal discussion between the groups to ensure that the views of each group were fairly represented in the negotiating position, and that everyone knew what the collective 'red lines' were.

Splitting the opposition

Once you are in negotiations, one of the things you might seek to do is to 'split' your opposition. Let's take an example to see how this might work in practice. In a factory, where production is expanding, you are negotiating on behalf of a union for a wage increase for the production workers. You meet with representatives of the employer, they bring along the managing director, the head of finance, the head of HR and the production manager. You can be certain that the person who has least sympathy for a pay increase is the head of finance because they can always use the money saved by a lower pay increase, either in reinvestment or in paying shareholders dividends. The managing director is most likely to lead the negotiations and one of their main concerns is to keep everyone on their side together. The production manager is likely to be the person most sympathetic to your claim as they work directly with your members and rely on them to get the job done, so a decent pay rise will make their job easier. You will also, in all probability, have more engagement with this person than the others, as you discuss new working practices, changes to overtime requirements, health and safety reviews and so on. In other words, the production manager has regular contact with you, and – hopefully, but not always – you will have built some rapport. Meanwhile, the director of HR is probably influenced by the level of staff turnover. If the company pays towards the bottom end of the pay scales in the local area, then people will regularly leave once they hear of a better job elsewhere. For HR, every time someone leaves, it is more work for them to recruit a replacement.

In the meeting, the employer side may lead with the head of finance explaining why the company can't, for financial reasons, agree the wage increase you have requested. As a negotiator you will likely have done your homework by studying the company's annual report and know what sort of dividend they are paying to their shareholders. A good figure to have in your head is the company's annual profit divided by the number of workers, it is a very rough figure that indicates how much profit they are making, on average from each worker. But, focussing on *inter-organisational bargaining*, you might want to ask the production manager about how much the staff have contributed to the success of the business this year and if they feel the workforce have earned a pay rise – this is the soft underbelly that you want to tease into being openly sympathetic to the union position (although it's likely they won't back it openly). Next you might want to move onto HR, perhaps asking them about the cost to the employer every time someone leaves for another job. They will, of course, have benchmarked the pay of your members against other companies, but you need to know whether these are appropriate comparators. Can you argue why, objectively, your members should be paid more than the going rate for similar jobs? Why does the local employment market require a higher rate if the company wants to retain staff? Engaging with the HR person will again be designed to suggest that there are other considerations beyond the 'simple' balance sheet. The workforce is, after all, the 'human resources' of the company. Moving onto the director of finance, your negotiators need to show that the company can afford a higher payment and it's a commercial choice whether it makes one.

Remember in negotiations your audience is not your colleagues on the negotiating committee. It's not these people you are aiming to impress. Your key audience is the different interests represented on the other side of the negotiating table. If you can reduce the focus on the finance director's concerns, you are more likely to reach agreement on your terms.

Creating division for your adversary

After the first introductory round of negotiations, you want to leave the director of HR and the production manager sympathetic to the employees' side, believing that their life would be easier if the company were to award a decent pay increase to the workers, and that the 'obstacle' to them having this easy life is the finance director.

Conversely, the employer side is also likely to want to split your team. You may have taken along a delegation that includes delivery drivers, the people who work on the production line, and supervisors. Although all part of the union, it's still likely that different sections may respond differently to any offer. A response from the employer after the first round of negotiations may be to say we have listened to your arguments, and we think we can move. This could be qualified by saying the company can't increase its offer for production line workers, but it accepts that the rates of pay for delivery drivers have gone up across the economy, so it is prepared to increase pay for this section of the workforce above the original offer. The first instinct of some of those union members offered the additional amount may be to accept, while those who have been offered no increase will want to stand firm. This is one reason why some employers have different unions recognised to negotiate on behalf of different grades, or trades. It avoids the internal union fights, but it doesn't make negotiations any easier.

From opening negotiations to closing the deal

We talked earlier about Arnie Graf and his exercise on the factory negotiations. One of the key things in negotiations is formulating three 'positions' – your opening position, your target position and your 'red line' position. Negotiating is a form of bargaining and you want to start by exploring what the other side is prepared to offer, so your opening offer is not your 'red line' or where you want to end up. A recent example of this is the British Medical Association's (BMA's) dispute with the UK government over pay. The NHS consultants demanded a pay increase of 33 per cent and took strike action in an attempt to force the government's hand in negotiations. More than 24,000 consultants in England voted in the BMA's ballot with a turnout of 71 per cent and, of those, 86 per cent voted for industrial action. It is unlikely that the BMA believed that consultants would have held out to get that level of increase, but it was an opening demand based on the fact that over the last 13 years, real pay for NHS consultants has fallen in value by 33 per cent. The argument of the BMA was that this demand was morally justified. Yet morality seldom wins disputes, and it is probable that both sides recognised that pay restoration wouldn't be achieved in one pay round. In reality, the 33 per cent claim probably bore little relationship to what

BMA members actually considered might be sufficient to bring the dispute to a close. As has been said, the opening negotiating position is more of a wish list, but a wish that has some material basis. By this we mean the negotiators are not plucking a figure of out thin air – there is an argument for why it should be this figure. In organisations with a long history of collective bargaining, the opening position might also be a signal to the other side as to what you will eventually settle for as negotiations take place. If a union wants a 6 per cent pay rise and it will not accept less than this it might ask for 12 or 9 per cent, recognising that the employer will settle for somewhere around the 6 per cent mark.

It is important for your members or constituency to understand that the opening position is not your target (otherwise they will be very disappointed when you recommend acceptance of a lower offer). Negotiation is also about managing the expectations of your members, but here lies a problem. You can't openly debate the target position, as to do so would be a clear indication to the employer that you will accept something less than you are asking. Indeed, in the above scenario, if a union newsletter stated that it was asking for 12 per cent but would accept 6 per cent, then the employer would interpret 6 per cent as your starting point and try to bargain you down.

Your target should be based on research that can be argued at the negotiating table and this should be reached on the basis of an analysis of what the employer can afford, what other employers in the sector are paying and so on. Finally, there is the 'red line' or 'resistance point', this is the figure below which you will not settle. It is, by definition, less than you would want, but it is better than the consequences of no agreement. In negotiating theory there is an acronym, BATNA, which stands for the best alternative to a negotiated agreement. Essentially, this concept asks, what are the consequences of walking away without an agreement? The Harvard Law School sums it up thus:

> It's a twist on the old 'bird in the hand' adage. If you've already got a golden goose, your negotiating partner has to offer even better terms to get you to say yes. But if all you're holding is a dead duck, you may

have to take whatever your counterpart offers you.
(Harvard Law School 2023)

In reality, all negotiations with any prospect of success take place within the boundaries of each side's resistance points. Let's use a wage negotiation again as an example. If an employer's aspiration is 5 per cent but their resistance point is 8 per cent, meanwhile the union's aspiration is 10 per cent, but their resistance point is 7 per cent, then the scope for agreement is somewhere between the two resistance points, that is between 7 per cent and 8 per cent. However, if an employer wants to give 3 per cent but their resistance point is 6 per cent, and the union wants 12 per cent, but its resistance point is 9 per cent, then there is nothing the negotiators can do, as there is no scope for agreement. While it is important to understand the consequences, or opportunities for your side if negotiations break down, it is also important to consider the consequences for the other side.

In the run-up to the 2012 London Olympics a number of transport unions were invited to attend a briefing from the Olympic Delivery Authority (ODA) to discuss issues related to public transport during the Games. Officially, the ODA had no power over the privatised bus companies, the London Underground or London Overground operators, but the unions recognised that public transport was vital to the success of the Games given the numbers that would be attending. As such, the unions took the opportunity to raise a whole series of grievances that had stalled in negotiations with the respective employers. The unions recognised that there was a change in the power dynamic as their members were crucial to the smooth running of the Olympics. The threat of a coordinated transport strike at a time when half a million overseas visitors were trying to get to the Olympic stadium considerably strengthened the negotiating position of the unions. The ODA wanted industrial peace and suggested the union had an almost patriotic duty to avoid disputes over that period. The unions responded by asking the ODA to use its influence to encourage the transport employers to move on a range of issues. In addition, the unions secured an attendance bonus whereby if workers turned up for work during the Olympic Games, they would automatically get the bonus.

The alternative for the ODA of no agreement was unacceptable, and they undoubtedly used their 'soft power' to influence the range of employers to resolve a range of issues. This movement was induced by the shift in the power balance and the need for transport to run smoothly throughout the Games.

To sum up, negotiations are sometimes viewed as the 'dirty end' of campaigning: the place where compromises are made. But genuine changemakers understand that all disputes end in negotiations of one sort or another, and that integrating the negotiating strand into your overall strategy is the way to get the best results. Compromise should not be a dirty word to campaigners, it is the practical job of translating the pressure we have generated in a campaign into agreements that take us forward, maybe not as far as we would like, but as far as is possible given the power our campaign has generated. Understanding the process of negotiations and developing the appropriate skills is one way in which we ensure our campaigns deliver measurable wins.

Devising a strategy for negotiations

Think of a dispute in which you are currently involved, or have been involved in the past.

Firstly, consider your 'side': what does success look like to different actors, or sections of your support? Try to create a grid, showing the different sections of your community and what they are most concerned about. For example, in the supermarket campaign we discussed earlier, the environmentalists were most concerned about the impact on wildlife in the nature reserve, the people whose homes were to be demolished had very different (although often overlapping) concerns, and the local shopkeepers were concerned about the impact on their businesses.

Now consider the other side. What are the various factions and what are the issues that they care about? Again, make a grid.

For your side, consider how you can tie all of these concerns into a negotiating position, remembering you will want to agree in advance a 'starting position' a 'target position' and a 'red line'. The 'starting position' will be easy, as it is literally your wish list, but agreeing on the priorities and compromises that might be acceptable is the challenge when discussing your target and your red line. To keep a coalition together, you need each section of the coalition to recognise that they are likely to win more together than they would addressing their concerns individually.

Consider the other side: you can guess what their opening position may be, but consider what different elements of their side might be prepared to give up. Finally, what can you 'trade' to entice at least sections of the other side to move towards your target position?

10

Disorganising: how opponents seek to disrupt

Those with a vested interest in the status quo will, almost inevitably, use their resources to seek to thwart our efforts. Therefore, if we want to win, we need to consider the disorganising that our opponents may seek to inflict on our campaigns and movements. If, for example, you were planning to win a game of football, you would likely not only plan your strategy, but you would also consider what moves you would expect your opponent to deploy. When lawyers are trained, they are encouraged to ask, 'what case is the other side going to advance, and what weaknesses are they going to try to exploit in yours?'. Yet campaigners all too rarely consider how their target will respond, and even more seldom consider the possibility that they might use underhand tactics. In contrast, in *Rules for Radicals*, Saul Alinsky always claimed that 'the real action is the enemy's reaction' – in other words, his tactics were often designed to generate a reaction from his target. Not only would he anticipate the response, but he would tailor his actions to provoke the reaction he wanted. Irrespective of what you think of Alinsky's approach, if you want to win your campaign then you need to consider how your target may try to disrupt and disorganise you. You will then need to think about how you will mitigate their attempts and inoculate your people from the anticipated manoeuvres.

Inoculation

In 1941 the Almanac Singers were a group of US pro-working-class folk singers that included Pete Seeger and Woody Guthrie.

They were an early example of the movement-orientated groups that would become common place in later years. That year, at a time when the US union movement was building a wave of 'sit-down' strikes, they wrote 'Talking Union Blues'. Woody Guthrie had always said that a song would travel further and faster than a leaflet, and the song was meant to be a guide to union organising, explaining that if workers want higher wages, then they've got to speak to their co-workers, produce a leaflet and get people along to a meeting, where they can elect a steering group. It then discusses the power of a strike. But perhaps the most powerful element of this song is the bit where he talks about how the boss will try to break the union's picket line by using the police and the National Guard. It's no coincidence that this union-organising song took time out to explain what the boss would do – organisers today call this *inoculation*. If we tell people in advance what the powerholders are likely to do, then it comes as no surprise and can be factored into the strategy.

Guthrie's lyrics list the common strategies used to defeat a union (such as red-baiting, stool pigeons, vigilantes, racism) so that the workers who go into struggle are prepared and will see it coming. They will then recognise the attempts to break them up, typically through alleging that the ringleaders are 'reds', through the actions of people acting on behalf of the employer ('stool pigeons'), and through the tactic of stirring up division and, in particular, racial tensions. It's essential for all serious campaigns that they consider what the likely reaction of the powerholders you are facing will be, so let's take a look at some historic and more recent examples.

Union busting

Suppose you were organising a union at a company that has a reputation for being anti-trade union. It's not difficult to conceive how a company might decide to do what it can to undermine your efforts. It may choose to organise a 'staff forum' to hear workers' views as a way of addressing the absence of any 'employee voice' within the company and which, on first appearances, might seem to be a way to address many of the concerns that the union raises. Perhaps it will tell workers that unions are an unnecessary distraction, that unions are 'dinosaurs', that they charge high subscription rates, and their leaders are well paid. The company might resort to name-calling, suggesting that union leaders are anti-business, or left-wing radicals. It may even organise and fund a network of anti-union employees to campaign against unionisation. We could debate which management union avoidance tactics are 'legitimate' and which are illegitimate, but we should not fool ourselves into expecting them to play by the rules.

Two multinational companies that have a reputation for being keen to ensure unions do not have a presence in their organisations are Starbucks (Shepardson and Russ 2023) and Amazon (Amazon 2018). In 2023, *The Guardian* newspaper reported that, in America: 'The National Labor Relations Board, the federal agency that polices labor-management relations, has accused Starbucks and Amazon of a slew of illegal anti-union practices, among them firing many workers in retaliation for backing a union' (Greenhouse 2023). While 'union busting' is very advanced and ingrained in the culture of American capitalism, it's less blatant in the UK. While there are plenty of companies that don't want effective trade unions, outside of the building industry there are relatively limited examples of criminal activity by employers preventing trade unions organising. For most workplaces, most of the time, employers will rely on an ideological, or narrative offensive to dismiss the effectiveness of unions. Companies may refer to their employees as 'partners' or issue company shares to staff to reinforce the message that 'when the company does well, we all do well' and so on, but some take a much more hard-line anti-union position. This has been common in the building industry in the UK. The deeply engrained employer hostility to trade unions in the building trades may in part be to do with the way the industry is organised, with most workers nominally self-employed through a series of subcontractors as part of a gig economy. It may also be because the industry is actually quite vulnerable to workplace stoppages.

In late 1972, building workers staged their first and only national dispute. Their concerns were about establishing a minimum wage for building workers, the abolition of the 'lump' system of payment, and to address the appalling health and safety issues on construction sites. During the dispute, Ricky Tomlinson and Des Warren organised a flying picket to a building site in the market town of Shrewsbury, 150 miles north-west of London. Despite a police presence, the pickets successfully persuaded the local building workers to join the strike. There was no trouble on the day, and no arrests were made. Ricky Tomlinson, who later became a film and TV star, recounted: 'In the 1970s, every day at least one person was killed or seriously injured on the sites – they were not called the "killing fields" for nothing. We won that industrial dispute and the bosses wanted revenge' (Tomlinson 2021).

Five months after the strike had been successfully concluded a police investigation led to charges against 24 of the Shrewsbury pickets, and they were convicted of 'conspiracy to intimidate', in a series of rigged trials. In 2015, it was revealed that a highly prejudicial TV documentary, 'Red Under the Bed', which was broadcast on the day the jury went out to consider their verdicts had been commissioned and promoted by: 'senior members of Heath's 1972 Conservative cabinet and members of the security services', according to *The Guardian* newspaper. In the film, 'two of the defendants are shown taking part in protest marches. The images are interspersed with footage of violence and damage on building sites alleged to have been caused by the pickets' (Boffey 2015).

With the help of the security services, the government had commissioned this film designed to paint the defendants in a bad light, and it was shown on TV during the late stages of their trial. It later transpired that the police had also destroyed evidence, and in 2021, nearly fifty years after the fact, the UK Court of Appeal finally overturned their convictions.

But this case was not an anomaly and to understand it, we have to go back to the Donovan Commission report, *Royal Commission on Trade Unions and Employers' Associations 1965–1968: Report*, published in 1968. The Commission concluded that trade unions had become too powerful and disruptive to industry and that while there were genuine grievances of workers, these should be raised and resolved through the use of professional trade union negotiators, not the threat of industrial action in the workplace. Subsequently, the Labour government produced a policy document in 1969, 'In Place of Strife: A Policy for Industrial Relations', which argued for a range of legal restraints on trade unions. The Labour government could not, however, reach consensus on these highly controversial proposals, and the planned legislation was dropped.

By February of 1972, the UK had a Conservative government, and it was facing the first national miners' strike since the 1920s. The miners' successful mass picket in 1972 at Saltley Gate near Birmingham was seen as a turning point in industrial relations, helping the National Union of Mineworkers (NUM) to win a major dispute, but cementing the government's determination to reduce the power of the union movement. The miners' pickets had been supported by an unofficial stoppage of about 50,000 workers in the engineering trade in Birmingham and somewhere between 15,000 to 30,000 of them marched to Saltley Gate coking plant to support the miners and blockade the entrance.

In 2003, the BBC reported that government papers released under the 30-year rule showed that:

> A 'volunteer force' was planned in Scotland to beat miners' pickets during the 1972 coal strike ... civil servants, police, local authorities and other organisations worked on a secret project to muster hundreds of drivers to supply the country's power stations. A Royal Air Force base was earmarked as a makeshift base for the unit, whose numbers were put at between 400 and 600 trucks and drivers. (BBC 2003)

This plan, to raise a volunteer 'army' of strike-breakers, had superseded another idea. According to the BBC report, 'Edward Heath's government had been working on plans to use the military to beat a strike since the summer of the previous year'. This massive strike-breaking plan was never put into action, in part because the picket at Saltley Gate brought the dispute to an abrupt end, but perhaps also because the government was concerned about the potential backlash that such unprecedented steps might provoke.

Within a hostile government, a strategy emerged that saw the use of both criminal and civil law to prevent unions from being effective. The Shrewsbury pickets were the first victims of this policy, which was ramped up during the 1976 Grunwick dispute at a photo-processing factory in North London. At Grunwick, the Freedom Association, an organisation set up in 1975 that gained public prominence through its anti-trade union campaigns, litigated against a postal workers union for showing solidarity with the Grunwick strikers. Labour was in power during the Grunwick dispute and, despite legislation that was meant to make union recognition a right if the majority of workers wanted it, the owners of the Grunwick factory simply refused to accept the recommendations of the government-established Advisory, Conciliation and Arbitration Service (ACAS) and secured a court order declaring the ACAS report 'ultra vires', or beyond their powers. This counter-attack against unions was in full swing by the time of the Conservative government of 1983 and Prime Minister Thatcher's planned revenge against the miners. During the first Thatcher government, from 1979 to 1983, a series of anti-union laws had been passed to reduce the power of trade unions, specifically outlawing 'sympathy strikes', or secondary picketing. But with the second term, came the provocation of a pit closure programme that sparked the infamous 1984–85 miners' strike. It is hard to describe the shock throughout the labour movement, as paramilitary policing of an industrial dispute suddenly became the norm. Folk singer Dick Gaughan wrote in his song 'The Ballad of '84' of blue-uniformed armies with truncheons and riot shields (see https://www.lyricsmania.com/ballad_of_84_lyrics_dick_gaughan.html). The showdown at the Orgreave coking plant at Rotherham, South Yorkshire, was the culmination of 20 years of planning by the rich and powerful, and their agents in the Conservative government.

The situation at Orgreave was very different to that at Saltley Gate – the state had planned well in advance to ensure the miners didn't win a second time. At Saltley, an estimated 15,000 to 30,000 Birmingham workers were physically present to support the miners' picket. The Birmingham police had no way to control that number of people and closed the gates. Attacking the pickets would have inflamed the situation, and the result would have been the closure of industry across Birmingham. However, at Orgreave, there were an estimated 8,000 pickets, almost all of them striking miners bussed in from all over the country and they were facing 6,000 paramilitary police. On this occasion the local working-class had simply not been mobilised. Gareth Peirce, a leading civil rights solicitor who defended a number of miners in subsequent court cases, takes up the story, describing a film that the police had made that day:

> In the film, you see how men arrived at Orgreave on a beautiful summer's day from all corners of the country. You see them from 6am onwards being escorted by police towards an open field; being brought by police over open ground from the motorway, being steered by police from below the coking plant to the field above. For two hours, you see only men standing in the sun, talking and laughing. And when the coking lorries arrive, you see a brief, good-humoured, and expected push against the police lines; it lasts for 38 seconds exactly.
>
> You also see – the film being shot from behind police lines – battalions of police in riot uniforms, phalanxes of mounted officers, squadrons of men with long shields, short shields, and batons. You see in the distance, in a cornfield, police horses waiting, and down a slope, on the other side, more police with dogs. Suddenly the ranks of the long-shield officers, 13 deep, open up and horses gallop through the densely-packed crowd. This manoeuvre repeats itself. In one of those charges you see a man being trampled by a police horse and brought back through the lines as a captive, to be charged with riot. You see squadrons of officers dressed in strange medieval battle dress with helmets and visors, round shields and overalls, ensuring anonymity and invulnerability, run after the cavalry and begin truncheoning pickets who have been slow to escape. (Peirce 2014)

That day, after being battered and bloodied, 95 pickets were charged with offences including riot and unlawful assembly. The police systematically lied in court, and eventually the trial collapsed. Michael Mansfield QC described the trial as: 'the worst example of a mass frame-up in this country this century', while the secretary of the Orgreave Truth and Justice Campaign said the country had witnessed 'a militarised police force at Orgreave beat up, fit up and lock up dozens of miners' (Sweeney 2016).

In 2016, over 30 years after the events, *The Guardian* reported:

> A review of the Orgreave prosecution court papers by the Independent Police Complaints Commission reported last June that there was evidence of excessive violence by police officers, a false narrative from police exaggerating violence by miners, perjury by officers giving evidence to prosecute the arrested men, and an apparent coverup of that perjury by senior officers. (Jones 2016)

The police riot at Orgreave was the culmination of a long-term plan to defeat militant trade unionism, and its success depended on trade unions not anticipating and planning for the aggressive response. The defeat of the miners set the context for a new era of industrial relations that has seen a major shift in power and, with it, a shift in what is known as the wage share. Put simply, workers across the economy today get paid less as a percentage of the value of their work than they did 40 years ago.

Blacklisting of construction workers

Union activists and members in the building trades have been subject to long-term surveillance and exclusion from work to prevent them organising their fellow workers. Companies held secret blacklists for decades – all of which is currently subject to a public enquiry. Dave Smith of the Blacklist Support Group takes up the story in his opening statement to the Undercover Policing Inquiry:

> In 1919, ex-military intelligence officers together with Conservative MPs and the captains of British industry set up the Economic League, to wage in their own words 'a crusade for capitalism' by keeping left wing

union activists under surveillance and denying them work. The Economic League had both direct formal and countless informal links with the police, that resulted in thousands of workers losing their jobs in sectors such as pharmaceuticals, mining, engineering, banking and local government. (Smith 2020)

The Economic League later became the Consulting Association.

When a blacklisted worker was elected as a union representative, raised concerns about safety on a building site, submitted an employment tribunal, or took part in a protest or strike, this was recorded on his or her blacklist file. Every job applicant on major building projects had their name checked against the blacklist and if there was a match, the worker would be refused work or dismissed. This includes workers engaged via sub-contractors and employment agencies. (Smith 2020)

Names on the blacklist were supplied, not only by employers, but, according to the Independent Police Complaints Commission:

Police officers across the country supplied information on workers to a blacklist operation run by Britain's biggest construction companies ... a Scotland Yard inquiry into police collusion has identified that it is 'likely that all special branches were involved in providing information' that kept certain individuals out of work. (Boffey 2015)

There is another twist to this story. In April 2022, Unite the union established a long overdue inquiry into the evidence that union officials had also contributed to the blacklisting of their own members. Given this history, it's no surprise that construction deaths, while not as high as in the 1970s, remain shockingly high. In 2022–23 there were 45 fatal injuries in the UK's construction sector, nearly one per week, and this was a third of all work-related deaths recorded that year (HSE 2023).

Yet the deaths of building workers can be avoided. In stark contrast to these figures the construction of the 2012 London Olympics recorded no fatalities. In fact, the frequency of accidents was less than a third of the construction industry average and substantially less than the all-industry average. In other words, working on the Olympic construction site was considerably safer than working in an average job in the economy. This was in part because the Olympic Delivery Authority was committed to minimising accidents, and crucially was prepared to work with rather than against trade unions.

Securing safe systems of work across the industry had always been one of the core objectives of blacklisted workers. While construction sites will inevitably have elevated risks of injury, the 2012 London Olympics construction project proved that managing those risks effectively is possible if employers are prepared to put adequate measures in place. However, winning safety across the construction sector remains substantially harder because of the on-going harassment, victimisation and blacklisting of building workers and, in particular, health and safety reps.

Corporate campaigns: the use of counter-narratives

There are many well-documented examples of powerful industrial companies seeking to undermine community or health campaigns related to either pollution or the safety of their products. We can start with the link between lung cancer and smoking. Medical journal articles linking smoking to lung cancer can be found from as early as 1854, in *The Boston Medical and Surgical Journal* (vol 49(26), pp. 527–32), and in 1912 Dr Isaac Adler noted that as smoking increased so did the incidence of lung cancer, a fatal condition that had previously been very rare (Proctor 2012). From then on, until the early 1950s, researchers using epidemiological studies noted how many sufferers of lung cancer either were or had been smokers. Cellular pathways studies provided evidence that cigarette smoke damaged the lining of the lungs. Research also identified known cancer-causing chemicals in cigarette smoke. Gradually, this mounting evidence created a strong consensus that there was a link between lung cancer and smoking. A longitudinal study published in 1954 demonstrated that smokers of 35 cigarettes a day increased their likelihood of dying from lung cancer by a factor of 40 (Proctor 2012). Internal documentation from the tobacco industry demonstrates that their own scientists recognised the link as early as 1953 (Teague 1953). Yet with each decade that the evidence of the harm caused by smoking increased, so the counter-narrative of the tobacco industry was ratcheted up. An internal memo from a PR company working on behalf of the tobacco industry stated in 1968: 'The most important type of story is that which casts doubt in the cause-and-effect theory of disease and smoking. Eye-grabbing headlines should strongly call out the point – Controversy! Contradiction! Other Factors! Unknowns!' (Rowell and Evans-Reeves 2017).

And so, while the science was settled as long ago as 1953, for decades the industry argued that there was 'no conclusive proof' of a link between smoking and ill-health. One way the industry perpetuated this myth was through the funding of research designed to 'look the other way', exploring everything but the link between smoking and lung cancer. It was a campaign of disinformation and the spreading of doubt when no real scientific doubt existed. Today, in the UK and in other advanced economies, the tobacco industry has largely lost the information war over the link to lung cancer. But it has migrated its business to emerging markets, and worldwide smoking continues to increase, with over one million people dying from lung cancer each year. There are currently an estimated 300 million smokers in China, a figure that may not yet have peaked.

The asbestos scandal

A similar pattern can be detected with the public health emergency caused by exposure to asbestos. In 1930, two public health professionals published a *Report on Effects of Asbestos Dust on the Lungs of Workers in the Asbestos Industry* (Merewether and Price 1930). They examined 364 asbestos workers, and found that a quarter had signs of asbestosis. For those who had worked in the industry for more than 20 years, the proportion was 80 per cent. They also noted that while manufacture of asbestos was a particularly important point of contamination, anywhere that asbestos was used, and dust was generated, would pose a risk. The government subsequently passed the Asbestos Regulations 1931 designed to reduce exposure. In 1939, an asbestos factory opened in Hebden Bridge, and closed in 1970. By 1976, a Parliamentary Ombudsman report by Sir Alan Mirre found that of the 2,200 workers who had ever worked in the factory 262 (12%) were reporting asbestosis and 77 had already died. Given that some of the workers were transient, it is possible that other deaths went unrecorded. This calamity became known as the 'Hebden Bridge Massacre'. But none of this was new, as the factory had been the subject of two previous TV exposures: 'Dust at Acre Mill' by *World in Action* in 1971, and 'The Killer Dust' by *Horizon* in 1975.

The asbestos industry's response was to dismiss the evidence. According to Alan Dalton, a leading safety campaigner of the era: 'the asbestos industry itself launched into a massive £500,000 advertising campaign to convince people that asbestos was safe' (Dalton 1979). The advertising campaign was pseudo-science. Alan Dalton takes up the story, saying that the Advertising Standards Authority, which he describes as not a particularly effective regulatory authority, found that, 'much of the information given in the advert was premature and unsubstantiated'. The *Sunday Times* (4 July 1976) criticised the advert, 'but the criticism was about one quarter the size of the original which appeared on another page' (Dalton 1979: 60) In March 1977, the journal *International Management* reported that 'Surveys prior to the advertising campaign showed that about one-fifth of the UK population thought asbestos should be banned. Several weeks after the last advertisement a survey indicated this number was halved' (quoted in Dalton 1979: 60).

The leading international academic critic of the asbestos industry at the time was Professor Irving Selikoff. His research used union records to demonstrate the real levels of fatalities within the asbestos industry. But in January 1977 he was provided with a significant grant, half of which came from the asbestos industry, to find a 'cure' for mesothelioma, the asbestos-related cancer. Dalton lamented the fact that Selikoff had now become indirectly employed by the very industry he had done so much to expose, saying: 'There is no suggestion that these doctors and scientists have deliberately sold themselves to the highest bidder, just that they are being used' (Dalton 1979: 95).

In August 1978, a working-class theatre company, Theatre Mobile, staged a play about the Hebden Bridge Massacre, which relied on a confidential internal memo 'Background notes on the anti-asbestos lobby', which had been sent to them by mistake. The theatre group were subsequently sacked by their sponsors and Cape Industries, owners of the asbestos works at Hebden Bridge, sued them for the return of the document.

According to *The Guardian* newspaper, as early as 1969, Cape's group medical advisor recognised that mesothelioma could be caused by 'short and possibly small' exposure to asbestos dust and the Asbestos Research Council (ARC), of which Cape was a founding member, concluded that the 'elimination of the dust hazard is therefore the only answer'. Yet in 1976 the Asbestos Information Committee, also founded by Cape, claimed: 'The normal use of asbestos products should not be a cause for anxiety.' This evidence of how much the industry knew, and how much they lied, emerged in 2022 as a result of court cases brought by relatives of people who had died of asbestos-related disease (Siddique 2022).

In 1979, after the publication of Dalton's book, his publishers were also sued by representatives of the asbestos industry and forced to remove a number of pages. The industry systematically used its funding power to control the output of scientific data, which helped it to frame the discussion about asbestos 'facts'. It deliberately misrepresented those facts to the public, and it bullied and sued critics while also seeking to co-opt critical voices it could not silence. A further documentary 'Alice – A Fight for Life' screened in 1982 finally conveyed to the British public the extent of the asbestos crisis. It featured 47-year-old Alice Jefferson, who had worked in the mill at Hebden Bridge for just nine months some 30 years earlier. When it was filmed, Alice was dying of mesothelioma. Perhaps it was the personal nature of the story, but this documentary successfully conveyed the true extent of the horror of the asbestos industry to the British public. But what was the reaction of the industry? In 2016, *The Independent* newspaper published evidence, some 33 years after the fact, that in 1983, as a response to 'Alice – A Fight for

Life', Turner & Newall, a former asbestos company, had spied on journalists and had put together a comprehensive strategy to discredit the documentary. Their dirty tricks campaign included allegations that the journalists, campaigners and industrial injury solicitors were 'communists', and the company wrote a pro-asbestos parliamentary speech and questions for a parliamentary select committee for the Rochdale MP Cyril Smith, while also revealing the home addresses of those behind the film. Cyril Smith publicly stated in the House of Commons that Turner & Newall should sue Yorkshire Television, and he was outspoken in his assertions that there was 'not the slightest health risk' associated with asbestos (Kirby 2016). Asked to comment on these revelations, in 2016 the chief executive officer of Friends of the Earth, Craig Bennett, was quoted as saying: 'It is clear that as long as people have campaigned for a better world, corrupt sections of the elite have tried to undermine their activities and misrepresent their arguments' (Kirby 2016).

According to Professor Sir Tony Newman Taylor (2018) from Imperial College, University of London, Britain has the highest rates of mesothelioma in the world, and because it can take up to 30 years to emerge, a further 50,000 cases are expected before the middle of this century. These rates would have been substantially lower if the industry had not deliberately misled the public for decades, and if the regulators had acted sooner to eliminate the killer dust. These examples show the extent to which companies and their intermediaries will go to undermine campaigns, even when they are around such serious health concerns as in the asbestos and tobacco industry.

State action: the extent of infiltration and surveillance

Yet it's not just private companies that will behave in this way. State intervention into campaign groups and political parties is a longstanding tactic to undermine and to create division. We have a great insight provided by historical internal documents of a number of secret police forces. In the early 1920s in post-revolutionary Russia, Victor Serge, a revolutionary Marxist, novelist, historian and member of the Bolshevik Party, studied the archives of the Czarist secret police and from this he wrote a short pamphlet titled 'What everyone should know about state repression'.

In the 1980s, the former Stasi archive – the records of the East German Ministry for State Security – was opened up to researchers revealing just how much the Stasi spied on almost every aspect of the daily lives of East Germans. Similarly, in America the Federal Bureau of Investigation (FBI) ran a special counter-intelligence programme from 1956 to 1971 called COINTELPRO to neutralise political dissidents. The papers on the COINTELPRO initiative were also made public and show the extent to which the FBI singled out the Communist Party and the Socialist Workers Party, among others. The Black Panther Party was specifically targeted and bore the brunt of the most damaging tactics.

These state agents keep records on the circles people mix in, the conversations they are having and the plans they are making. Agent provocateurs are used to disrupt organisations, individuals are targeted and harassed, and personal rivalries are exacerbated. On a more mundane level, if you seek to organise for social change, the people with power may well send someone along to your meetings to hear the plans, they may also try to create a narrative that your proposals will hurt the very people you are trying to support, and they may attempt to disrupt in insidious and open ways. The scale and, at times, the success of some of these operations is staggering.

In the Troubles in Northern Ireland, there were two leading paramilitary organisations, the Irish Republican Army and the Ulster Defence Association. The British intelligence agencies had a group called the Force Intelligence Agency, and it ran an agent known as 'Stakeknife', who was actually the head of the IRA's Internal Security Unit, known as the 'nutting squad'. This unit was responsible for the torture and execution of suspected informers within the IRA's ranks. Stakeknife was believed to be involved in up to 40 murders in that role. It is widely assumed that among those murders, he framed and killed genuine republicans to maintain his cover. It is hard to overstate this level of subterfuge. The head of internal security who had the power of life and death over the organisation's members was working for the British state (Harding, Oliver and O'Neill 2003).

Meanwhile, the intelligence chief of the Ulster Defence Association, Brian Nelson, was also an agent of the British state. He had a card index on potential targets for loyalist assassinations and would hand out cards from this index to assassins. When loyalists began talking about executing Stakeknife, Nelson allegedly diverted attention from the British Intelligence asset by arranging the murder of another republican who had not been active in many years. Nelson was also implicated in the murder of Pat Finucane, a leading human rights lawyer in the north of Ireland, who was murdered in his home just three weeks after British MP Douglas Hogg told parliament that in the view of the intelligence services there were a number of lawyers in Northern Ireland 'unduly sympathetic to the IRA'. There is very little doubt that during the Troubles at least some of the sectarian murders and internal executions were at the behest of the British security services. In a similar vein, Victor Serge uncovered evidence that the leader of the Bolshevik Party in the pre-revolutionary Russian parliament, the Duma, was in fact a Czarist state agent.

In America in the late 1960s, after the assassination of both Malcolm X and Martin Luther King, the Black Panther Party for Self Defense emerged as a leading militant organisation. It grew out of a student group at Merrill College in Oakland, California, and according to reports, the third member to join was an infiltrator. Later, the CIA field officers were expected to subvert local chapters and at particular times use agents provocateurs to initiate bloody feuds. Sometimes these feuds were between Panther chapters and other Black nationalist organisations, or local gangs. In other cases, they were designed to initiate feuds between different elements of the Panther leadership.

We might expect the state faced with self-proclaimed revolutionary organisations, or paramilitary groups, to have a counter-insurgency strategy, even if we might have a variety of views on exactly which tactics are legitimate or not. But the very same strategies, to varying degrees of intensity, are used routinely on entirely peaceful, sometimes mainstream, organisations.

The Spycops Scandal

In 2010, a state secret slowly began to unravel. The UK Special Demonstration Squad was established by the Greater London Metropolitan Police Service in 1968 to infiltrate Vietnam War protesters, yet it wasn't disbanded after the war. While it used similar tactics – infiltration, disruption, provocation and the fanning of conflict – to those used against 'enemies of the state', it now used these tactics against perfectly legitimate pressure groups, such as the Anti-Apartheid Movement, the Anti-Nazi League and the Greenham Common Women's Peace Camp. Trade unions such as the Communication Workers Union, the Fire Brigades Union, the National Union of Teachers and the National Union of Students were all subjected to police infiltration. Campaigns demanding justice for people murdered in racist attacks, or who died after interactions with the police, appear to have been systematically infiltrated, including campaigns seeking justice for people such as Blair Peach, Brian Douglas, Cherry Groce, Harry Stanley, Jean Charles de Menezes, Ricky Reel, Roger Sylvester, Rolan Adams, Joy Gardner, Trevor Monerville and, most notoriously, the Stephen Lawrence campaign. Groups seeking accountability of the police, such as the Newham Monitoring Project and the Southall Monitoring Group, were also targeted. It is alleged that five democratically elected politicians were also spied upon by the undercover operations.

For over 40 years, the police operated a systematic spying operation, in which over 140 spycops infiltrated more than 1,000 groups (Evans and Lewis 2023). There was no public scrutiny of these operations, and it is not clear who, if anyone, had any oversight of what was described by even one of its participants as a 'black operation'. In recent years, the story has emerged through a combination of confessions by former spycops, covers being blown through carelessness, the research of investigative journalists and the incredible research of spied-upon activists, some of them women tricked into intimate relationships with these spycops. An Undercover Policing Inquiry was announced by Theresa May, the UK Home Secretary, in 2015 and this is on-going in 2024. It may well reveal even darker secrets of this operation.

During deployments that typically lasted four years, undercover Metropolitan Police officers pretended to be committed activists, but behind the scenes they were relaying details of groups and the individuals within them to their superiors. In some cases, they were actually inciting criminal activity. At least 20 of the spycops deceived women into long-term sexual relationships, living with them as partners – in some cases despite having their own wives and children – and a number of them fathered children with the women that were under their surveillance. To date, 12 women have been awarded compensation for these abuses by the courts. It has been shown that in criminal prosecutions spycops concealed evidence that would have assisted the defence cases. Spycop Carlo Neri (real name Carlo Soracchi) was alleged to have unsuccessfully sought to incite members of the Socialist Party to firebomb a charity shop with alleged connections to a far-right organisation (Undercover Research Group 2023).

To date, campaigners have identified 50 examples of protesters being wrongly convicted or prosecuted as a result of evidence relating to the activities of the spycops being concealed (Undercover Research Group 2023). In February 2023, the counsel to the inquiry set up by the government into undercover policing produced a closing statement to tranche one of the inquiry, which concluded:

> Reporting on groups sought to build up as full a picture as possible of a given group's activities. Everything from a group's constitution, policies, literature, membership details, financial affairs, leadership, factions, inter-personal dynamics, aims, conferences, social events, meetings, demonstrations and other political activities were reported upon. Very long and detailed reports on the proceedings at national conferences were common and often drew praise.
>
> We do not suggest that detailed, professional, reporting on a group or an individual by an undercover police office is in principle wrong. But the threat posed by the group or individual must be sufficiently serious to justify such reporting on them. It is one thing to infiltrate an organised crime gang and report

relevant intelligence. It is quite another to infiltrate a law-abiding political party or protest group which is neither a threat to public order nor threatens the safety or wellbeing of the State. (Undercover Policing Inquiry: Counsel to the Inquiry's Closing Statement for Tranche One)

In response, the Blacklist Support Group issued a statement:

A few years ago, we were slated as conspiracy theorists for suggesting that undercover police infiltrated trade unions and blacklisted activists. This week, the spycops public inquiry has acknowledged that it did happen.

Counsel to the Inquiry's closing statement admits that the SDS [Special Demonstration Squad] political policing was unjustified and that undercover police officers joined trade unions to spy on internal union meetings. ... Information about what trade unionists said at union meetings was gathered by undercover police officers claiming to be union members. This intelligence was sent back to Special Branch. This is spying on trade union activities: plain and simple.

Counsel to the Inquiry also accepts that intelligence was shared with employers to blacklist British citizens because of their perfectly lawful political and trade union activities. This is state-sponsored blacklisting: plain and simple. (Institute of Employment Rights 2023)

Infiltration of anti-apartheid protesters: Stop the Seventy Tour campaign

This state-sponsored spying was also evident in the anti-apartheid movement in the 1970s – and again details of this have been revealed recently in the Undercover Policing Inquiry. Peter Hain, now Lord Peter Hain, was born in Nairobi, Kenya, to White South African parents who were staunch opponents of the South African apartheid regime. Because of their opposition to apartheid and, in particular, their leafleting for the release of

Nelson Mandela, they were banned, imprisoned and prevented from working. They emigrated to the UK when Peter was 16. He became a leading figure in the anti-apartheid movement in the UK and, in particular, in the Stop the Seventy Tour campaign. The campaign forced the cancellation of the all-White Springbok cricket series in June 1970. At the time, apartheid South Africa only fielded White teams in international competitions such as rugby and cricket. It is worth taking some time over his reflections on the role of the undercover policing he was the subject of, because not only was he a political activist but he went on to become a senior politician holding important cabinet positions and was instrumental in the negotiations that brought 'the Troubles' to an end in Northern Ireland. In his statement to the Undercover Policing Inquiry, he says:

> I was a political activist involved in non-violent activities and organising against some of the most abhorrent and appalling manifestations of racism and prejudice that existed during the 20th century, in particular the apartheid regime in South Africa. I believe history has vindicated the position that many of us took in protesting against apartheid. (Hain 2020)

Describing the evidence of undercover policing disclosed to him, he said that it's hard not to be struck by the sense that such activity was out of control. Worse, it shows the UK police had entirely the wrong focus. They were preoccupied with gathering information on peaceful non-violent activists through inappropriate covert means, while sharing information with and showing far less concern about the activities of those who supported racist and far-right ideologies. He says he is not a victim, in the way so many others were, including the women tricked into intimate sexual relationships, or the grieving families spied upon, but:

> ... although I am not a victim I am appalled at the activities revealed in these documents. The potential threat such activity had to the struggle against racism and apartheid and the lives of those committed to

peaceful democratic change is almost impossible to define, it is a chilling reminder of how hard those struggles had to be fought with officers of our own state treating us with suspicion and without proper respect for our rights, our privacy and our lives.

The Stop the Seventy Tour campaign achieved remarkable success, it grew from a handful of people meeting in Peter Hain's home to a network of 100,000 people prepared to be involved in non-violent direct action. As a result, the racist tour was cancelled. In the light of our previous discussions on organisational structure, it is worth noting that the Stop the Seventy Tour campaign was:

> ... a very loose movement where spontaneity, independence and local autonomy were the driving principles. It consisted of local groups often focused upon the 25 matches in the Springbok rugby tour of October 1969 to January 1970 and then around the dozen matches planned for the 1970 cricket tour, e.g. in local student unions, local anti-apartheid groups, YL groups, socialist groups, United Nations Groups, church groups, trade union groups, anti-racist groups etc.

Despite this loose structure it had a very clear DNA. The campaign was 'committed to non-violent direct action (NVDA) – in the tradition of the Suffragettes and Gandhi's struggle for India's independence – to oppose apartheid and stop all-white sports tours'. As Stop the Seventy Tour (STST) campaign leader Hain said, he was always:

> completely open about that. I said this in media interviews and speeches, and this was repeated by other STST activists at public meetings. Anyone engaged in the campaign understood this. ... There was no command and control structure, disciplinary processes, rules etc and it was not even a membership organisation.

Commenting on disclosure obtained in the inquiry, Hain notes that an undercover officer 'Mike Ferguson', concerned to protect his cover, actively deflected suspicion away from himself and onto an innocent and genuine campaigner. It's interesting, reading Peter Hain's statement, just how much of the 'intelligence' seems to have been made up by the undercover officers to impress their superiors, and how little of it was of any real value: 'There is a considerable degree of sheer fabrication and exaggerated self-importance in Mike Ferguson's claims'. One example is when one undercover officer reports that he was told of a planned non-violent direct action event over the phone by Peter's mother. The suggestion that she, a previously active opponent of apartheid in South Africa, would have shared this information informally with a stranger over what she assumed was a bugged phone is simply not credible. It seems that infiltrators are inherently unreliable, which is why organisations are often infiltrated by multiple individuals who are unknown to each other, so that their handlers can cross-check their versions of events.

Peter Hain also comments on the infiltration of Anti-Apartheid Movement (AAM) meetings:

> I am struck by the pointlessness of UCOs [undercover officers] attending, reporting on, and keeping reports of these meetings. The AAM was a mainstream democratic organisation, rather than one focussed on protesting. It had bishops as its presidents – such as the Right Reverend Ambrose Reeves and the Right Reverend Trevor Huddleston.

The organisational base from which Peter Hain operated at the time was the Young Liberals. He was asked about reports of a group called 'Croydon Commitment', or CC. He described them as 'a self-styled militant faction within the Yls' and that he 'always thought that CC were trying to disrupt the Yls. They seemed to recommend more and more outlandish things. This raised my suspicions.' This again feels like a familiar tactic, a successful non-violent direct-action campaign that attracts growing support is suddenly faced with a more 'militant' but ineffective grouping seeking to draw away at least some of its base.

The media, the police and corruption: the phone-hacking scandal

It isn't just the security services that are involved in the undermining of legitimate campaigning organisations, there is also evidence of the involvement of corrupt police officers. The activities of the so-called 'fourth estate', the media, have long played a role by framing issues in ways that distort and marginalise campaigners. In 1987 a private detective was murdered in a South London pub car park. Daniel Morgan had reportedly been working on exposing police corruption and the inquest into his death was told that Morgan's business partner, Jonathan Rees, had said that Daniel would be killed in a murder arranged by officers at Catford Police Station (Dodd and Laville 2011). The officer in charge of the case had been working unofficially for Rees and would subsequently leave the police to become his new business partner. Meanwhile, a detective, John Davidson, reportedly attached to the original investigation, was later accused of corruption in the sabotaged investigation into the Stephen Lawrence murder. While no one has been convicted in the Morgan killing, as long ago as 2006, during a third investigation, the officer leading the investigation, DS David Cook, said the identity of the murderers was 'one of the worst-kept secrets in south-east London'. Despite this, in 1993 Jonathan Rees, Morgan's former partner, began working for Rupert Murdoch's *News of the World* and other newspapers as a source of stories obtained through a network of corrupt police officers. In 2000 Rees was convicted, along with a corrupt police officer, after planning to plant cocaine on a woman in order to discredit her during a custody battle with her ex-partner. Rees was sentenced to seven years' imprisonment, but upon his release in 2005, he was back on the payroll of the *News of the World*, recruited by its editor, Andy Coulson, who within two years was himself recruited as the communications director for soon-to-be prime minister David Cameron, and upon the Conservative Party victory in the 2010 general election became the government's director of communications.

In 2008 Rees, along with others, was charged with the murder of Daniel Morgan, but the case collapsed in 2011 after lengthy legal arguments about the admissibility of evidence. *The Guardian* sums up Rees's modus operandi:

> His numerous targets included members of the royal family whose bank accounts he penetrated; political figures including Peter Mandelson and Alastair Campbell; rock stars such as Eric Clapton, Mick Jagger and George Michael; the Olympic athlete Linford Christie and former England footballer Gary Lineker; TV presenters Richard Madeley and Judy Finnigan; and people associated with tabloid story topics, including the daughter of the former miners' leader Arthur Scargill and the family of the Yorkshire Ripper, Peter Sutcliffe. (Davies and Dodd 2011)

Jonathan Rees paid a network of corrupt police officers who sold him confidential records. He boasted of other corrupt contacts in banks and government organisations; hired specialists to 'blag' confidential data from targets' current accounts, phone records and car registration; allegedly used 'Trojan horse' emails to extract information from computers; and – according to two sources – commissioned burglaries to obtain material for journalists (Davies and Dodd 2011). In 2021, an independent review described the Metropolitan Police as 'institutionally corrupt' and the Police Commissioner, Cressida Dick, was personally criticised in the report of the Daniel Morgan Independent Panel:

> The Metropolitan Police's lack of candour manifested itself in the hurdles placed in the path of the Panel, such as AC Cressida Dick's initial refusal to recognise the necessity for the Panel to have access to HOLMES (the data system which provides safeguards for the integrity of investigations and also enables independent scrutiny to identify failures), as well as limiting access to the most sensitive information. (National Archives 2021)

Following the publication of this report, both the Conservative Home Secretary and the Labour Mayor of London expressed full support for Police Commissioner Cressida Dick.

Incitement to violence: the discrediting of the animal rights movement

The animal rights movement in the early 1980s was seeing its campaigns of non-violent direct action, and particularly those focussing on animal experimentation, beginning to have a significant impact on public opinion. The images of monkeys or beagles in research laboratories didn't sit right with the wider public, and pictures of people 'raiding' laboratories to rescue these animals – for example, the high-profile rescue in 1975 of beagle dogs forced by ICI (Imperial Chemical Industries) to inhale cigarette smoke – was leading to a wave of support for non-violent direct action. In 1982, a number of headline-grabbing 'raids' on animal experimentation establishments – and in particular a mass trespass at Porton Down, the Ministry of Defence establishment where animals were subjected to experiments designed to increase our efficiently in killing humans – saw non-violent direct action increasingly becoming the norm among supporters of animal rights. A movement of potentially self-sacrificing militants were undertaking 'actions' designed to both free individual animals and publicise the wider plight.

However, just as the movement experienced 'take off', unknown people were suddenly poisoning Mars Bars, sending letter bombs and issuing bloodcurdling threats. None of this appeared to have originated from within the animal rights movement, and it's only possible to speculate on the extent to which it was undertaken by agent provocateurs. However, what is now undisputed is the actions of the 'Special Demonstration Squad' – the rogue police unit that infiltrated groups such as London Greenpeace and allegedly organised the fire-bombing of a number of Debenhams stores in 1987.

London Greenpeace was a small, anarchist-inspired group with no organisational links to the more famous Greenpeace International. Established in the 1970s, it was pretty much moribund until a sudden surge in participants in the early 1980s. These included two spycops, Bob Lambert and John Dines. In 1986, the group produced what was to become a notorious leaflet: 'What's Wrong with McDonald's: Everything They Don't Want You to Know'. It was later revealed that the leaflet had, in part, been written by Bob Lambert, the police informer. John Dines had, in the meantime, manipulated himself into an intimate relationship with London Greenpeace member Helen Steel, and become the treasurer of London Greenpeace.

It wasn't long after the production of the McDonald's leaflet, that seven private sector infiltrators from two firms hired by McDonald's joined the group and, according to some of those who were there, it later transpired that often there were more infiltrators than there were legitimate group members in meetings. As a result of information gathered, McDonald's began issuing injunctions against London Greenpeace activists due to the impact of the McDonald's leaflet. Thanks to the heroic resistance of Helen Steel and Dave Morris, two of the very few genuine activists within the group, who stood up to McDonald's, and to the pro bono work of a then largely unknown lawyer (at least outside of the legal profession), Keir Starmer, the subsequent legal case that lasted ten years, resulted in a pyrrhic victory for McDonald's. The judge found that the leaflet had contained some libels, but that certain of its allegations with regard to the accusations of misleading advertisements, unnecessary cruelty to animals and paying low wages were not libellous. Steel and Morris appealed to the European Court of Human Rights which found:

> in a democratic society even small and informal campaign groups, such as London Greenpeace, must be able to carry on their activities effectively and that there exists a strong public interest in enabling such groups and individuals outside the mainstream to contribute to the public debate by disseminating information and ideas on matters of general public interest such as health and the environment. (*Case of Steel and Morris v. The United Kingdom (Application No. 68416/01)*, para 89)

The European Court ordered the UK government to pay compensation to Steel and Morris, who also sued the Metropolitan Police for sharing information they had gathered with McDonald's private investigators, which was settled out of court. The 'McLibel story' shows two things: first, the horrendous extent to which business and the state will silence perfectly legitimate criticism of business interests, and second, how ineffective this can be when faced with determined resistance. There can be no doubt whatsoever, that if they had their time again, McDonald's would not have sued this tiny group of peaceful activists.

There is another twist to this story. The Animal Liberation Front (ALF) was an organisation that, while nominally committed to non-violence, had no compunction about damage to property. In 1987, the ALF's press officer, Ronnie Lee, was sentenced to ten years in prison, creating a vacuum in the organisation. At precisely this time, spycop Bob Lambert is alleged to have moved his focus to infiltrating the ALF. In July 1987, three incendiary devices were planted in Debenhams stores designed to cause fire damage, or at the very least massive water damage to stock, nominally in protest at the department store selling furs. The incendiary devices caused estimated damage costs of £9 million. Two former London Greenpeace activists, Geoff Sheppard and Andrew Clarke, were quickly arrested for the attacks, and sentenced to long prison sentences. After Bob Lambert was exposed as a state agent, both Sheppard and Clarke identified him as the third member of the ALF cell, and claimed he had, in fact, instigated the campaign and planted the incendiary device in the Luton store. In 2012, Caroline Lucas MP used parliamentary privilege to name Bob Lambert and to call for an inquiry into his involvement in the attack.

It is important to note that in 1982, when the animal rights movement hit 'take off', there were no activists advocating for violence. The direct action that did take place, although militant, and at times aimed at destroying property – particularly cages, or instruments used to experiment on animals – was inspired by narratives of peace and justice. While many hunt sabs were prepared to use force in self-defence if attacked, they were not engaged in provoking fights with the hunt or its supporters. Yet very quickly, once the movement was infiltrated, anonymous new groups sprang up promoting extreme violence, even terrorism, as a tactic. Some people within the movement were influenced by this new, more violent 'militancy', and made the mistake of undertaking the dirty work that the spycops urged them to do.

In the 1980s, this 'turn to violence' saw the so-called Animal Rights Militia send letter bombs through the post, food bars laced with poison, and car bombs planted under the vehicles of alleged opponents. In the absence of any convictions at the time, how many of these actions were initiated by agent provocateurs can only be guessed. John Curtin, himself a lifelong animal rights militant, convicted for (among other things) action in the Hunt Retribution Squad, was interviewed in 2022 on a sympathetic podcast where he described his concerns (Curtin 2022). He recounted how some activists had resorted to what he described as 'old-style mafia tactics' which, despite acknowledging their effectiveness, he felt was going too far: 'Are we meant to adopt mafia-style tactics then, which are ugly, sinister and violent?'. It was a long way from the idealism that had inspired so many in the early evolution of the movement. The question is: would anyone in the animal rights movement have taken that journey to violent extremes without the actions of provocateurs sent into the movement?

The state's frustration of legitimate campaigning

What these examples show is that if we want to organise for social justice, we should expect that there will be attempts to disrupt, spy upon, misrepresent and disorganise us. The state, far from guaranteeing our freedoms, will at times conspire to frustrate them. The connections between the state, business, organised criminals and the so-called 'free' press are many and varied, but can create the circumstances in which criminal acts are perpetrated to frustrate legitimate campaigning. Whether we are seeking to reduce the incidence of workplace injuries, to achieve justice for the families of murder victims like Stephen Lawrence or Daniel Morgan, whether it be wider issues of peace and nuclear disarmament, or opposition to the apartheid regime of South Africa, history shows us that a combination of the state, the 'free press' and business will, at times, go way beyond anything that should be considered acceptable in a democracy, and will seek to sabotage and disorganise.

While this, of course, should be of some concern to us, it should not deter us. Many of the campaigns, including those to end the Vietnam War, and apartheid in South Africa, have been phenomenally successful. But if we want to maximise our effectiveness, then part of our planning should include considering the likely actions targeted at us, and how we can minimise their impacts.

Scale

We hope it is clear from the examples we have discussed that every campaign needs to think about the steps that will be taken to misrepresent, undermine and disorganise it. But, of course, not every campaign will be faced with the extent of the dirty tricks we have outlined. If, for example, you are campaigning for some repairs to be done on the estate where you live, or to have extra lighting put in to deter antisocial behaviour, it is unlikely (but not impossible) that you will have Special Branch lining up to infiltrate your tenants' association. Far more likely is that the landlord will assert that the costs of these repairs will mean that the rent will need to go up, or that they will suggest the need for repairs has been exaggerated.

In the London borough of Hackney, when Sunstone, a women's gym, closed and the women tried to prevent the sale of the building by having it declared an 'asset of community value', accusations were made by a senior local politician that the women were antisemitic, but the gym and its future was as important to the Jewish women who used it as any others, and the allegation fell flat. During a campaign against a supermarket development, a previously unheard-of Twitter account posted constantly about how the majority of people in the area wanted the new store, and how the campaign was simply the loudmouth moanings of a bunch of 'nimbys'; and a candidate for the local council made it his mission to demonise the campaign at every opportunity. When seeking to ensure that the name C.L.R. James was retained on the local library, there were dark mutterings about 'left-wing agitators who are always looking backwards preventing the borough from moving forward'.

As we said in the beginning, whatever scale you are acting at, those who oppose the change you are seeking to create will use their resources, legitimately or illegitimately, to counter you. It's part of the role of an organiser to be aware of this and mindful about how to limit the ability to disrupt and undermine our campaigns.

Devising a risk register for your campaign

Consider a campaign that you are part of (this exercise works best as a group exercise, but can also be done individually).

Ask yourself who opposes the campaign. This might be because they object to the outcome you are seeking, or it could be because, even though they aspire to the same objective, they feel that this issue belongs to 'them' and they don't want you organising around it.

Write a list of these people, institutions and organisations.

Next write a list of the key things your campaign must do before it can win. For example, it might need to raise some money, it might need to win majority support among a particular group, it might need to win at least nominal support from a range of groups across your community, and it might need some people to move from opposing you to becoming neutral.

For each of the above elements, ask yourself: what could the opponents do to undermine us?

This might be in terms of narrative, telling a story about you or your issue in a way that makes people less sympathetic; in terms of changing rules, for example an employer who wanted to undermine the influence of an emerging trade union might make a rule that says use of the company's email system for anything other than company business is a disciplinary offence (thereby preventing people sharing union information via email); it could be in terms of physically disrupting your meetings; or it might involve removing a person with power (for example a local councillor) who is sympathetic to your cause.

For each of these disruptions, score them, on a scale of one to five: firstly, for how likely they are to materialise; and secondly, for how damaging they would be. A score of one means that something is unlikely to happen or is not going to have much impact, while something scored five is very likely to happen or very likely to have a significant impact.

Finally, select those disruptions that are likely to happen and likely to have a significant impact (anything that scores three or above in both columns) and consider what you can do to minimise the impact if they materialise.

11

Rethinking and remaking organisations

The way we organise is crucial. Not only does the choice of organisational structure impact on our ability to marshal and channel the resources we have, but it can also redefine who 'we' are. It is often said that people who want to see a better world should try to live the values that are inherent in their vision. The way we organise, the relationships we build and the care we show to each other are all choices that have a material impact on the outcomes of our campaigns. Too many purportedly progressive groups value their supporters solely on the basis of how much activity can be extracted from them, and as a consequence supporters end up burnt out, disillusioned and demoralised. This is not the way to build a bright, inclusive and fairer future!

This chapter will explore the insights of centralised and decentralised organisational forms through the analogy of 'the spider and the starfish'. This approach to thinking about the way organisations operate adopts an interesting perspective on control and power within organisations (Brafman and Beckstrom 2006). Essentially, the spider represents traditional hierarchical structures, while the starfish represents decentralised, self-organising groups. In this chapter we will reflect on the puzzling question of how it is that some organisations with the least resources are able to do the most effective work. Brafman and Beckstrom, the authors of *The Starfish and the Spider: The Unstoppable Power of Leaderless Organizations*, consider the benefits and drawbacks of leaderless organisations and compare this with the more hierarchical structures of more traditional centralised organisations. What we want to do in this chapter is to draw upon our direct experience of both working for and being members of social movement groups to explore how we avoid the so-called 'iron law of oligarchy' that suggests that all organisations, sooner or later, become agents of their own bureaucracies rather than agents of change. This will be contrasted with a prescient essay, 'The Tyranny of Structurelessness' (Freeman 1971), on power relations within feminist collectives. The essay explores how even in organisations that appear 'flat', there are always hidden power dynamics at work.

The chapter will delve into some of the insights gleaned from social movement theory, and in particular the study of the African American freedom movement, to explore how organisations stimulate movements and, conversely, how they can stifle them. Specific examples used will be the Hunt Saboteurs Association, which is very much a starfish-type organisation where decision making is more consensus-based or decentralised, contrasted with trade unions, which are too often 'spider'-like, or overly bureaucratic organisations.

If we want to change the world, then one question soon arises: How can we best organise our forces to achieve this? Or, put another way, what is the best structure to harness and direct the energy for change? One common approach is to establish a national coordinating organisation and recruit supporters through a membership scheme. But how do we turn support into power? Let's go back to the old adage about the sources of power: organised people or organised money. We generally don't have the money to outspend our opponents, and their power is almost always contingent on their access to resources. Without wishing to be too circular, our adversaries have power because they have access to resources, and they maintain access to those resources because they have power.

To start with, we must distinguish between supporters, followers and changemakers. Supporters are people who want to see the goal you have set achieved but they may, or may not, actually contribute to achieving those goals. Think of the football fan that only watches their team on the television: they cheer them on, but they don't contribute materially to the development of the team's achievements. However, a fan who buys a season ticket might be compared to someone who joins an organisation, becoming a member and paying an annual membership fee to help sustain the organisation's efforts. Yet there are also other ways that a supporter could help: by creating a fanzine, or helping to run a children's league team, and so on.

In the field of social change, supporters can also be either followers or changemakers – or they might be a bit of both. Followers are – almost by definition – not organised, and their potential is not developed. An example of this on a grand scale is when Jeremy Corbyn MP stood for election as leader of the Labour Party in the UK in 2015. There was a significant increase in Labour Party membership following his election, and a huge mailing list of followers was created through the Corbyn support group Momentum. The sheer numbers meant that there was potential power here, but the majority were a largely passive group of followers who might attend a rally or vote for a particular set of candidates in internal party elections but who did, and were asked to do, little more. While Momentum aspired to create a huge movement for social change, it largely failed to equip its followers with the skills, experience, analysis or *permission* for them to do so. And as often happens when this groundwork isn't done, support for a cause dwindles as the project hits successive challenges.

Initially, when Momentum was formed, local groups were set up, but there was little horizontal networking, and even less decentralised setting of objectives. It's true that during key parliamentary elections, Momentum was effective at delivering busloads of canvassers to marginal constituencies yet, as we have seen in earlier chapters, mobilising is not the same as organising and it's difficult to sustain mobilisations without building the base of your movement – otherwise you are continually relying on the already committed, who eventually become less active over time. We talked about theory of change in Chapter 2, where we asserted that what social movement organisations need is a clear and compelling strategy, with a credible way forward, that can convince supporters that they can win. This appeared to be missing in Momentum. Instead of systematic engagement with supporters, month in, month out, over issues that a community cared about, there was a flawed theory of change that implied that the way to change the way people voted was through relatively shallow levels of engagement. It was as if it was assumed that the electorate would share the same perception that the majority of Momentum members held of Corbyn as a secular messiah. While Momentum bussed in people to knock on doors during election campaigns and some local groups did community organising, its focus was primarily inward-looking with a focus on the next internal Labour Party election cycle, and tragically, supporters weren't developed into community builders.

An alternative theory of change could be based on a distributive organising approach. Distributed organising can be distinguished from traditional political organising in that it aims to activate a network of campaigners who may be spread across different interest/cultural groups and/or geographical boundaries. In this approach to organising, it draws upon the initiatives and energies of grassroots campaigners to lead the people around them with a degree of autonomy. It's a more horizontal form of organising compared to much organising in trade unions, which tend to adopt a more 'command and control' form of leadership. Instead, distributed organising often relies on a central coordination group to launch the network and to drive it towards common goals via an agreed strategy. An advantage of distributed organising is that it can help a movement or campaign scale rapidly and channel huge amounts of collective power. Adopting this would likely have had two effects in Momentum. One would be that people in organised communities may not have seen Corbyn as a candidate in the mode of 'saviour' but instead as a spokesperson – or, to use the language of the starfish model, a 'champion' – and secondly, people would have been inoculated against the avalanche of character assassination against him in the run-up to the 2019 election. Isolated individulas are more susceptible to being fooled by dominant narratives – as we discussed in Chapter 8 – but when people are organised, they are able to check the 'dominant' narrative against their own and other people's experience.

Before we dive too deeply into a discussion about the best structures for social movement organisations, perhaps we should think a little about what outcomes these structures are expected to deliver. There's a great deal written about how change happens and how it can be hastened. A report by the Sheila McKechnie Foundation (2018) 'Social Power: How Civil Society Can "Play Big" and Truly Create Change' is one example. This report looks at the activities that civil society groups initiate in an attempt to influence change. It visualises this through a mapping process consisting of four quadrants:

- community, including community organising, community development, and so on;
- public sphere, including protests, media stunts and online activism;
- service provision, including volunteering and service delivery; and
- institutional power, including advocacy, lobbying and policy recommendations.

Sometimes movements will rely on one organisation to try to work in all of these very different segments, but it may be that different structures are better suited to different tasks. For example, if you want to produce policy recommendations you might want a highly centralised, research-driven organisation with professionally qualified staff, but if you want to create pressure for change, you might want a diffuse volunteer-led organisation that is steered by the collective learning of trial and error across the base. If, as the Foundation's report suggests, you need policy recommendations, evidence-based reports *and* pressure for change, then you might want to have different organisations within the ecology of the movement to focus on different elements of the overall task.

Another influential recent report on changemaking is 'Making Change: What Works?' (Laybourn-Langton et al, 2021), in a collaboration between the Institute for Public Policy Research (IPPR) and the Runnymede Trust. This research found that a common belief was that the way change can be achieved is by evidencing the need for change. In this view of the world, people with power (or the public) simply lack evidence of the problem and how to solve it. This is what we call the 'information deficit' approach.

This approach, they say, is:

> fundamentally flawed. Instead, successful movements seek to close what we call the 'salience deficit', where the public or power-holders do not think the issue is

important or see it through a different frame, and the 'power deficit', where the people wanting change are not in positions of power or have limited influence on those who are.

The report concludes, having studied the LGBTQ+, race equality and environmental justice movements, that movements work best when they comprise: 'a wide range of groups undertaking different activities: an "ecosystem of influence". If the movement is sufficiently well developed, this ecosystem will, together, cover the bases needed to close information, salience, and power deficits, and to effectively shift leverage points.'

Effective ecosystems of influence they say, have three main characteristics.

1. Breadth (diversity): The ecosystem has a broad range of different types of groups and activities, ranging from research through campaigning to frontline services.
2. Depth (capability): The ecosystem's groups have sufficient resources and ability to identify and move leverage points, including money, talent and knowledge.
3. Inter-connection (community): The ecosystem is well connected, whether tangible (for example, formal convening organisations) or intangible (for example, trust and shared language).

We are not suggesting that either of these reports provides a blueprint for social movement architecture, but what they do is to raise important questions about what organisations within movements are hoping to achieve, and if those organisations are fit for purpose. This question of the fit between structure and purpose is one that is all too familiar to trade unionists. One exercise that we've delivered in trade union education is to ask a group of trade unionists to imagine they had permission to completely overhaul and reinvent their trade union's structures, and democratic processes, to make them relevant to the tasks they are designed to address. This might seem a relatively easy task – to have the freedom to start from scratch – but participants have found it surprisingly difficult to re-imagine alternative structures.

We are sometimes strongly wedded to structures that have largely been inherited from previous generations, or the result of unholy compromises between power brokers in union merger talks, but we can and must think carefully about which structures are the most appropriate to help us achieve our aims. Next, let's think a little more deeply about the stages a movement goes through and the tasks that are required at different stages.

The movement action plan

Bill Moyer, a US social movement activist in the 1970s, developed a theory known as the 'Movement Action Plan' that suggests movements move through eight distinct stages. There are, of course, competing theories of how movements evolve and the stages they develop through, as well as a number of critiques of Moyer's approach. We use it here, not because it is necessarily the best approach, but merely because it is a great starting point for a discussion about how, at different points in a movement's evolution, the internal and external environments change and the opportunities, and consequently the tasks necessary, to move forward also change. As a movement progresses towards success, there will be a need for different outputs, and different relationships, suggesting perhaps that groups need to be flexible – almost chameleon-like – constantly adapting to the needs of the movement, or perhaps there just need to be a number of organisations, whereby individual groups are able to move in and out of prominence depending on the specific needs of the overall movement at any particular time. What is clear and acknowledged by Moyer, even if the articulation of his theory suggests otherwise, is that movements are not linear: there are times of advance and times of setback. With that caveat, let's dive into Moyer's Movement Action Plan.

Stage one: critical social problem exists (normal times)

At this stage the issue exists, but opposition to it is limited and weak. There are three typical responses to this early stage of a campaign. Firstly, there are the professional lobbying groups – often with a hierarchical structure and little direct accountability to the group they are advocating on behalf of. Secondly, there are 'principled dissent groups': these are people determined to do what is right, even though they have little support and even less evidence of progress. They are a moral compass, but are, for the moment, seemingly largely irrelevant. Thirdly, there are the grassroots groups who at this stage are, more than anything, providing a level of support to the 'victims' of this injustice (we choose the word deliberately, despite its negative context, because at this stage it is often an accurate description). At stage one of the Movement Action Plan the key objectives of the 'movement' are to show that there's a serious problem, and to start to network and maintain active opposition – despite the lack of widespread support – and of course to prepare for the future stages.

It takes a certain level of resolve to be active at this stage of a campaign because the social justice campaign group doesn't have the power to force change, and quite likely the powerholders opposing you are relatively unconcerned by the emerging opposition to their plans. Meanwhile, the public are largely disinterested in the issue. However, society isn't static, and despite the apparent impregnability of the powerholders and their commitment to the status quo, the contradictions between what is right and what is happening will ripen, providing the opportunity to move to stage two.

Stage two: showing how official institutions are failing

For a genuinely transformative movement to arise, there needs to be widespread public perception that current practices violate widely held beliefs and views of what is 'right'. It is worth mentioning one of Saul Alinsky's 'rules for radicals' here: 'make the enemy live up to its own book of rules', because it is often government or institutional malpractice in defending the status quo that drives public perception towards opposition. People who are neutral can very soon become sympathetic to social justice causes if they believe that those in power are being underhand or deceitful. In this stage of Moyer's Movement Action Plan, a social justice movement needs to expose the problem and the unwillingness of those in power to respond to the concerns. In some senses, the task at hand is to exhaust the possibilities of achieving change through official channels, so as to demonstrate that only mass action will create the change. The grassroots organisation needs to deepen and broaden its appeal within its communities; it needs to move from advocating on behalf of victims to organising 'communities of resistance'. This is the stage where a counter-narrative is growing and becoming normalised, expressing clearly that there is something wrong and something should be done about it, but it's not yet effecting any change.

Stage three: ripening conditions

It's at this stage of the Movement Action Plan that history intervenes. While most of the time the status quo seems stable, unchanging and unchangeable, in reality social conditions are the result of complex social forces and these forces are very rarely under the complete control of powerholders. Sometimes the status quo, or rather the power balance that maintains the status quo, is disrupted by innovation – a classic example would be the invention of the spinning jenny and the steam engine that drove the industrial revolution and destroyed the centuries-old hold on power of the landed aristocracy. Sometimes, it is quarrels among the elite that unsettle the existing state of affairs: for example, the American Civil War brought slavery to an end because there were contrasting interests amongst the divided powerholders in the pre-Civil War consensus. Sometimes it can just be because of rising expectations – the growth in student numbers in the 1960s created student-led movements demanding racial justice, an end to war, and equal rights for women – precisely because the education of these students created within them a sense of power, and a feeling of moral obligation, to put their knowledge to some use for the communities from which they came.

In stage three some newly activated people mistakenly see no value in more established organisations, and those more established, advocacy and lobbying-based organisations tend to see little value in the protest culture of newly established groups. Older groups are to some extent still stuck in the past, while their activity is still bringing new people towards the movement. The newly activated are already impatient with the slow pace of change. New groups emerge, largely independently, and old networks are repurposed to provide support for the emerging movement, which remains in its embryonic state. For those who recognise it, the most important task now is to prepare for the acceleration of interest that will hopefully come. The base of the movement must develop a deeper understanding of the problem and the power structures that maintain it, and an ability to analyse and consider tactics.

But more than anything there is the need to celebrate the emerging potential for change, even if it is delivering few results yet. The necessary, although at times hard to justify, optimism of this period is perhaps best captured by this quote from Arundhati Roy:

> Our strategy should be not only to confront empire, but to lay siege to it. To deprive it of oxygen. To shame it. To mock it. With our art, our music, our literature, our stubbornness, our joy, our brilliance, our sheer relentlessness – and our ability to tell our own stories. Stories that are different from the ones we're being brainwashed to believe. The corporate revolution will collapse if we refuse to buy what they are selling – their ideas, their version of history, their wars, their weapons, their notion of inevitability. Remember this: We be many and they be few. They need us more than we need them. Another world is not only possible, she is on her way. On a quiet day, I can hear her breathing. (Roy 2003)

This is a militant optimism, a determination that we will not continue to live the way we have lived, we will not be silent, and more than anything: we will win. This is not the optimism of the fool, who believes against all evidence to the contrary, but the optimism of the reflective activist who sees the tectonic plates of our society shifting, and knows that opportunities will arise which, if seized and used strategically, will deliver the desired goals.

Stage four: social movement take-off

Movements do not grow incrementally; indeed, they tend to surprise even the most ardent of their activists when they reach their take-off phase. It's often as if people have been slowly becoming aware of the issue, and then, something provokes a national discussion of it. This could be a particularly horrible example of the problem, or it could be that the movement has choreographed a protest that reaches beyond its usual base. Today, these events are often referred to as 'moments of the whirlwind', when the usual rules of social movements are suspended, and everything seems possible. It is widely accepted that it's impossible to confidently predict which spark may lead to a whirlwind moment.

The killing of George Floyd clearly was one such moment, but the equally brutal deaths of Eric Garner, Michael Brown, Tamir Rice, Walter Scott, Alton Sterling, Philando Castile, Stephon Clark and Breonna Taylor, while marked by protests, didn't lead to the massive international mobilisations that accompanied the murder of George Floyd. Perhaps it was the incessant drip, drip, drip of yet another Black person murdered by the police without any evidence that the authorities understood the need for systematic change that meant, for some reason, George Floyd's murder was the point at which large numbers of people, way beyond the usual protesters, felt 'things have got to change, and they have to change now'.

But it doesn't have to be an outrage that triggers the moment of the whirlwind; it could be an action by the movement that captures the imagination. In 1982 in the UK, an animal rights organisation's non-violent visit to a vivisection laboratory in the county of Essex saw tabloid papers carrying front-page pictures of balaclava-clad animal rights activists breaking out beagle dogs from the research centre. For some reason the national mood was overwhelmingly with those rescuing the dogs from their fate and instinctively against the use of animals in research. The militant anti-vivisection movement mushroomed over the coming months. In those early months of 1982 it felt to many, way beyond the limits of the movement, as if the lawbreakers were on the right side of history. This brings us to a very important point. The moment of the whirlwind is almost always a collective emotional response. It's not caused by an intellectual response to the incident but, as a society, people suddenly feel differently about the issue.

This moment of the whirlwind is often fleeting, and if not harnessed, the energy may dissipate. For a brief moment the nation's attention is captured and people are crying out to know what they can do. Unfortunately, too often, the movement doesn't have a sufficient answer. Both #MeToo and #BlackLivesMatter were huge moments in the UK and elsewhere, yet the energy and potential to drive systemic change largely dissipated within a short period of time. The lack of a plan to move people from protest to systematic work meant that town hall steps protests became less frequent and ever more poorly attended. Eventually, the anger and the opportunity were gone.

Another example of missing the moment was in 2006, when a far-right neo-Nazi party stood for election in the borough of Barking and Dagenham in East London. Local anti-racists and a national anti-fascist campaign knew they needed to do everything they could to persuade people not to vote for the far-right candidates. On the night of the election count, 12 of the 13 far-right candidates got elected to the council and became the official opposition. It sent a shockwave across the country and there was an immediate outpouring of desire to stop the far-right in their tracks. The national anti-fascist organisation found its answer-machine and email inboxes flooded with offers of help. This was clearly an emotional response to the news that a far-right group had managed to exploit people's fears so successfully. But without a plan for what to do in the event of such a far-right breakthrough, there was no way to utilise this newly activated anti-fascist support. In fact, it was four years before that desire to do something was focussed, and in 2010, a brilliant on-the-ground campaign swept every one of the far-right councillors in Barking and Dagenham out of office.

In contrast, in early 2021, anti-racist organisation the Runnymede Trust knew that a report by the UK government's Commission on Race and Ethnic Disparities (CRED) ('the Sewell Report') was due to land. This was a time when the government was suggesting that anti-racism was the 'metropolitan elite' engaged in special pleading. It was anticipated to be a damaging report given that the government had chosen as the chair someone who denied the existence of institutional racism. As such, it was expected that the content of the Sewell Report would be ideologically rather than evidence-driven. As part of its ever-widening 'culture war' and its then repositioning itself as the party of the 'White' working-class, the government wanted to create a backlash against advocates for racial justice, and the *Daily Mail* and the Murdoch press were set to be willing accomplices.

The Runnymede Trust anticipated the publication of the report would see a howl of anguish from racialised communities in the UK. It needed a plan to challenge the narrative of the Sewell Report, as well as a means to harness the anger of the community. After several delays it became clear when the government was going to launch its report and ideological offensive. Runnymede Trust staff set up an online discussion with leading advocates of race equality to go live the night the report was published. The government, however, made a mistake. It issued a press release with key 'findings' the day before the report was published, and headlines were written saying that the UK was a post-racial society devoid of institutional racism. For advocates of race equality, this was a 'moment of the whirlwind' when vast numbers of people, Black and White, were stunned that the government was now claiming the UK was a post-racial society despite all the evidence of institutional racism. By issuing the press release before the long-awaited report, the government had complete control of the narrative on day one. However, the following day, reporters who had written stories from the government press release saw the full report and recognised how weak its conclusions were. The evening the first press stories were published, the Runnymede Trust held its online meeting with an attendance of around a thousand people – many having only become aware of the meeting during that afternoon as a social media storm took place. The meeting itself was a sombre affair with some great activists and intellectuals dismissing the report's findings and outlining a way forward. Many press were also present, and eagerly reported the counter-narrative, which was that institutional racism was far from dead. Soon, people who had been part of the government's Commission were issuing their own statements distancing themselves from the Sewell Report's unevidenced conclusions.

The government's next step was even more counter-productive. A group of MPs supportive of the government wrote to the UK's Charity Commission demanding an investigation into whether the Runnymede Trust had been acting outside of its charitable remit. The government had long weaponised the Charity Commission, with attacks on groups like War on Want, the National Trust and even Barnardo's, so the whole race equality and charities sectors lined up in support of the Runnymede Trust. Six months later, the Commission published its findings which said: 'following careful assessment of the concerns raised, the Commission says that it was within the charity's purposes to engage with and take a position on the CRED report and has found no breach of its guidance' (Gov UK 2021).

The Runnymede Trust had seen the storm approaching, had strategised how it would respond both to the ideological attack and to the emotional impact on its community, and had reaped the benefits of engaging with the whirlwind. Among these benefits were, incidentally, some significant sums of money arising from new partnerships with businesses who had decided that, when it came to race equality, they were going to be on the right side of history, and trusted Runnymede not only to advance the cause of race equality, but to navigate the hostile environment with a high degree of skill.

Among the key strategic tasks at these movements of the whirlwind are to clearly expose the duplicity and complicity of powerholders and to align social justice movements with deeply felt values. As we have said previously, while the vast majority of the population in the UK aren't actively anti-racist and many people may accept and internalise racist stereotypes, it's only a minority that are comfortable with overt racism. The government's narrative that the UK was a post-racist society didn't fit even within the lived experience of the majority of White people. The government was widely perceived as adopting intentional ignorance to the self-evident racism in society. Meanwhile, the evidence-driven, moderate, but resolute, Runnymede Trust was perceived to be speaking truth to power.

'Take-off' is potentially one of the most exhilarating stages in campaigning, yet people who have been long-established campaigners who have perhaps carried the movement through the lean years can sometime be unwelcoming to newcomers as they feel: 'where were they when there was just a few of us?'. People who have merged their identity with that of the campaign can sometimes find it hard to change gear when circumstances require it. Indeed, sometimes they act as 'gatekeepers' of knowledge and power within the movement preventing the new influx of activists reaching full potential. There is also the threat that we covered in Chapter 10 – the risk of disrupters entering the movement during the moment of the whirlwind, whose aim is to undermine the progress that is now genuinely possible.

Stage five: perception of failure

The next stage, according to Bill Moyer, is a perception of failure. Despite the surge when campaigns hit take-off, and regardless that the campaign has started to win the hearts and minds of large sections of the public, not enough has changed. Given the huge amount of effort and personal sacrifice that people have made to bring the social justice movement to this stage, and the excitement about the new possibilities that arise in the take-off stage, it's inevitable that people want to see concrete change and they want to see it now. While it is not a golden rule, there will often be a time lag between when a movement acquires significant support to build real power and when it achieves important changes. This is because the powerholders will want to decide if any shift in power away from them is just a temporary blip. They will only move fundamentally when they are convinced that they must. Think of the leaders of the repugnant apartheid South Africa. Despite an incredible military machine, which included a nuclear arsenal, there came a point where they realised that while they could kill almost at will, in the long term, they could not govern, and they moved. Apartheid was dismantled, but it took time. It is precisely at the point when a movement's goals seem realisable that people begin to become impatient. When they are protesting in the belief that someone has to speak out, there is often little sense of urgency, or hope of fundamental change, but when the movement grows, success feels close and inevitable, and when it doesn't urgently materialise, this can create a crisis.

With the passing of the take-off stage and the accompanying growth in large protests, riotous meetings, and the frenetic activity of the newly energised, people can begin to feel that 'our moment has passed'. In this phase not only may there be the perception of failure, but there may also be inevitable setbacks. Campaigns don't follow a linear path, and setbacks are part of the movement's learning opportunities; as the old boxing saying goes: 'it is not how often you get knocked down that counts, it is how often you get back up again'.

There are a range of responses to this crisis. One such response is to have built into the movement's DNA an inoculation against despair based on studying how other social movements have advanced over time (and noting that there are inevitably setbacks, or 'fallow periods') and the need to move from protest to strategic interventions. One all-too-familiar response is a decision by a militant minority – frustrated at the slow pace of change, believing that the public are not concerned enough and that they therefore must 'go it alone' – to act as a vanguard, and often to adopt extreme tactics. Examples are the American Weathermen, who grew out of the group Students for a Democratic Society, and advocated violence and the planting of bombs; and the rise of armed insurrection groups in the African American freedom movement, the Angry Brigade in the UK, and the Animal Rights Militia – although they may have been a 'false flag' operation, as we explored in Chapter 10.

A more familiar example might be within trade unions, where there is often an 'oppositionist' tendency that dismisses the strategic work of building power, and instead advocates that militant minorities are capable of winning more than a broad coalition of workers. It's precisely in this 'perception of failure' stage, that a group of self-selecting, self-declared activists are able to convince themselves that the mass of ordinary members are irredeemably backward and that they will need to be led into what often turns out to be poorly supported and poorly planned action. As has been said elsewhere:

The primary problem with the militant minority tendency is it misunderstands the central premise of unionism, which is that in order to win meaningful gains as the working-class it's necessary to organize a militant majority. Unionism, in this way, requires one to adopt an attitude that believes in both the capacity of any ordinary worker and their ability to change over time. (Riccio 2023)

Another frequent failing at this stage is for the movement to remain 'stuck in protest'. In other words, as a movement begins to gain power, it needs to move from protesting, to beginning the process of forcing and negotiating change. There is a contradiction here: the movement does not, yet, have sufficient power to achieve all the change it wants, but it has sufficient power to negotiate some important change. There comes a dilemma when some are not satisfied with anything other than the full realisation of their demands. To remain a purist protest movement when real, albeit sometimes small, changes are possible is to duck the responsibility of leadership, and to avoid the necessity of an evolving strategy. What is necessary at this stage is a strategy that recognises what is possible today, while continuing to build the power necessary to win even more tomorrow.

There's an important insight into how to progress negotiations during this stage. As campaigners, your group shouldn't agree to anything that is in contradiction with your overall vision – although some concessions may be forced upon you. For example, a campaign for the regularisation of undocumented migrants might want a total amnesty, but there might be, within the government of the time, an emerging difference of approach between maintaining the current hostile environment or, for example, a suspension of deportations for those who had been in the country for five years. The movement would be 'stuck in protest' if it didn't realise that this partial amnesty, if it could be secured, would be a significant win.

Perhaps the most frequent challenge of this stage of a campaign is internal dissent. As people become disillusioned with the perceived failure, a blame culture can erupt with different groups blaming each other for perceived failures of the campaign. Of course, our opponents can and do contribute to this and capitalise upon it. Perhaps the most extreme examples of this – combining both the turn to militancy and exploiting internal movement dissent – was when the Los Angeles Police Department and the FBI in the early 1970s fermented a blood feud between two Black militant organisations, a local chapter of the Black Panther Party and the US Organisation. The Los Angeles Police Department and the FBI allegedly provided financial and material support to the US Organisation, including advising them of the time and location of Black Panther Party meetings at a time when the two rival groups were involved in deadly clashes. In 1976, *The New York Times* reported on the findings of a Senate Select Committee on Intelligence Activities that found: 'The Federal Bureau of Investigation carried out a secret, nationwide effort to "destroy" the Black Panthers, including attempts to stir bloody "gang warfare" between the Panthers and other groups and to create factional splits within the party' (*The New York Times* 1976).

The newspaper reported that after three fatalities in a dispute between the US Organisation and the Black Panther Party, the San Diego office had proudly sent a message to FBI headquarters claiming: 'Shootings, beatings and a high degree of unrest continues to prevail in the ghetto area of southeast San Diego.'

It takes a level of collective reflection to recognise, and seize, the (albeit, limited) opportunities of this stage of a movement. Organisations need to hold their nerve, avoid a turn to a misguided cult of militancy and to keep their 'eyes on the prize'. But reflection and the practice of 'securing what we can', when it does happen, is an opportunity for important learning as social justice movements approach the next phase of movement building.

Stage six: majority public opinion

The next stage – at least in the theory – is when the movement gains majority public support. At this stage the strategy requires a whole new rethink. The organisation must shift gear from semi-spontaneous protests designed to create a short-term crisis for the opposition to a long-term struggle to press home the advantage of majority support. Particularly in a democracy – but it is also true under autocracy – if the powerholders persistently frustrate the will of the people, they will weaken, and occasionally lose, their grip on power. The purpose of action during this stage is to redraw the balance of power, so that a new consensus may arise. What was considered legitimate previously will increasingly become unacceptable, not because activists don't like it but because the majority of the population are opposed to it, and every time the opposition seek to use their power to prop up the existing state of affairs, they lose power and credibility.

At this stage while the balance of power is not yet with the organisation or group, it has fundamentally shifted from where it was in the earlier stages. Suddenly groups who were patiently lobbying with little headway are finding themselves courted by politicians and are reaping the benefits of the work at the grassroots (although they may convince themselves that it is the eloquence of their advocacy that has attracted this additional interest). What's needed at this stage is to encourage the participation of the majority of the public to increasingly move people from passive supporter to active supporter. At this moment, the campaigners of the earlier phases might find it difficult to re-orientate. The days of heroic 'lone wolf' protest activism are largely past, and there needs to be a selection of targets who can realistically be 'flipped'. While some of these might appear token, for example, a declaration by local authorities that they are 'nuclear-free zones', such declarations have two effects: they further isolate powerbrokers who continue to defend the status quo, and further normalise campaigners' demands. It is this work of ensuring that the current shift in public opinion becomes permanent and of converting that support into measurable gains that holds the key to victory. At this stage, local initiatives leading to local wins can contribute to a sense that 'the tide is turning' on the national stage.

This stage often involves consolidation, and that may require a move away from the more spontaneous loose structure, which was essential for the days when the campaign was mobilising a few committed people, and the creation of a structure capable of holding the aspirations of far larger numbers who are often less personally committed. These are people who agree with you that things should change, but they do relatively little to help.

Truth be told, the majority of them aren't going to identify with Nelson Mandela's famous words 'the struggle is my life', nor be attracted to his assertion that: 'only through hardship, sacrifice and militant action can freedom be won'. Fortunately, a mass movement doesn't need to be made up entirely of heroic people; it can be the sheer numbers of supporters, not the individual levels of commitment, that makes movements decisive.

Stage seven: success

While a movement might find itself oscillating between some of these stages, particularly stages five and six, in the theory at least, there comes a point where the movement succeeds. Success comes in different guises. Sometimes there will be a trigger event, which initiates a crisis, and a showdown at a time when the opposition no longer have the stomach for a fight. A good example is for the African American freedom movement in the US, where the violent police attacks on the Selma March televised on news reports across the world created an international crisis of confidence for the US. This crisis spurred on the passage of the Voting Rights Act of 1965.

Then there is the quiet showdown (or slowdown), where powerholders simply adopt all – or more often some – of the key demands of the movement. In the example in Chapter 4 where we talked about when the local council in Dalston in East London decided to remove the name 'C.L.R. James' from a newly rebuilt library, they provoked a massive campaign of opposition as the move was seen as 'whitewashing' Dalston's radical past, and its role as a key centre in the UK's Caribbean cultural and political history. The campaign was successful, and when it came to the opening of the library, the Cabinet Member responsible for library services in his opening speech, affirmed, to everyone's mild surprise, that he had always believed the library should retain the name of this Caribbean Marxist, and how glad he was for the community's support that had made this possible. Far from being the target of that community's opposition to the name change, it seemed he had reinvented his role as leading (somewhat quietly) the campaign to retain the name.

Success can also come through a long, slow process of attrition, perhaps most easily recognised by looking at how bad things were in the past. An example might be the fight for LGBTQ+ rights in the UK. It's very easy to count the progressive steps forward over this issue: the abolition of the government's Section 28 provisions – a clause in the 1988 Local Government Act, which prohibited the teaching in schools 'of the acceptability of homosexuality' until its repeal in 2003; the slow and evolving process by which LGBTQ+ couples finally, in 2017, attained equal rights to pensions; or the 2013 decision to allow same-sex couples to marry in the eyes of the law. But while these are momentous steps forward, few LGBTQ+ campaigners would feel that they have achieved equality. In this example, looking back at how much the campaign has achieved doesn't mean that current levels of discrimination are any more acceptable – indeed, it might increase the demand for more action as a better future seems genuinely possible.

In this period, the drive for change is less likely to be propelled by the social justice movement and far more likely to be driven by the existing powerholders as they seek to rapidly distance themselves from their former behaviours and policies that are now widely considered unacceptable. This century, for example, business has often been ahead of government in proclaiming its support for equality in the workplace. Many businesses have finally realised that discriminating against whole sections of their customer base is not a smart business move. Once companies start to promote concepts of equality within their workforce, even in a relatively token way, it can help normalise the seemingly mild, but undoubtedly radical notion that equal treatment is a right, and this can become a dominant narrative within the workforce. Of course, there's a difference between words and deeds, and between policies and practices. Nevertheless, this doesn't take away from a cultural shift where discriminatory practices are widely perceived as not acceptable – not just by those who experience those practices, but by a large majority of the workforce.

Perhaps surprisingly, one of the challenges for any movement is to recognise success. When you are locked into a bitter conflict with powerholders, the moment they move, there is a tendency to dismiss their movement. It is either a 'clever trick', or the content of their change (however fundamental) is dismissed as insufficient. In organising, we use the concepts of a fixed or change mindset. Most people, most of the time, assume that things stay as they are. If your boss is a pain, they will always be a pain; if a colleague won't join the union, then they will never join the union. This fixed mindset allows us to categorise who is for and who is against and, of course, who is neutral or not interested, but when we make the mistake of thinking that people's views and actions are static, we can lose the ability to accurately assess a situation. Perhaps the most dramatic examples of people changing their positions were the rulers and business backers of apartheid in South Africa. In the 1970s and 1980s, anti-apartheid activists would picket a high-street bank in the UK, asserting that its extensive business dealings in South Africa made it the 'Bank of Apartheid'; later the diehard White supremacists labelled the same bank the 'Bank of the ANC' because it had begun to argue for ending apartheid. When F.W. de Klerk became the President of South Africa in August 1989, he was a long-established and hard-line supporter of apartheid. Leading anti-apartheid campaigner Bishop Desmond Tutu dismissed any suggestions that his presidency would lead to change: 'I don't think we've got to even begin to pretend that there is any reason for thinking that we are entering a new phase. It's just musical chairs' (Allen 2006). Yet within six months de Klerk had announced plans for reforms, and had released Nelson Mandela from prison and opened the door to a peaceful transition.

Unless we are attuned to the way that change takes place, including the way that people and their attitudes change, then we risk being stuck in the past using strategies and tactics that would have been appropriate previously, but which are now out of date. Without the ability to recognise when change is taking place, not just in terms of the power available to both sides, but the change that is taking place within the ranks of the powerholders, it's difficult to seize the opportunities that arise. Equally, without a clear point at which victory can be declared, it can be hard for people to celebrate progress. In general, there can a problem with movements recognising progress and celebrating the steps forward. This is one of many reasons why activists suffer burnout.

Stage eight: continuation

Myles Horton argues that as you build a movement, so your goals inevitably get wider. As you begin to create the possibility of change more people will be motivated to support your movement and so, in a virtuous circle, the scale of potential change increases. Success breeds not only success, but a new vision of what success might be. However, what has been won can also be lost. The history of the working-class movement is one of successes followed by counter-offensives by the employers and their supporters, whether these are about the severely limited right to strike, about narratives of unions as 'dinosaurs' or 'wreckers', or the most substantial of all union issues, the wage share – the percentage of the money generated by work that goes to wages as compared to profits. A movement that fails to keep its 'eyes on the prize' even at the point of success can see that success rolled backwards.

Perhaps one of the most dramatic examples of failing to continue has been mentioned earlier. The Obama 2008 election campaign built an incredible grassroots voter mobilisation movement, but after the historic victory of electing the first Black President of the USA the movement was demobilised and the path left clear for the emergence of the Tea Party and the subsequent rise of Donald Trump.

In contrast, after the historic passage of the UK's Hunting Act 2004, which partially outlawed hunting with hounds, the Hunt Saboteurs Association repositioned themselves as hunt monitors, seeking to ensure that hunts did not breach the law, and if they did, the evidence was recorded. On a wider scale, the anti-apartheid movement, having seen South Africa transition to democracy, evolved into Action for Southern Africa with the ambition of ensuring that 'the legacies of colonialism, racism and apartheid are replaced with justice, human rights and peace' (ACTSA 2023) and continues to campaign on a variety of issues, including cancelling unfair debt, LGBTQ+ rights, workers' rights, particularly around occupational health, democracy, HIV and so on.

Social change ecosystem

Irrespective of whether you accept Bill Moyer's assertions about stages of campaigns, it is clear that there are different tasks or outputs required at different times. The question therefore is: which structures are most efficient at motivating and supporting your people to deliver on those tasks? Another way of thinking about this has been developed by Deepa Iyer, who identifies as a South Asian American writer, lawyer, strategist, facilitator and activist. In her social change ecosystem framework, there are shared values at the centre of activism and a range of roles that people need to perform within social change activism. She describes these as follows:

- Weavers: who see the lines of connection between people, places, organizations, ideas, and movements.
- Experimenters: who innovate, pioneer, and invent. These are people who take measured risks.
- Frontline responders: who are active in addressing immediate issues and who marshal and organize resources, networks, and messages.
- Visionaries: who imagine and generate the boldest possibilities, hopes and dreams, and who remind us of our direction;
- Builders: who develop, organize, and implement ideas, practices, people, and resources in service of a collective vision.
- Caregivers: who nurture and nourish the people around them by creating and sustaining a community of care, joy, and connection.
- Disruptors: who take uncomfortable and risky actions to shake up the status quo, to raise awareness, and to build power.
- Healers: who recognize and tend to the generational and current traumas caused by oppressive systems, institutions, policies, and practices.
- Storytellers: who craft and share our community stories, cultures, experiences, histories, and possibilities through art, music, media, and movement.

- Guides: who teach, counsel, and advise, using their gifts of well-earned discernment and wisdom.

Again, you may dispute the importance of some of these roles, or you may feel that there are many other roles in a movement. For example, we might want to add advocates or negotiators, but this framework is a good place to start a discussion about the roles of organisations within a movement, because it illustrates that a successful movement needs to have an ecosystem that provides a way of focussing the efforts of supporters performing many different roles.

Let's move on to think of some examples of traditional social change movement including trade unions, NGOs, charities and perhaps some of the looser groupings. Trade unions are very hierarchical, often with a structure that starts with a workplace rep, through departmental stewards' committees, branch committees, regional committees and national committees. They also invariably have annual, or biannual, conferences where policy is set. This structure is pretty ubiquitous across the UK trade union movement, and it is often criticised for being unchanged over the last 100 years despite the ways the world of work has changed. An exception to this structure is the development of 'self-organised groups' for Black, women, LGBTQ+ and disabled members – although when these committees do exist, they are almost always a direct copy of and a bolt-on to the pre-existing structures. Trade unions traditionally mirrored employer structures, but the modern workplace is increasingly complex: people can be working together in the same location despite having different employers, and indeed, with the gig economy, lots of people are nominally self-employed. While there is scope for drawing members into activity in trade unions, it's normally in a very functional way; this could be recruiting a member to be a departmental rep responsible for raising local issues with local management, or a 'caseworker' supporting members in grievance, disciplinary or related hearings, a health and safety rep responsible for carrying out statutory inspections for health hazards, and so on.

Applying Deepa Iyer's typical roles to trade unions we might think of the local reps' structure as involving frontline responders, but it is hard to see how the traditional trade union structure makes space for those weavers, experimenters, visionaries, caregivers, healers, storytellers, and guides to step forward and contribute. Instead, most union structures tend to be highly centralised, with the roles of guide (training officers), storytellers (media and spokespeople), and builders (union organisers) being formal employed staff roles. This isn't really the best structure for involving members in their unions. Often union members have evolved informal lay structures to circumnavigate the formal ones so as to increase participation. This has been evident in cross-employer and cross-union networks, or 'combines', all operating outside of formal structures. And, in times of dispute, informal strike committees are often established, which undertake the responsibility to organise the members' activity during a dispute – the picket lines, and the 'get out the vote' campaigns, and so on.

Taking a different example, we can look at a fairly typical campaigning charity. These often have only limited staff, of whom the majority will either be working on the organisation's infrastructure (press officer, finance, management and so on) or on research. They will have some form of supporters list, with perhaps one person whose role it is to either activate those people, or mine them for donations. Supporters are generally asked to undertake tasks that support the centre, for example organising fundraising events or participating in campaigns that are centrally convened – although some groups may have no role for supporters other than to send donations to head office. If the organisation is a think tank, they may ask supporters to write letters to the local paper about a recent publication, or to organise a talk locally about its implications, but there's very little scope for local groups to act on their own initiative; indeed, it's often hard to see what added value supporters are asked to contribute to the organisation's plans.

A great example of an alternative approach would be the Jo Cox Foundation, which came into existence in the UK after the terrorist murder of Jo Cox MP. Taking inspiration from her life, the organisation coordinates a 'Great Get Together' once a year close to the anniversary of her death. By simply encouraging supporters to arrange something, anything, that brings their community together they are able to achieve so much. Up and down the country small community groups, sometimes based in a street, or a couple of streets, arrange a street party. Others take over community halls and venues to create something special for their community to share, and of course there are some huge parties, including for example, recently in the Olympic Park in East London. The foundation also organises a winter get together, but its primary focus is on encouraging this once-a-year coming-together of people, and it works, because to put on even a small event, you have to go out and speak to your neighbours, engage with the local authority to get the street closed for the day, arrange someone to bring a PA, organise the games for the children and ensure that people will bring food for the pot-luck dinner. This focus on a simple, but flexible, objective allows almost anyone to initiate something that contributes to the national focus. Yet to organise even small events successfully and to their full potential you need a steering group that can involve all the talents, all the offers, and in all probability many of the various roles in Deepa Iyer's model. This then allows us to consider how organisations sometimes are able to build power by ceding control. This concept may be an anathema to some people who perceive themselves as 'leaders' but who find it difficult to cede control and who fail to distinguish between control and power.

Leaderless organisations

In their groundbreaking book, *The Starfish and the Spider: The Unstoppable Power of Leaderless Organizations*, Ori Brafman and Rod Beckstrom explore how power can be built by unleashing the potential of supporters. Their analogy is between a spider and a starfish. If you were to cut off the head of a spider you are removing its brain, its central nervous system, and it dies. But a starfish, which doesn't have a well-defined central nervous system, is different. If you were to cut off one of its legs then the starfish will grow a replacement, and even more impressively, the leg will grow a replacement body. The authors then use this metaphor to explore organisations, defining them as either spider-like or starfish-like. One example of a starfish-like organisation is perhaps Wikipedia, which is a highly decentralised and immensely successful online encyclopaedia, written and quality checked by an army of volunteers. It's reputedly as reliable as many traditional encyclopaedias – although its critics dispute this.

Brafman and Beckstrom may overstate the ubiquitous value of the starfish model as there may be occasions when a stable, well-financed, hierarchical model – a spider-like organisation – is more suited to a particular set of needs for a movement, perhaps when lobbying or developing evidence-based research. However, the authors' central thesis, that starfish models are better able to unleash the potential of supporters, is compelling. What then are the key features of a starfish model? Five key themes are identified – perhaps deliberately playing with the idea that starfish have five legs. The authors identify the five 'legs' as: circles, the catalyst, ideology, a pre-existing network, and a champion. We will explore these five concepts below.

Circles

The concept of circles is simple. In most meetings you may find that the chairs are facing the front, and at the front there is a 'top table', consisting of important people – usually a panel of speakers. At such a meeting, it's likely that most of the discussion is directed and emanates from this top table. But if you were to attend, for example, a Quaker meeting, you would find that there is no top table, and that people speak when they are moved to speak. At Alcoholics Anonymous, a similar non-hierarchical organisation, everyone is equally valued, and everyone is expected to be concerned about the welfare and sobriety of the whole group. A circle is a group without a hierarchical structure. The authors of *The Starfish and the Spider* don't consider the informal hierarchies that might arise in circle groups, but they argue convincingly that circles create an environment in which participants have to take responsibility for each other, and that circles create inclusivity, with members accepting a high level of responsibility for the welfare of the group and the advancement of its objectives. The authors explain that, unlike more formally structured groups, there are often few 'rules', but a deep sense of acceptable behaviour or 'norms' that evolve from the group. They argue that:

> norms can be even more powerful than rules. Rules are someone else's idea of what you should do. If you break a rule, just don't get caught and you'll be okay. But with norms, it's about what you as a member have signed up for, and what you've created. (Brafman and Beckstrom 2006: 89)

Put another way, the authors argued that members of circles have a very strong sense of ownership, and a deep commitment to maintaining the culture within the group. The circle then, is the basis of any starfish organisation. They also consider online communities, such as open-source programming communities, which tend to operate as virtual circles, but there are a number of challenges – not least that you don't tend to meet other members of the circle and the nature of interactions can be fleeting, leading to less accountability. Nonetheless it is noted how effective these online communities can become.

The catalyst

Brafman and Beckstrom (2006: 91) place a great deal of focus on the role of a catalyst. The essence is captured when they say they recognise a regular pattern across decentralised organisations: a catalyst gets the organisation going and then cedes control to the members. The role of the catalyst is to make a start, to set a vision and to involve people. They are lighting a fuse, and the organisation will then take its course when they step away: 'In letting go of the leadership role, the catalyst transfers ownership and responsibility to the circle. ... A catalyst isn't usually in it for praise and accolades. When his or her job is done, a catalyst knows it's time to move on' (Brafman and Beckstrom 2006: 92).

The catalyst is the antithesis of a traditional CEO for whom control is important. Remember earlier, in Chapter 6, when we talked about Marshall Ganz's assertion that in organising theory you build power by ceding control.

Ideology

The term ideology is contested; in one sense it means a coherent ordering of our knowledge into a system of thought that helps us to understand and predict reality. In other contexts, ideology is understood as a set of false beliefs, sometimes propagated to defend unfair systems. For example, the notion of a 'free market' in capitalism inherently has to ignore the fact that some people are wealthy enough to control the market, and some people are poor enough that they are at the mercy of the market. As an anarchist once said, 'a theory is something you have, but an ideology is something that has you'.

Setting that aside, for Brafman and Beckstrom there's something more than a transactional relationship going on – there's a sense of 'us'. One interesting example of this approach they draw upon is the 'tribe' that attends the Burning Man festival. This is a cultural, arts and self-reliance festival held in Nevada's Black Rock Desert and attracts up to 20,000 people with no evident sense of structure. It is based on ten principles: 'radical inclusion, gifting, decommodification, radical self-reliance, radical self-expression, communal effort, civic responsibility, leaving no trace, participation, and immediacy' (Harvey 2004). Equally, in Alcoholics Anonymous, there's a radical philosophy and the 'Twelve-step Programme'. Perhaps it would be best to describe this not as ideology, but as a shared belief system and set of values: what Marshall Ganz would refer to as 'a story of us' (see Chapter 7).

The pre-existing network

Brafman and Beckstrom are not alone in arguing that everything has a history, and that movements evolve out of that history. The backbone to the anti-slavery movement in the UK was built upon the Quaker circles, and those circles served the new movement well: 'The Quakers weren't just decentralized themselves: they served as the decentralized platform upon which the antislavery movement was built. This piggybacking effect enabled the abolitionist movement to take off' (Brafman and Beckstrom 2006: 95). Perhaps the best example of this, and we have mentioned it in Chapter 4, is the African American freedom movement, where the National Association for the Advancement of Colored People (NAACP) built its network on the network of Black Churches, and the relatively small number of Black-owned and -orientated businesses, such as newspapers and hairdressers. The Southern Christian Leadership Conference (SCLC) piggy-backed on the NAACP branches, and later the Student Non-violent Coordinating Committee (SNCC), when it organised voter registration and desegregation drives in the Deep South – built upon these pre-existing networks.

When COVID-19 struck in Britain in 2020, a small group of anarchists got publicity for a concept known as 'mutual aid'. They asserted that we couldn't rely on the state to provide us with care in the crisis, and that communities must organise to 'do for self'. No doubt to their complete surprise, a mass movement of COVID mutual aid groups rapidly sprung up across the country. However, they didn't arise entirely out of nowhere. Local community groups, and the connections between people involved in them, were the base upon which the biggest decentralised organising drive in a generation was built. Tenants' associations, church groups, ethnic minority community groups, community centres, even trade union branches, became the backbone of a mass, inclusive, decentralised network that saw neighbours looking out for neighbours, collecting food and medicine for those who were isolating, and creating online community chats for people who had previously just passed each other in the street with a nod and a 'good morning'.

There are two reasons why pre-existing networks are so important: the first is that they create a shortcut that means that not every connection needs to be built from scratch, but equally importantly, they are a source of people with experience in organising. People who, because of their experience, know what needs to be done, people who are recognised and perhaps trusted in their communities, the organic leaders who have already been surfaced.

The champion

The final leg of Brafman and Beckstrom's structure is 'the champion'. They distinguish between the catalyst, the person who get things up and running, and the champion, someone who is 'relentless in promoting a new idea ... champions take it to the next level' (2006: 98). Perhaps a good person who fits the description of catalyst is Ella Baker, whose lifetime of organising created the networks across the rural South that the African American freedom movement was based on, but Martin Luther King was the champion. However important his speeches were to the congregations that first heard them, he was often speaking to wider America, making the case for racial justice. Imprisoned in Birmingham Jail, he wrote a letter – nominally in response to local clergy demanding restraint and an end to the campaign of non-violent direct action – but in reality, it was addressed to the nation, and in particular that group he refers to as 'white moderates', who nominally supported race equality but opposed the non-violent direct action initiated by King and his supporters. As with so much of his oratory, it is worth revisiting an extract because this 'Letter from Birmingham Jail' was transformational in its impact on the audience it targeted. To use the language of transformative conversations, it asked 'white moderates' the 'difficult question':

> We know through painful experience that freedom is never voluntarily given by the oppressor; it must be demanded by the oppressed. Frankly, I have yet to engage in a direct-action campaign that was 'well timed' in the view of those who have not suffered unduly from the disease of segregation. For years now I have heard the word 'Wait!' It rings in the ear of every Negro with piercing familiarity. This 'Wait' has almost always meant 'Never.' ... I must confess that over the past few years I have been gravely disappointed with the white moderate. I have almost reached the regrettable conclusion that the Negro's great stumbling block in his stride toward freedom is not the White Citizen's Councillor or the Ku Klux Klanner, but

the white moderate, who is more devoted to 'order' than to justice; who prefers a negative peace which is the absence of tension to a positive peace which is the presence of justice; who constantly says: 'I agree with you in the goal you seek, but I cannot agree with your methods of direct action'; who paternalistically believes he can set the timetable for another man's freedom; who lives by a mythical concept of time and who constantly advises the Negro to wait for a 'more convenient season'.

This proclamation was designed to challenge the 'white moderate' to choose sides: they must either support the freedom movement or get out of the way, because their pleas for restraint are making progress more difficult. It was persuasive and effective.

Whether you find the detail of Brafman and Beckstrom's analysis convincing, it's a helpful distinction to consider when thinking about structure and organisations. Do you want a spider-type organisation, with a headquarters, a command-and-control centre, and a centralisation of power, or a starfish organisation that relies so much more on the activity and the creativity of activists at the base? Starfish organisations like the Hunt Saboteurs Association turn supporters into active agents of change, and it's this process that explains why it is that so often large, well-financed organisations with significant staffing resources are unable to match the contribution of a diffuse network of groups that rely wholly on the activity of supporters while operating on a shoestring. Sadly, funders for social justice have been slow to learn this lesson and continue to fund large unwieldy organisations that have often proven incapable of equipping their supporters with the skills and analysis necessary for them to become active changemakers. Yet, as with any tool of analysis, the starfish/spider definitions shouldn't blind us to the fact that most organisational structures contain elements of both.

Consider your organisational structure: is it working?

Think of a campaign or movement in which you are involved.

Next consider the different groupings within your organisation's ecosystem. Try to evaluate these – are they spider-like, or starfish-like?

Give a highly centralised spider organisation a score of one, and a highly decentralised starfish group a score of five, with some groups scoring somewhere between the two poles. Then consider how each of the groups seeks to advance your cause, using the definition in the IPPR/ Runnymede Trust report. Ask yourself, which deficit are they primarily seeking to address:

• the information deficit;
• the salience deficit; or
• the power deficit?

Do you think they have got the balance right?

Now consider the stages outlined in Bill Moyer's 'Movement Action Plan', and ask yourself: Which of the eight stages is the movement or campaign you are considering experiencing now?

Finally, consider what should be the strategic objectives for the movement at this moment, and to what extent the movement's structures are enabling these activities?

Final reflections

When we were teenagers back in the 1970s, we believed that life would get better, that society would become fairer and that what we did would accelerate that process of bending the arc of history towards social justice. We had no sense that, actually, social justice could be rolled backwards. We may have been misguided and naive, but we were not alone. As the 1960s drew to a close, there was hope in the world, a belief that emerging technology would be harnessed to eliminate poverty at home and starvation abroad, that we would all work less hours and have more leisure. Despite some important steps, what we have largely seen is life has got harder, the UK, in particular, is far more unequal, and for many people there is a sense of disempowerment in the face not just of growing economic and societal problems but of the poisoning of our very planet.

The tide began to turn in the 1970s, imperceptibly at first, but the change accelerated, and it has not reversed. From the 1970s and 1980s there have been repeated legislative steps taken to ensure that it was harder for trade unions to organise. This process has been revisited in recent years with new rules about ballot thresholds and proposals for 'minimum service guarantees' (the almost laughable idea being that if you go on strike, you will be obliged to minimise the disruption to your employer's business). Throughout the same period, there has also been a concerted whittling away at the right to protest, and again, we are now facing renewed attempts to minimise our right to organise. As we were writing this book, we had a Home Secretary who, in genuinely Orwellian terms, described peace protesters as 'hate marchers', and the police were issuing leaflets telling protesters which slogans they considered acceptable.

The then Conservative government openly planned legislation to override our human rights, as it demonised asylum seekers and in so doing green-lighted the far-right thugs who were to launch anti-migrant racist attacks in the weeks after the Conservative Party's defeat. The COP28 climate summit was coming to an end without any sense of the necessary urgency, and in recent years, life expectancy had shortened, the world of work had become less and less secure, our prison population was reaching bursting point and homelessness in all its forms rose.

We now have a new, government, but one which is timid in its proposals to address the problems we face: it's going to be down to ordinary people to save the planet, and to do that we need to get organised. The crisis is now: on the international stage, as we write this, the World Health Organization reports that a child dies every ten minutes in the catastrophic war in Gaza (Nichols 2023).

Yet, even amid this despair, everywhere we look there are also signs of hope. The incredible mutual aid movement that sprang up during the COVID-19 pandemic shows that there are great wells of human agency ready to reach out and to work together to make a difference. When people are faced with the opportunity to act with a confidence that their actions will make a difference, they move. Our job as changemakers is to help our people remember a truth that they already know but have been persuaded to bury: that when we act together, there is no force that can stop us. We have both the power and a duty to remake the world.

What this book has tried to show is that organised people can beat organised money every time, but only if we are genuinely organised, inclusive, curious and strategic. In these pages, we have tried to pass on to you, that which was passed down to us, a sense of what is possible. Please do not treat anything we have written as received wisdom, but take the ideas and play with them, introduce them into your organising and test them, keep what works and discard what does not.

And finally...

The building blocks of solidarity are community, whether that be a faith organisation, a darts team, a union branch or a kids' football squad: the spaces where we interact and come to know each other as human. If you do nothing else, find ways to bring people together, to share their hopes and their dreams. When we share our dreams, we can transform the world.

References

ACTSA. 2023. 'Action for South Africa' (https://actsa.org/) (last accessed 6 December 2023).

Alinsky, Saul. 1972. *Rules for Radicals: A Pragmatic Primer for Realistic Radicals*. New York: Vintage.

Alinsky, Saul. 1989 [1949]. *Reveille for Radicals*. New York: Random House.

Allen, John. 2006. *Rabble-Rouser for Peace: The Authorised Biography of Desmond Tutu*. London: Rider.

Amazon. 2018. 'Amazon's Union-Busting Training Video' (www.youtube.com/watch?v=AQeGBHxIyHw) (last accessed 7 December 2023).

Baker, Ella. 1969. 'The Black Woman in the Civil Rights Struggle'. Speech given at the Institute of the Black World, Atlanta, Georgia (https://awpc.cattcenter.iastate.edu/2019/08/09/the-black-woman-in-the-civil-rights-struggle-1969/#:~:text=I%20use%20the%20term%20radical,is%20easier%20said%20than%20done) (last accessed 3 September 2024).

BBC. 2003. 'Striking miners faced "volunteer force"' (http://news.bbc.co.uk/1/hi/scotland/2617565.stm) (last accessed 21 December 2023).

BBC. 2022. 'Glasgow City Council to pay £770m to settle equal pay dispute' (https://docs.google.com/document/d/1UKE4fjHl0eQfE4yHttu3CHFKe2FAiI8P/edit?usp=sharing&ouid=106411158561149365287&rtpof=true&sd=true) (last accessed 16 July 2024).

Blueprints for Change. 2023. 'How to guides' (https://blueprintsfc.org/) (last accessed 3 September 2024).

Boffey, Daniel. 2015. 'Revealed: Ted Heath behind TV documentary used to sway jury in trial of Shrewsbury trade unionists' (www.theguardian.com/politics/2015/dec/05/ted-heath-used-tv-film-to-sway-jury-to-convict-building-strike-pickets) (last accessed 7 December 2023).

Brafman, O. and R.A. Beckstrom. 2006. *The Starfish and the Spider: The Unstoppable Power of Leaderless Organizations*. Portfolio.

Clegg, Stewart, David Courpasson and Nelson Philips. 2010. *Power and Organisations*. London: Sage.

Combahee River Collective. 1988. 'The Combahee River Collective Statement' in *How We Get Free*, ed. Keeanga-Yamahtta Taylor. Chicago: Haymarket Books.

Commission on Race and Ethnic Disparities. 2021. *Commission on Race and Ethnic Disparities: The Report*. London: HMG.

Curtin, John. 2022. 'Radicals and Revolutionaries, Episode 13: John Curtin (Part 2)' (https://directory.libsyn.com/episode/index/show/cf519327–60e5–4b89-b237-ef4cca8dbfcd/id/23275457) (last accessed 9 December 2023).

Dalton, Alan. 1979. *Asbestos Killer Dust: A Worker/Community Guide: How to Fight the Hazards of Asbestos and Its Substitutes*. BSSR Publications Limited.

Davies, Nick, and Vikram Dodd. 2011. 'Murder trial collapse exposes News of the World links to police corruption' (www.theguardian.com/media/2011/mar/11/news-of-the-world-police-corruption) (last accessed 21 December 2023).

Debs, E.V. 1908. *Debs: His Life, Writings and Speeches: With a Department of Appreciations*. Girard, Kansas: Appeal to Reason.

Dodd, Vikram, and Sandra Laville. 2011. 'Scotland Yard admits Daniel Morgan's killers shielded by corruption' (www.theguardian.com/uk/2011/mar/11/scotland-yard-daniel-morgan-killers?intcmp=239) (last accessed 8 December 2023).

Draper, Hal. 1966. *The Two Souls of Socialism*. Berkeley, California: Independent Socialist Committee.

Edwards, Paul. 2006. 'Power and ideology in the workplace: going beyond even the second version of the three-dimensional view'. *Work, Employment and Society* 20(3): 571–81.

Ella Baker School of Organising. 2023. 'Training and education resources for organisers' (www.ellabakerorganising.org.uk/resources) (last accessed 22 November 2023).

Evans, Rob, and Paul Lewis. 2023. 'The true story of Britain's secret police undercover' (www.spycops.co.uk/the-story/) (last accessed 8 December 2023).

Foot, Matt, and Morag Livingstone. 2022. *Charged: How the Police Try to Suppress Protest*. London: Verso.

Fox Piven, Frances, and Richard Cloward. 1977. *Poor People's Movements: Why They Succeed, How They Fail*. New York: Vintage Books.

Freeman, Jo. 1971. 'The Tyranny of Structurelessness.' (www.jofreeman.com/joreen/tyranny.htm) (last accessed 4 December 2023).

Freire, Paulo. 2005. *The Pedagogy of the Oppressed*. New York: Continuum.

Ganz, Marshall. 2009a. 'Telling your public story: Self, Us, Now. Worksheet' (https://philstesthomepage.files.wordpress.com/2014/05/public-story-worksheet07ganz.pdf) (last accessed 21 November 2023).

Ganz, Marshall. 2009b. *Why David Sometimes Wins: Leadership, Organization and Strategy in the California Farm Workers Movement*. Oxford: Oxford University Press.

Ganz, Marshall. 2010. 'Leading Change. Leadership, Organization, and Social Movements' in *Handbook of Leadership Theory and Practice: A Harvard Business School Centennial Colloquium*, eds. Nitin Nohria and Rakesh Khurana: Harvard Business School Publishing Corporation.

Ganz, Marshall. 2011a. 'Organizing notes'. Boston: Harvard University.

Ganz, Marshall. 2011b. 'Public narrative, collective action, and power', pp. 273–89 in *Accountability Through Public Opinion: From Inertia to Public Action*, eds Sina Odugbemi and Taeku Lee. Washington DC: The World Bank.

Ganz, Marshall. 2016a. 'Public narrative' in *Organizing: People, Power & Change*. Harvard (https://projects.iq.harvard.edu/files/ganzorganizing/files/what_is_public_narrative.pdf) (last accessed 10 November 2023).

Ganz, Marshall. 2016b. 'Resources and resourcefulness: Strategic capacity in the unionization of California agriculture'. *American Journal of Sociology* 105(4): 1003–62.

Ganz, Marshall. nd. *Marshall Ganz' Framework: People, Power and Change*. Harvard Kennedy School. (https://wcl.nwf.org/wp-content/uploads/2018/09/Marshall-Ganz-People-Power-and-Change.pdf) (last accessed 24 July 2024).

Gill, Oliver. 2023. 'How the Tories nationalised almost half of Britain's railway network by stealth' (www.telegraph.co.uk/business/2023/05/12/tories-nationalised-half-britains-railway-transpennine/) (last accessed 26 July 2023).

Gov UK. 2021. 'Charity Commission concludes compliance case involving The Runnymede Trust' (www.gov.uk/government/news/charity-commission-concludes-compliance-case-involving-the-runnymede-trust) (last accessed 5 December 2023).

Graf, Arnie. 2020. *Lessons Learnt: Stories for a Lifetime of Organising*. Chicago: ACTA Publications.

Gramsci, Antonio. 1971. *Selections from the Prison Notebooks*. New York: Harper and Row.

Greenhouse, Steven. 2023. '"Old-school union busting": how US corporations are quashing the new wave of organizing' (www.theguardian.com/us-news/2023/feb/26/amazon-trader-joes-starbucks-anti-union-measures) (last accessed 7 December 2023).

Hain, Peter. 2020. 'Undercover policing inquiry. First witness statement of the Right Honourable Lord Peter Hain' (www.ucpi.org.uk/wp-content/uploads/2021/04/UCPI0000034091.pdf) (last accessed 8 December 2023).

Han, Hahrie. 2014. *How Organizations Develop Activists: Civic Associations and Leadership in the 21st Century*. Oxford: Oxford University Press.

Harding, Thomas, Ted Oliver, and Sean O'Neill. 2003. 'Murder fear after naming of IRA spy' (www.telegraph.co.uk/news/uknews/1429810/Murder-fear-after-naming-of-IRA-spy.html) (last accessed 8 December 2023).

Harvard Law School. 2023. 'The program on negotiation' (www.pon.harvard.edu/tag/best-alternative-to-a-negotiated-agreement/) (last accessed 1 December 2023).

Harvey, Larry. 2004. 'The 10 principles of Burning Man.' (https://burningman.org/about/10-principles/) (last accessed 7 December 2023).

Holgate, J. 2021. *Arise: Power, Strategy and Union Resurgence*. London: Pluto.

Holgate, Jane, Melanie Simms, and Maite Tapia. 2018. 'The limitations of the theory and practice of mobilization in trade union organizing'. *Economic and Industrial Democracy* 39(4): 599–616.

Horton, M., and P. Freire. 1990. *We Make the Road by Walking. Conversations on Education and Social Change.* Philadelphia: Temple University Press.

Horton, Myles, Judith Kohl, and Herbert R. Kohl. 1990. *The Long Haul: An Autobiography.* Doubleday.

HSE. 2023. 'Work-related fatal injuries in Great Britain' (www. hse.gov.uk/statistics/fatals.htm) (last accessed 8 December 2023).

Institute of Employment Rights. 2023. 'Spycops inquiry confirms spying on unions and blacklisting' (www.ier.org.uk/news/ spycops-inquiry-confirms-spying-on-unions-and-blacklisting/) (last accessed 8 December 2023).

Jones, Dave. 2016. 'South Yorkshire interim police chief welcomes Orgreave inquiry' (www.theguardian.com/uk-news/2016/ may/06/south-yorkshire-interim-police-chief-welcomes-orgreave-inquiry) (last accessed 8 December 2023).

Kelly, J. 1998. *Rethinking Industrial Relations. Mobilization, Collectivism and Long Waves.* London: Routledge.

King, Martin Luther. 1962. 'Dr. Martin Luther King's visit to Cornell College', ed. Cornell College News Centre (https:// news.cornellcollege.edu/dr-martin-luther-kings-visit-to-cornell-college/) (last accessed 2023).

Kirby, Dean. 2016. 'How the world's biggest asbestos factory tried to stop campaigners exposing the killer dust's dangers' (www. independent.co.uk/news/uk/home-news/how-the-world-s-biggest-asbestos-factory-tried-to-stop-campaigners-exposing-the-killer-dust-s-dangers-a6798236.html) (last accessed 8 December 2023).

Laybourn-Langton, L., H. Quilter-Pinner, and N. Treloar. 2021. *Making Change: What Works.* London: IPPR and Runnymede.

Lorde, Audre. 1982. 'Learning from the 60s' in Presentation at Harvard University in celebration of a Malcolm X weekend.

Lukes, S. 2005. *Power: A Radical View.* London: Palgrave.

MacAskill, Ewen, and Julian Borger. 2004. 'Iraq war was illegal and breached UN charter, says Annan' (www.theguardian.com/ world/2004/sep/16/iraq.iraq) (last accessed 4 August 2023).

Marx, Karl, and Friedrich Engels. 1987. *The German Ideology: Introduction to a Critique of Political Economy*. London: Lawrence and Wishart.

McAdam, D. 1982. *Political Process and the Development of Black Insurgency, 1930–1970*. Chicago: University of Chicago Press.

McAlevey, Jane. 2016. *No Shortcuts: Organizing for Power in the New Gilded Age*. Oxford: Oxford University Press.

Merewether, E.R.A., and C.W. Price. 1930. *Report on Effects of Asbestos Dust on the Lungs and Dust Suppression in the Asbestos Industry*. London: His Majesty's Stationery Office.

National Archives. 2021. 'The Report of the Daniel Morgan Independent Panel', House of Commons (https://webarchive.nationalarchives.gov.uk/ukgwa/20220331103928/https://www.danielmorganpanel.independent.gov.uk//wp-content/uploads/2021/06/CCS0220047602–001_Daniel_Morgan_Report_Volume_3.pdf) (last accessed 8 December 2023).

New York Times. 1976. 'FBI sought doom of Panther Party' (www.nytimes.com/1976/05/09/archives/fbi-sought-doom-of-panther-party-senate-study-says-plot-led-to.html) (last accessed 5 December 2023).

Nichols, M. 2023. 'A child killed on average every 10 minutes in Gaza, says WHO chief' (https://www.reuters.com/world/middle-east/child-killed-average-every-10-minutes-gaza-says-who-chief-2023-11-10/) (last accessed 3 September 2024).

Obama, Barack. 2004. 'Barack Obama's Keynote Address at the 2004 Democratic National Convention' (www.pbs.org/newshour/show/barack-obamas-keynote-address-at-the-2004-democratic-national-convention) (last accessed 21 November 2023).

Orwell, George. 1946. 'Politics and the English Language' (www.orwell.ru/library/essays/politics/english/e_polit/) (last accessed 14 December 2023).

Peirce, Gareth. 2014. 'Archive, 12 August 1985: How they rewrote the law at Orgreave' (www.theguardian.com/politics/from-the-archive-blog/2014/jun/17/orgreave-how-they-rewrote-the-law-1985) (last accessed 8 December 2023).

Piggot, Robert. 1994. 'Dozens unlawfully jailed for failing to pay their poll tax: Councils still threaten prison as punishment' (www.independent.co.uk/news/uk/home-news/dozens-unlawfully-jailed-for-failing-to-pay-their-poll-tax-councils-still-threaten-prison-as-punishment-1384870.html) (last accessed 4 August 2023).

Politico. 2016. 'Sanders raises $33M in final quarter, $73M total for 2015' (www.politico.com/story/2016/01/sanders-fundraising-final-quarter-2015-217288).

Proctor, R.N. 2012. 'The history of the discovery of the cigarette-lung cancer link: Evidentiary traditions, corporate denial, global toll'. *Tobacco Control* 21: 87–91.

Reid, James 1972. 'Alienation, Rectorial Address.' Delivered in the University of Glasgow on Friday, 28 April 1972, by James Reid. University of Glasgow Publications.

Riccio, Alex. 2023. 'The militant minority will not save the labor movement.' *Organising Work* (https://organizing.work/2023/09/the-militant-minority-will-not-save-the-labor-movement/) (last accessed 5 December 2023).

Rowell, Andrew, and Karen Evans-Reeves. 2017. 'It was Big Tobacco, not Trump, that wrote the post-truth rule book.' (https://theconversation.com/it-was-big-tobacco-not-trump-that-wrote-the-post-truth-rule-book-75782) (last accessed 8 December 2023).

Roy, Arundhati. 2003. Excerpt from Arundhati Roy's talk at the closing rally of the World Social Forum in Porto Alegre, Brazil, 27 January.

Scargill, Arthur. 1975. 'The New Unionism.' (https://newleftreview.org/issues/i92/articles/arthur-scargill-the-new-unionism) (last accessed 1 November 2023).

Schutz, Aaron, and Mike Miller (eds). 2015. *People Power. The Community Organizing Tradition of Saul Alinsky*. Nashville, Tennessee: Vanderbilt University Press.

Seton, Craig. 1985. 'Miners' strike aftermath'. *The Times. No. 62263*. 8 October. London, p 4.

Sheila McKechnie Foundation. 2018. 'Social power: How civil society can 'Play Big' and truly create change' (www.lloydsbankfoundation.org.uk/media/a0hph1kf/social-power.pdf) (last accessed 4 December 2023).

Shepardson, David, and Hilary Russ. 2023. 'Starbucks' ex-CEO Schultz resists "union busting" claims by U.S. Senators' (www. reuters.com/markets/us/us-senators-slam-starbucks-ex-ceo-schultz-over-union-busting-2023–03–29/) (last accessed 7 December 2023).

Siddique, Haroon. 2022. 'UK asbestos maker withheld information on material's risks, court papers show' (www. theguardian.com/uk-news/2022/mar/20/uk-asbestos-maker-withheld-information-on-material-risks-court-papers-show) (last accessed 15 December 2023).

Smith, Dave. 2020. 'In the matter of the undercover policing inquiry. Opening statement' (www.ucpi.org.uk/wp-content/uploads/2020/11/20201105-Opening_Statement-Blacklist_Support_Group.pdf) (last accessed 8 December 2023).

Sweeney, Steve. 2016. 'Orgreave activists take fight to Rudd. Hundreds gather outside Home Office to demand an inquiry.' (https://morningstaronline.co.uk/a-bc5a-orgreave-activists-take-fight-to-rudd-1) (last accessed 8 December 2023).

Taylor, Anthony Newman. 2018. 'The Asbestos Story: a tale of public health and politics'. *Imperial Medicine Blog* (https://blogs.imperial.ac.uk/imperial-medicine/2018/02/02/the-asbestos-story-a-tale-of-public-health-and-politics/) (last accessed 8 December 2023).

Teague, C. 1953. 'Survey of cancer research with emphasis upon possible carcinogens from tobacco', Ness Motley law firm documents. (www.industrydocuments.ucsf.edu/docs/ymch0045) (last accessed 24 July 2024).

Tomlinson, Ricky. 2021. 'We were convicted in 1973 after a political trial – it was a nonsense' (www.theguardian.com/law/2021/mar/23/we-were-convicted-in-1973-after-a-political-trial-it-was-a-nonsense) (last accessed 7 December 2023).

Undercover Research Group. 2023. 'Carlo Neri (alias)' (https://powerbase.info/index.php/Carlo_Neri_(alias)#cite_note-j.email.1–7) (last accessed 8 December 2023).

Waddington, J., and Allan Kerr. 2015. 'Joining UNISON: Does the reform of a union organising strategy change how members perceive their recruitment?'. *Industrial Relations Journal* 46(3): 187–207.

Walton, Richard, and Robert McKersie. 1965. *A Behavioral Theory of Labor Negotiations: An Analysis of a Social Interaction System.* Ithaca: ILR Press.

Washington Post. 2015. 'This Bernie Sanders crowd shot should make Hillary Clinton a little jittery' (www.washingtonpost.com/news/the-fix/wp/2015/08/10/this-bernie-sanders-crowd-shot-should-make-hillary-clinton-a-little-jittery) (last accessed 24 July 2024).

Yates, J. 2021. *Fractured: Why Our Societies Are Coming Apart and How We Put Them Back Together Again.* Manchester, HarperNorth.

Index

Index